# SOURCES FOR THE HISTORY OF LONDON 1939–45

## A GUIDE AND BIBLIOGRAPHY

GW00391409

## Heather Creaton

Deputy Director, Centre for Metropolitan History
Institute of Historical Research
University of London

*British Records Association*

*Archives and the User No. 9*

**1998**

*For Eva and Joe*
*who remember it all*

*Cover illustration*:

A Ministry of Health poster reinforces the message about child evacuation
*(PRO INF 13/171/2)*

ISBN 0 900222 12 3

© British Records Association, 1998
40 Northampton Road
London EC1R 0HB

Printed in Great Britain by Quorn Litho, Loughborough LE11 1HH

# Contents

Shelterers' bedding storage system at Leicester Square underground station.
*(London Transport Museum U/33116)*

# List of Illustrations

Crown copyright material in the Public Record Office and the RAF Museum, Hendon is reproduced by permission of the Controller of Her Majesty's Stationery Office. Mass-Observation material is reproduced with the permission of Curtis Brown Ltd London, copyright the Trustees of the Mass-Observation Archive at the University of Sussex. The Fougasse cartoon is reproduced with the permission of *Punch* Ltd. Thanks are due to London Metropolitan Archives, Corporation of London, to Guildhall Library, Corporation of London, to the Imperial War Museum, to the London Transport Museum, to the Dean and Chapter of Westminster, to the Senate of the University of London, to the NatWest Group Archives, to the Trustees of the Bishopsgate Foundation, and to Camden Local Studies and Archives Centre for their kind permission to reproduce items from their collections. Forest Heath District Council allowed the use of the letter from Newmarket Rural District Council, now among papers at the PRO. Due acknowledgement is also made for the short newspaper and periodical extracts used.

# Preface

The British Records Association worked hard through the war to ensure the safe survival of historical documents for the future. The major repositories naturally made careful evacuation arrangements for the records in their care. The greatest danger was to smaller collections and working archives, and it came not only from bomb, fire and water damage, but also from over-enthusiastic salvage drives. The BRA's Record Preservation Section organised a group of 'local referees' who checked documents sent to salvage dumps and rescued those of archival importance. The chief instigator of this work and much else was the redoubtable Ethel Stokes (a founder-member of the BRA and its archivist for many years), who unfortunately died in October 1944 as a result of an accident in the blackout.

As the end of the war approached, the BRA became concerned that very recent records might be destroyed now that the emergency was over. 'It is for the present generation to see to it that records worthy of the great struggle of 1939–45 take their place alongside the Retinue Rolls for Agincourt and the lists and plans for defence against the Spanish Armada and Napoleon Bonaparte...', they wrote in a memorandum of May 1945, mentioning particularly Home Guard, Civil Defence and War Emergency Committee records, but also the Red Cross, St John's Ambulance Brigade and the Women's Voluntary Service. That the BRA's exhortations bore some fruit is shown by the contents of this guide.

The British Record Association's own archives are in the care of London Metropolitan Archives, in ACC/3162.

Heather Creaton
*Centre for Metropolitan History*
*November 1998*

Anthony Heap, a local government officer, records a difficult day in his diary, 1941

*(LMA ACC 2243/15/1)*

# Abbreviations

| | |
|---|---|
| AFS | Auxiliary Fire Service |
| ARP | Air Raid Precautions |
| BBC | British Broadcasting Corporation |
| BFI | British Film Institute |
| BMA | British Medical Association |
| BRA | British Records Association |
| CC | County Council |
| CD | Civil Defence |
| CEMA | Council for the Encouragement of Music and the Arts |
| CID | Criminal Investigation Department |
| CLRO | Corporation of London Records Office |
| COI | Central Office of Information |
| ENSA | Entertainments National Services Association |
| FAP | First Aid Post |
| GLAN | Greater London Archives Network |
| GPO | General Post Office |
| HE | High explosive (bomb) |
| HMSO | His/Her Majesty's Stationery Office |
| HO | Home Office |
| IB | Incendiary bomb |
| ITMA | It's That Man Again (radio programme) |
| IWM | Imperial War Museum |
| LAUF | London Archive Users' Forum |
| LCC | London County Council |
| LFB | London Fire Brigade |
| LFCDA | London Fire and Civil Defence Authority |
| LMA | London Metropolitan Archives (formerly Greater London Record Office) |
| LPTB | London Passenger Transport Board |
| LWT | London Weekend Television |
| MBC | Metropolitan Borough Council |
| MCC | Middlesex County Council |
| MH | Ministry of Health |

| | |
|---|---|
| M-O | Mass-Observation |
| MOH | Medical Officer of Health |
| MOI | Ministry of Information |
| MP | Member of Parliament |
| NAAFI | Navy Army and Air Force Institute |
| PLA | Port of London Authority |
| PRO | Public Record Office |
| RAF | Royal Air Force |
| RAMC | Royal Army Medical Corps |
| REME | Royal Electrical and Mechanical Engineers |
| RE | Royal Engineers |
| RNVR | Royal Naval Volunteer Reserve |
| SA | Salvation Army |
| SOE | Special Operations Executive |
| UDC | Urban District Council |
| UP | University Press |
| UXB | Unexploded bomb |
| VAD | Voluntary Aid Detachment (nurses) |
| VD | Venereal disease |
| WAAC | Women's Army Auxiliary Corps |
| WAAF | Women's Auxiliary Air Force |
| WRNS | Women's Royal Naval Service |
| WVS | Women's Voluntary Service (now WRVS) |
| YMCA | Young Men's Christian Association |
| YWCA | Young Women's Christian Association |

# London Local Government Boundaries, 1939

Adapted from *London Statistics, 1936–38* (LCC, 1939)

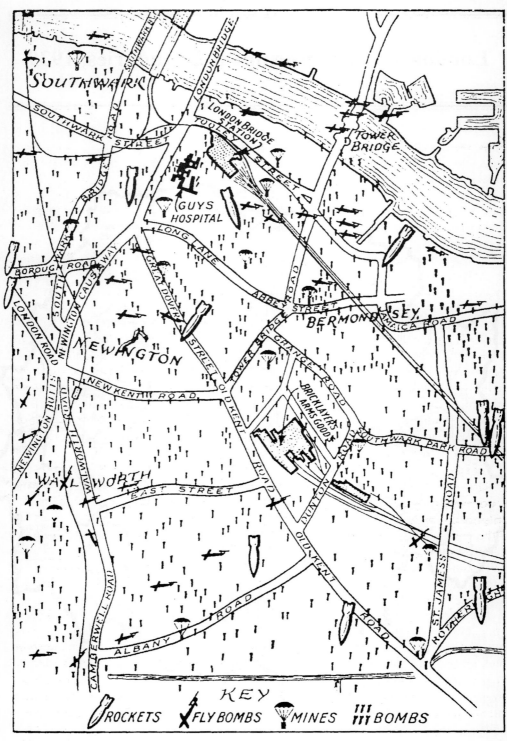

Casualty incident map prepared by Guy's Hospital.
*(Guy's Hospital Gazette, n.s.59, 1945, p. 210.)*

# 1. Introduction

Millions of words must have been written about London during the Second World War. The subject exerts a continuing fascination upon the general public and historians alike, and celebrations in 1995 of the fiftieth anniversary of victory sparked off still more interest. A special London at War Study Group has recently been established. Yet some of the published offerings constantly recycle the same material, rather than re-examining the original sources. This guide is an attempt to remind the reader of the enormous variety of primary sources available to the historian of this period, covering every aspect of London life, and to list as many as possible of the printed works likely to be useful for information and analysis. It cannot claim to be comprehensive, given the sheer quantity of surviving material, but aims to provide a starting point which will stimulate others to further investigations.

'London in 1939 was the greatest city in the world', says Philip Ziegler in the first chapter of his excellent *London at War, 1939–1945*, going on to justify this claim in terms of the city's importance nationally and globally, and its consequent vulnerability — real and perceived — to enemy attack. Over eight million people lived in Greater London. The capital was pivotal to national and international trade and at the heart of the country's political, cultural and social life. A definitive strike at London, the government feared, would demoralise the whole country and indeed the Empire. As the international situation deteriorated in the late 1930s the British authorities paid special attention to the problems of London in their emergency planning.

'What do you mean by "London"?' is a familiar question to those working on the capital. It is answered in various ways, depending on the historian's period or specialism. For the purposes of this guide 'London' comprises what the late twentieth-century reader customarily thinks of as 'Greater London', covering the area of the former Greater London Council. Probably wartime residents of the outer areas, like rural Rainham or Pinner did not think of themselves as 'Londoners' then. Some still do not, but the definition is well-understood and its diversity permits an extension of the range of relevant topics considered here beyond those applicable mostly to the inner city, such as deep shelters, to those affecting the outer reaches, like farming, and market gardening.

The guide is arranged by topic. First, I look at the great and obvious changes the war brought to London life, such as Air Raid Precautions (ARP), bombs and evacuation. Next come the efforts to continue normal life in difficult circumstances — schooling, transport, food, leisure activities and so on. Relevant records are spread among a great variety of repositories, and some degree of overlap is inevitable for the effects of the war were all-pervasive. This overlap is well-illustrated by ARP and evacuation matters. These were national policies administered by government departments through local authorities and voluntary organisations. As a consequence, source material may be found at the PRO, at LMA, in the appropriate county and borough record offices, or in other collections, like the IWM, and London Transport, as well as still in private hands. I have tried to indicate the full range of possibilities under each section. Many of the records mentioned have their out-of-London equivalents also, so readers interested in the war's effect on other parts of the country may still find useful guidance here.

It became clear during the compilation of this guide that some wartime material survives in almost every repository, however unlikely it seems on first enquiry. It is always worth asking advice from the staff, who can often lead the enquirer to sources not immediately obvious to the new visitor. Not all the potential material is in document form, of course. Maps, photographs, drawings, paintings, posters, film, sound recordings, artefacts and costume can also provide valuable evidence for this period, and some examples are covered here. Some original sources are now available on microfiches, including the Home Intelligence reports 1940–44 and sections of the Mass-Observation archive.

Useful source material is not solely confined to repositories in the London area, though they form the focus of this guide. Specialist collections have holdings relevant to London — the Modern Records Centre at the University of Warwick, for example, contains trade union and employment records of London significance. Diaries and letters written in London, or recording wartime visits there, may crop up in any collection in this country or abroad. Allied troops wrote memoirs later, diplomats sent reports back to their home governments. Papers of wartime governments in exile contain descriptions of their practical, day-to-day problems in London as well as matters of high politics. So while it is safe to say the bulk of the likely sources are still housed in and around London, valuable additional material may be found almost anywhere. One other general point to bear in mind is that some files containing personal information about individuals may still be closed to most enquirers.

The compilation of this guide has taken several years, alternating with my other duties at the Centre for Metropolitan History. My sincere thanks are due to friends and colleagues in libraries and record offices across London and well beyond who have, as always, been helpful, hospitable and encouraging. Several of them have been kind enough to read parts of this guide in draft and to offer advice and suggestions. I am particularly grateful to Janet Foster, general editor of this series, for her skill and patience in dealing with the text, and to Olwen Myhill of the Centre for Metropolitan History for the typesetting. Any remaining errors are, of course, entirely my responsibility as editor.

# 2. London's War: a brief outline of events

As the bibliography (Chapter 7, below) shows, there are many detailed histories of the progress of the war. Philip Ziegler's *London at War* (1995) makes a particularly informative and readable introduction. Nevertheless, it may be helpful to give a short resumé of events here for ease of reference.

Plans for national defence in the event of another war had been drawn up and reviewed at intervals throughout the 1920s and 1930s, but the Munich crisis in 1938 jolted the authorities into practical action. Construction of air raid shelters of various kinds began, more training was provided for ARP volunteers, sandbags were filled, gas masks and identity papers issued, evacuation plans rehearsed. When Chamberlain returned from his talks with Hitler to announce 'peace in our time' the general relief was manifest, and many Londoners were glad to forget the recent emergency preparations. Others, including Home Office staff, treated the news as a purely temporary respite giving an opportunity to remedy some weak links, especially through the provision of more shelters, the recruitment of extra ARP wardens, and the rehearsal of emergency drills. Barrage balloons were hoisted, blackout preparations made. The Ministry of Home Security appointed Regional Commissioners to be responsible for Civil Defence throughout the country; London — 'Region 5' — had Sir Ernest Gowers and Admiral Sir Edward Evans. If desperate times came, they were empowered to take over civil government in their region, with near dictatorial powers. War began to seem unavoidable.

**1939**  Evacuation of mothers and children began on 1 September. On 3 September war was declared, but apart from an immediate false alarm, nothing much happened and the 'phoney war' began, when the only bombs were planted by the IRA, and there was widespread criticism of 'overpaid' and apparently idle firemen and air raid wardens. 'Enemy' aliens were interned. By Christmas many evacuees had drifted back to London. Food rationing began. The quiet spell lasted until the summer of 1940.

**1940**  The fall of Norway, Belgium, Holland and France heralded the 'fifth columnist' scare about foreign spies, quantities of civilian refugees, invasion fears, the setting up of the Home Guard, the arrival of large numbers of Allied and Colonial troops, and the aerial 'Battle of Britain', clearly viewed by suburban South Londoners in August. On 23 August came the start of the Blitz, building up to a terrible autumn of heavy, nightly raids. Mercifully, pessimistic official forecasts about gas attacks and extremely severe physical and psychiatric bomb casualties proved ill-founded, but London suffered greatly. A particularly destructive incendiary raid on the City on 29 December prompted new regulations about regular overnight firewatching, and there was a terrible direct hit on Bank underground station in January 1941.

**1941**  The attacks became less regular for a while though there were dreadful incidents like the destruction of the Café de Paris in early March. March and April were very bad, and on 10–11 May came the severest raid yet on London, during which the House of Commons was almost destroyed. More prosaically, clothing was put on ration at this time, and a scrap metal drive led to many London park and garden railings being removed.

**1942**  passed without major incident in London. The city grew shabbier, there was a campaign to encourage 'holidays at home', with entertainments of all kinds in the parks, to dissuade Londoners from unnecessary travel. Various shortages irritated the public, and rationing was extended. American troops arrived, with money to spend and an aura of Hollywood glamour. But a general sense of tedium set in, as people coped with the restrictions of life and began to regard further bombing as unlikely. Victory at El Alamein in October turned the tide of war in the Allies' favour and boosted public morale. However, Allied bombing of Germany, and especially of Berlin, brought tit for tat raiding from early 1943.

**1943**  Shelterers caught up in the tragic accident at Bethnal Green tube station in March, when 173 people were suffocated in a fall down the entrance stairs, had hurried there precisely because they were expecting a reprisal raid after a heavy Allied attack on Berlin the night before. Spasmodic nocturnal and daylight raids continued throughout the year, including machine gun attacks on schools in London; in January thirty-eight children and six teachers died at an LCC school in Catford. The winter was very severe.

**1944**  Early in the year the German bombers returned for the 'Little Blitz'. There were fourteen major raids between January and April with incendiaries the main threat. Housing stock suffered badly; among other varied targets were the Surrey Docks and the London Library. The strain of more than four years of war was beginning to tell on Londoners, who felt that victory was very close and that they had suffered enough. Morale improved with a lull in air attacks during April and May and news of the successful D-Day landings in early June. But German revenge on London was expected, and duly came from 13 June with the V1s, pilotless planes known as 'Doodlebugs' that bumbled overhead, cut out and dropped with devastating effect. South London took the brunt of these attacks, with Croydon particularly badly hit. One of the most damaging V1 hits was on the Guards' Chapel during a service in June, killing 119 and injuring 102.

A new wave of evacuees left London at this time. Adjustment to the unnerving new menace was difficult, but at least people could hear the engine approaching and had a few moments in which to dive for cover. The V2 rockets, launched from September, gave no warning at all, could not be intercepted, and caused dreadful carnage like the hit on Smithfield market, and the destruction of New Cross Road Woolworths in December. Many V2s fell in East London and its suburbs, wiping out whole streets at once.

**1945**  The last V-weapons landed in March at a stage when victory was known to be very near. There was a gradual relaxation of blackout regulations. Londoners celebrated VE Day on 8 May, and VJ Day on 14 August. In between, in July, came the General Election, returning a Labour government. London settled down to a long period of postwar austerity and a very slow programme of rebuilding and restoration.

# 3. Locating the Sources

## NATIONAL GOVERNMENT RECORDS

Government control was all-pervasive during the Second World War. The military campaign had to be backed up by economic controls and the defence of the civilian population; this brought an unavoidable quota of regulations, directives and bureaucracy. The government, of course, was responsible for the entire country, but London was so central to national life and so vulnerable to enemy attack that its needs and problems occasioned great official attention which is reflected in government records. These are kept in the Public Record Office (PRO) which has published a helpful guide by John Cantwell, *The Second World War: A Guide to Documents in the Public Record Office*. It conveniently summarises the Office's holdings, with a brief introduction to the work of each department, the names of its main officials and a listing of its surviving records. The index yields eleven headings for London, but further information about London and Londoners occurs in a wide range of other documents. Reports on bomb damage, or morale, or food supply nationwide frequently contain a lengthy section on London; departmental correspondence on routine matters often includes incidental comment about wartime staffing and accommodation problems in the capital. All government departments made shelter and evacuation plans for their London staff. So material concerning London may crop up in almost any PRO file of wartime date, though some classes are more productive than others.

The War Cabinet took over the reins of government from the day war was declared, supported by an array of committees, military and civil. John Cantwell's book reproduces a useful flow chart showing the way these committees reported to the War Cabinet. Wartime requirements also increased the number of interdepartmental committees, necessary to coordinate overlapping responsibilities, for the Ministries of Home Security, Health and the Home Office were all concerned with Civil Defence matters, for example; and the Ministries of Education and Health both dealt with aspects of evacuation. Most departments were themselves evacuated to the provinces for at least part of the war. The Ministry of Food went to Colwyn Bay; the Ministry of Labour to Southport, for instance. However the War Cabinet had an extensive warren of underground offices beneath Whitehall from which it could operate in comparative safety. If invasion came, they were to move to a bunker in Neasden called The Paddock, camouflaged to look like part of Gladstone Park, with room for 200 staff. It was never used.

The work of all government departments was affected by the war. For most this meant carrying out an extension of the functions that they had had in peacetime. The Foreign Office, Treasury and Inland Revenue are obvious examples. However, many new departments were set up to deal with wartime needs. They included the Ministries of Aircraft Production, Economic Warfare, Food, Fuel and Power, Home Security, Information, Production, Supply and War Transport. Among the most fruitful quarries for London material are the records of the Ministry of Home Security for Civil Defence papers, the Ministry of Information's Home Intelligence reports, the Metropolitan Police, and the

War Damage Commission which dealt with compensation claims for war-damaged property. Conscious of the unprecedented nature of the 'total war' effort, the government required each Ministry or Department to gather material for a future history of its wartime work. Many of these were published a few years after the war, in the *Official History of the Second World War UK Civil Series*. They are magnificent sources of detailed information, fully documented and surprisingly readable as narrative. Several contain extensive information about London. The notes upon which they were based, with extra information and drafts, survive in the PRO, either with Cabinet papers at CAB 102 or among the appropriate departmental papers, or both. Notes for the official history of wartime education, for instance, are in CAB 102/238–9 and in ED 138. These are of extra importance because the planned volume was never published, due to the editor's death. Other series of the *Official History* covered military and medical matters.

The usual weeding process took place before the departmental records reached the PRO, so what survives is a deliberately chosen cross-section. Their nature varies with the work concerned, but typically they consist of files of reports, memos and other correspondence under subject headings, such as the Ministry of Health file 'Tube Shelters — London region. Reports on vermin at stations' in MH 76/538, or the Ministry of Information folder 'Home morale: report on decline of public confidence' in HO 262/12. Plans, photographs and contemporary information leaflets and pamphlets sometimes survive with the files. Some preserve letters and postcards from members of the public commenting on current issues, or complaining about government regulations. Examples of material to be found in PRO files follow later, under topic headings.

For varied historical reasons, some government records were never passed to the Public Record Office for preservation, but were retained by their producing department, like those of the Post Office, and Parliament. Other 'national' records, such as some court records — like Quarter Sessions — are traditionally kept locally in county record offices or their equivalent. National records of all kinds may contain caches of material for the local historian at any period. While national government records deal with policy matters and decisions affecting the whole country, they also contain considerable information about specific localities. The importance of London to the war effort makes the city feature even more prominently in documentation of this period, and the possibilities should not be overlooked by the researcher.

## LOCAL GOVERNMENT RECORDS

The government relied on local authorities to administer many aspects of its wartime functions, with the result that records of these authorities contain enormous quantities of material on the capital as a whole and about its constituent boroughs. There were two levels of local administration at this period for what is now thought of as 'Greater London'. These were the county councils, and within them, the boroughs. Twenty-nine inner London boroughs fell within the remit of the London County Council, with its seat at County Hall, just across the river from the Houses of Parliament. The twenty-six other central London boroughs belonged to the area of the Middlesex County Council, with its own Guildhall near Westminster Abbey. The records of both the LCC and the MCC are now housed in the London Metropolitan Archives (LMA). The remainder of outer London still belonged to the neighbouring counties of Surrey, Essex, Kent or Hertfordshire, whose County Record Offices retain quantities of relevant wartime material. More distant CROs may also have useful material on the reception of London evacuees in their area. At the heart of the ancient city, the Corporation of London retained its autonomy over the 'square mile'; its records are kept in the Corporation of London Record Office (CLRO). Records of individual boroughs are the responsibility of the appropriate local authority, often a successor body to the wartime borough because of later local government reorganisations.

All these councils kept copious wartime records, though varying policies and later changes of administrative responsibility mean that some collections have survived better than others. GLAN's *London Local Archives: A Directory of Local Authority Record Offices and Libraries* provides a list of these repositories, with more detail than can be included in the list at the end of this book. GLAN is also producing a series of guides to the contents of the London local authority record offices, to appear in stages from 1998, which will aid research for this as for all other periods. The Royal Commission on Historical Manuscripts' regular *Record Repositories in Great Britain: A Geographical Directory* covers the country as a whole. *British Archives*, by Janet Foster and Julia Sheppard (3rd ed., Macmillan, 1995; 4th ed. now in preparation), with its large London section of information and addresses, is an invaluable reference work dealing with local authority holdings as well as a wide range of other institutions.

Just as the war affected the normal working of long-established government departments at a national level, so it impinged on that of local government committees such as Housing, or Highways, or Libraries, and is reflected in their records. In addition, just as national government set up extra departments to deal with the emergency, so local government established special committees to cope with wartime problems. And they, too, needed to liaise with each other, leading to a crop of inter-departmental working groups to ensure coordination of measures.

The most significant of these new council committees were the Emergency ARP, later called CD, committees created under the Air Raid Precautions Act of 1937, which obliged all local authorities to make plans for dealing with the effects of enemy action on the civil population of their area. So among the records of the county councils and the boroughs are found agendas, minutes and papers of their ARP Committees from 1938 onwards, at first full of information about advance planning, later showing how the arrangements were working in practice. These emergency committees, usually chaired by the Town Clerk, were empowered to act on behalf of their council in a crisis, if enemy action should prevent normal business being carried out. Among the duties imposed on them was the drawing up of a local invasion defence scheme designed to keep civil government going as long as possible and to impede enemy advance through their area.

The official minutes of the county councils and boroughs, usually printed or typed, and sometimes indexed, are easy to use. Concise and formal, they do not give much indication of the discussions that led to the decisions recorded, but they will give the researcher dates and subject headings to pursue through individual committee minutes, and beyond that through departmental records — correspondence, internal reports and memos and miscellaneous paperwork. Typically, council minutes will merely record the presentation of a report from its ARP Committee. The report itself will contain a concise account of matters discussed and decisions recommended, but the departmental papers, if they survive, may have draft reports from council officers on the matter in question, external correspondence about it, photographs, plans and newspaper cuttings if relevant, and internal memos of varying levels of indiscretion. Apparently straightforward decisions sometimes turn out to have a tangled history.

An enormous level of extra work was generated for local authorities by these new wartime responsibilities. Many rose heroically to the challenge, others were less competent. In May 1940 Mass-Observation reported on the problem in M-O file 152. ARP and evacuation had created the most work. Dealing with them had caused overwork for local staff who had had to cope with them on top of their usual workload, giving up holidays and weekends for considerable periods. Other related problems were the confusion caused by conflicting instructions from separate government departments, the slowness of national government to reimburse local authorities for financial outlay, delays in the arrival of essential equipment, and lack of materials. The health services were especially overburdened, dealing with expectant mothers and infectious diseases. But on the whole, the report concluded, the work had gone ahead reasonably smoothly, given the circumstances.

Augmenting the evidence from these official papers is a variety of visual evidence. Maps, photographs and plans were needed by local authorities for various purposes. LMA, for example, has a good collection of bomb damage maps drawn up for the LCC towards the end of the war for assessing potential postwar development sites. Other authorities kept similar records, including the boroughs. Most local collections have photographs of their area during the war years. Some would have been produced by their own council to record war damage, others by Ministry of Information photographers, showing departing evacuees, people queueing for air raid shelters, mobile canteens at bomb incidents and other local scenes. Guildhall Library and the Museum of London both have sets of prints of a remarkable series of photographs of bomb damage to the City, taken by a policeman who recorded the scene after each raid.

Redevelopment plans for parts of the local authority area or of individual buildings can often be found among the papers of architects', engineers' and planning departments. If they relate to a particular kind of building, such as a school, they may also be found in the records of the education department. Plans are not usually listed separately, they need to be located through a subject search. Some local collections have film showing their area in wartime, like Hounslow Local Studies Centre's footage of bomb damage and fund-raising events in Heston and Isleworth.

Luck can even lead the researcher to the 'inside story' of working for local government in the war. Anthony Heap, whose diary is held in LMA ACC 2243/15/1, worked for the borough of St Pancras. 'Fewer rents for me to collect on Monday...', he commented dourly in January 1941 when tenants had been evacuated from a damaged block of flats. Local authority collections frequently contain non-official primary sources relating to the war, like Heap's journal. Enthusiastic local archivists and librarians have actively collected unpublished diaries and encouraged the writing of memoirs by people who lived in the area at that period, and have made audio tapes of local residents talking about their memories. They may vary in quality and depth, but can provide most useful additional evidence for the historian.

## INSTITUTIONAL AND BUSINESS RECORDS

The all-pervading nature of wartime regulations and requirements means that every London-based institution may contain some reflection of contemporary conditions in its archives, if they survive. This applies to museums, hospitals, schools, churches, libraries, businesses, learned societies, the BBC, the Port of London Authority, sports clubs, housing associations and numerous other organisations. All were affected by the war to some extent, sometimes dramatically. At the very least, they were obliged to provide for the safety of their staff and visitors in the event of an air raid. They also faced the loss of staff to the call-up and the need to find replacements, often women, who had to be trained as quickly as possible. This could lead to friction with the trade unions, and heated debate over equal pay entitlement. Welfare matters, personnel files, canteen provision, shortages of essential supplies, transport difficulties, evacuation of people and objects to safer zones, repair of bomb damaged buildings, fire-watching and Home Guard units are all subjects to be found among institutional records, as well as details of their usual activities.

Many such records have been deposited with the Modern Records Centre at Warwick, London Metropolitan Archives, Guildhall Library's Manuscript Department, and the borough collections. Others remain with the firm or institution that created them. Access to them is usually no problem for bona fide researchers, though some restrictions may apply where personal information is held about individuals. Of course the nature of the records varies immensely from case to case, as the following brief examples will demonstrate.

J. Lyons & Co., the catering firm famous for its popular 'Corner House' restaurants, has deposited its archives in LMA ACC 3527. The firm had branches countrywide, but its headquarters and factory were in Hammersmith. It had restaurants all over London and a thriving social club in Greenford. The records reflect all these aspects of the business, including, for example, an account book of meals served per day at the Oxford Street Corner House. Wartime menu cards survive, emblazoned with the slogan 'Food is a munition of war, don't waste it', and there is a collection of letters from former 'Nippy' waitresses, many of whom worked in London branches. Among the LMA's wide range of other commercial records are those of the Fulham manufacturing chemists, Whiffen & Son Ltd., in B/WHF, with files of incoming orders, correspondence illustrating salesmen's travel problems, the loss of trade through bomb damage to provincial factories, and ARP data such as a ledger of payments to firewatchers. Ledgers, correspondence files and order books comprise typical archives of commercial firms.

Bank records illuminate a rather different form of trading activity, one that affected so wide a cross-section of the public that the records provide plentiful general economic and social information, as well as business details. The modern 'big four' High Street banks' archives preserve the records of former banks they have taken over, so the National Westminster Bank archive contains the records of the Westminster Bank and the National Provincial Bank and their predecessors, Barclays has those of Martins, and so on. All these clearing banks operated across the whole country, but they had many London branches — the National Provincial had 170 — and all had their headquarters in the City. Typical of their holdings are reports and correspondence about air raid damage, including post-raid reciprocal banking arrangements with 'rival' banks, air raid damage ledgers and branch folders, with photographs of the staff at work clearing up, and ARP expenditure and personnel. Some archives contain reminiscences sent in by former staff describing their wartime service in general, or perhaps bomb damage to a specific branch.

Some London hospital records survive for the war period, at LMA or still with the hospital concerned. They vary greatly, but may include minutes, reports, correspondence, patients' registers, case books, operations registers, admission and discharge papers, staff registers, photographs, and architects' drawings. As well as general and teaching hospitals LMA has records of mental, maternity and children's hospitals, and specialist establishments like the Royal Eye Hospital, all with wartime coverage.

The National Portrait Gallery's wartime records, housed in their Heinz Archive and Library, provide an example of what happened to an art collection at this period. Most of the paintings were evacuated to Mentmore House in Buckinghamshire, but the London premises were used for temporary exhibitions and there was a storage area in the reinforced basement 'dugout'. The archive contains a draft 'National Portrait Gallery History, 1939–43'; nightwatchmen's patrol diaries; typed lists of 'rats killed and trapped, 1940–3', memos about storage conditions and humidity in the basement; correspondence with donors, and photographs of staff at Mentmore, as well as ARP material with some duty rotas, staff lists and a range of official pamphlets, training bulletins and newsletters.

The City and Guilds of London Institute's records are with Guildhall Library Manuscripts Department, in MS 21, 935/75. This organisation set professional examinations and validated the results for a cross-section of vocational courses. Their correspondence file 'War service, 1939–45' contains information on staff structure at the outbreak of war and the position since; a list of staff still on war service in August 1945; a memo dated 27 October 1939 about staff and salaries which includes details of the changed arrangements for the office since the outbreak of war, and hardship cases among their staff — 'father died as result of service in the Great War. Lives with and is main support of mother and household'.

Mass-Observation, a very different kind of institution from those so far mentioned, was set up in the late 1930s to apply the techniques of anthropological investigation to social research in Britain. Its reports, diaries and papers, housed now at the University of Sussex, provide a wealth of primary evidence about public attitudes, behaviour and morale. Mass-Observation monitored the whole country, but London samples were frequently used and the resulting data on subjects as varied as reading habits, religious belief, anti-Italian riots in Soho, reactions to billeting, and the behaviour of women in pubs provide a rich quarry for the social historian.

Voluntary organisations played a very active part in wartime life, often undertaking work at the request of government departments. The Women's Voluntary Service was particularly prominent in this role, and its records reflect its extensive London activities, especially in its 'narrative histories', the regular reports from London branches. The Red Cross and St John's Ambulance Brigade archives are also full of useful material from this period, as are those of the Young Women's Christian Association (YWCA), at the Modern Records Centre of the University of Warwick.

The range of institutional records available to the researcher is very broad, and the examples used here represent only the tip of an iceberg of potentially useful material. The topic sections later in this guide contain many more samples.

## RECORDS OF PERSONAL EXPERIENCE

A wide range of sources do not fall directly into the previous categories of administrative records generated by national or local government, or by institutions of some kind as part of their wartime activities. Instead, they reflect personal experience in some sense and include diaries, letters, sound recordings, oral history interviews, film, and drawings and paintings. Ephemera, and artefacts can also be considered here. This sort of material may occur in almost any collection, whether a record office, library, museum or in private hands.

Unpublished diaries and collections of letters, can provide revealing additional sources for the history of wartime London, both in terms of factual information and as an indication of attitudes, expectations and morale at different stages of the war, and in varying social circles. Facing an unknown future and unprecedented upheaval in their personal lives, many Londoners felt the need to keep a day-to-day record of their experience of history in the making. Some had a hopeful eye on eventual publication, especially if they were politicians and journalists, others wrote for their future children and grandchildren, or found it helpful to let off steam in private in this way. The Mass-Observation organisation harnessed the diary-keeping urge for official purposes and this guide's section on morale (p. 63, below) examines this more fully, but many more people kept personal journals recording their everyday lives.

The bibliography shows the large quantity of diaries that were eventually published. At their best, they are very valuable records, but inevitably they have been polished up for public view, edited and pruned. Unpublished diaries present the raw material, still exactly as written and carrying much of the atmosphere and strain of the events described. Examples are cited under many headings later in this guide, for diarists wrote about everything including daily work, air raids and bomb damage, theatre visits, filmgoing, and personal relationships. Letters have similar immediacy and interest, illuminating the problems of everyday life, rationing, travel and family news. Those written to family and friends overseas are particularly valuable because they tend to describe and clarify matters that would not need explanation to those at home. Later reminiscences can also supply useful information, otherwise hard to find.

The historian of London in wartime is fortunate in the survival of so much written documentation. Non-written evidence can also provide practical, detailed information on many points as well as conveying the 'feel' of life at the time. Luckily this material is also widely available. It can take many forms. Sound recordings of various kinds are available in several collections, notably the British Library National Sound Archive, the Imperial War Museum Sound Archive and the Museum of London. Some of the recordings were made during the war, for broadcasting, others have been made for recent radio and television series, such as the LWT programmes *The Making of Modern London, 1939–45* in which the interviewees cover a wide range of topics. Some people also contributed letters and photographs which are of considerable interest. The material is kept in the Museum of London's Oral History Department. Oral history projects, both local and national have generated tape collections in a variety of repositories. Among the many interviewees in the IWM Sound Archive's collection, for example, are politicians, policemen, munitions workers, dance band musicians, conscientious objectors, cameramen, artists, rescue workers, mobile canteen drivers, refugees, evacuees and internees. The National Sound Archive avoids covering the same ground as the IWM, but various of its tapes, especially the National Life Story collections, and the 'Living memory of the Jewish community', 'Labour oral history project' and 'City lives' series, contain wartime reminiscences as part of wider interviews. Some institutions and firms have set out to record staff memories; the London Transport Museum, for example, has tapes of former employees remembering the problems of wartime service. Transcripts exist for some recordings, a useful additional tool but no substitute for hearing the original voices which carry so many nuances of emphasis, accent and intonation.

Even the popular music of the day gives clues to contemporary preoccupations and morale.The National Sound Archive has a rich collection, including Florence Desmond's splendidly suggestive 'I've got the deepest shelter in town' — 'I've got a cosy flat, there's a place for your hat/I'll wear a pink chiffon negligee gown/ And do I know my stuff, but if that's not enough/ I've got the deepest shelter in town' — recorded in 1941. The Sound

Archive of the IWM also has thousands of recordings of popular wartime entertainment material, and makes available BBC wartime broadcasts.

Film coverage of London during the war is extensive, if patchy. Film of the Blitz itself is scarce, for technical difficulties made it hard to record under such conditions. Cinema newsreels filmed extensively, often for morale-boosting purposes, so shots of cheerful Londoners abound, 'carrying on' as normal amid bomb damage or waiting stoically in tube shelters. The National Film and Television Archive at the BFI has an extensive collection of newsreel film as well as other footage of London in the war. In September 1939 the Ministry of Information enlisted the services of the GPO Film Unit, soon renamed the Crown Film Unit, which had a distinguished history of documentary-making. They made films such as *The First Days* (1939), a valuable record of Londoners preparing for war, showing shelters, barrage balloons, sandbags, wardens, evacuation of people and art treasures to the country. *London Can Take It* (1940) is presented as a film despatch by the American reporter Quentin Reynolds, and shows one night of the Blitz, from sunset to sunrise. It played a big part in swinging US popular opinion behind the British war effort. Other films with useful material include *London, Autumn 1941* (1941), *City of Progress* (1941), *London 1942* (1942), *London Terminus* (1944) which shows Waterloo Station at work in wartime, and *Piccadilly Roundabout* (1944). All are in the BFI's collection. The IWM Film and Video Archive has Army and RAF film of their activities in wartime London, showing troops clearing bomb-damaged sites, V1 damage and the like, and Fire Brigade film of the great City raid of 29–30 December 1940. It holds collections from the Southern Railway and the London Fire Brigade showing damage, as well as privately shot colour film of the Auxiliary Fire Service in action. It also has German newsreel film, with Portuguese commentary, of a raid on London, filmed from the bombers. Businesses sometimes recorded their wartime activities on film. Both the Westminster and Barclays Banks made films of everyday life at their London headquarters, including ARP procedures, early in the war. Some amateur footage taken by people who had owned home movie cameras prewar and saved some film survives here and there, and feature films sometimes contain useful footage of wartime London. *Waterloo Bridge* (1940) and *Waterloo Road* (1944) are good examples. Bomb sites and damage are clearly visible too in a succession of films made just after the war, notably *Hue and Cry* (1946).

Contemporary paintings and drawings provide factual information and a wide range of emotional responses to the experience of war. The Ministry of Information set up the War Artists' Scheme, commissioning several thousand paintings and drawings recording the war effort at home and abroad. Many are now in the collection of the Imperial War Museum. The Scheme suggested subjects to the artists, some of whom chose to record the look of wartime London, especially after bomb damage. These included, for instance, Anthony Gross' *Sandbags in Bethnal Green* (1940), Graham Sutherland's *Devastation in the City* (1941) and *The City: A Fallen Lift Shaft* (1941), John Minton's drawings of devastated Poplar, and post-raid studies by Muirhead Bone and John Piper.

Artists tackled indoor subjects too. Henry Moore's series of drawings of sleeping shelterers is well-known; Feliks Topolski also painted tube shelter interiors. Edward Ardizzone chose to paint the Home Guard in training in *A Day with the Home Guard: Battle Rages for the Bank of England*. Eric Ravilious' *Room 29, Home Security Control Room*, and Meredith Frampton's *London Regional Civil Defence Control Room* all take their distinctive approaches to similar themes. Frampton's CD Control Room painting not only accurately depicts the look of this vital communications centre, with its wall maps and charts, files, telephones and the essential teacup and milk bottle, but provides perceptive portraits of Sir Ernest Gowers, the Senior Regional Commissioner, his Director of Operations and Intelligence, Lt-Col. A.J. Child, and his Deputy Chief Administrative Officer, K.A.L. Parker, at work in the room. Interest in new art was high during the war, with exhibitions a popular diversion for Londoners and visitors. The Firemen Artists exhibited regularly, usually showing the work of trained artists who had joined the Fire Service for war work. They painted training sessions, life at the Fire Station, and portraits of their fellow firefighters. Some examples appear in William Sansom's *Jim Braidy*. The London Transport Museum has examples of the work of Henry Stockley, one of their bus drivers, who worked throughout the war and painted in his spare time. His work includes a series on the Blitz, including *Blitz: the Shell Building, 1941* and *London Saved, 1941*.

Photographers recorded wartime London for a variety of reasons. Some took pictures of bomb damage to buildings and equipment for official reference purposes and later compensation claims; these are mainly to be found among national and local government archives. Firms and institutions recorded their wartime conditions and activities, too. But the photographs that played so large a part in the propaganda battle, and which influence our view of wartime London to this day, are the black and white stills taken by agency photographers for the Ministry of Information, for publication in the press at home and overseas. Copies survive in many collections; the Imperial War Museum and Museum of London have extensive runs. They begin in 1939 with a spate of shots of cheerful Londoners taping up their windows, filling sandbags and wearing gasmasks in unlikely circumstances, such as the chorus girl wearing feathers, gasmask and nothing else, and a dance band playing with their masks on. During the Blitz, pictures of Londoners battling on in spite of the damage were popular — scenes such as a tin-hatted postman trying to deliver mail to a bomb-damaged house, and smiling housewives collecting clean washing from a mobile laundry among rubble and debris. However, the agency photographers did not ignore the grimmer side of events — the IWM collection also has a picture of a wrapped body being removed from a bomb-site, and of canvas body bags in the playground of the LCC school at Catford after the severe raid of January 1943. This is stamped by the censor 'Not for use in GB'. Late in 1940 the Ministry commissioned the well-known photographer Bill Brandt, and an unnamed colleague, to record life in the air raid shelters. The result was a distinguished series of which the Imperial War Museum has the negatives, and the Museum of London a set of the vintage prints. Copies of these photographs were appended to the Wendell Willkie report of 1941 and played their part in persuading the American government into the Lend-lease agreement. The photographs show the wide variety of shelter arrangements, some very basic, others quite comfortable, the people who used them and the ways in which they passed the time. Photographs were sometimes appended to official reports and correspondence and survive among those records. Some of Hackney's Civil Defence War Diaries, for example, contain photographs of bomb incidents, such as H/A/30. PRO class HO 192 has many photographs of bomb-damaged premises among its written material; AIR 34/741–5 includes photographs of Chislehurst Caves in use as an air raid shelter. IR 83/198 records daily life at Chelsea tax office in 1941–2 in sixty-six photographs. An indexed guide to its photographic holdings is available in the PRO, but the compilers stress that it is not complete.

Cartoons can act as barometers of the prevailing concerns and states of mind. *Punch* is a good source for this as for other periods, and the British Institute for Cartoon Research at the University of Kent has an extensive collection, including Sydney Strube's cartoons from the *Daily Express*, and Neb's from the *Daily Mail*. Many concern wartime conditions and shortages that applied nationwide, commenting on the latest war news or joking about the blackout, or rationing. Some refer to London specifically, like E.H. Shepard's famous appeal to Herbert Morrison to open the deep shelters to the public during the Blitz, 'Open Sesame'. Cartoons in the London evening newspapers, particularly David Low's cartoons in the *Evening Standard* and Lee's 'London Laughs' and 'Smiling Through' series from the *Evening News,* have special London relevance.

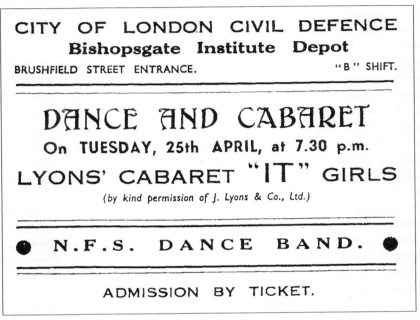

**CITY OF LONDON CIVIL DEFENCE**
**Bishopsgate Institute Depot**
BRUSHFIELD STREET ENTRANCE.          "B" SHIFT.

**DANCE AND CABARET**
**On TUESDAY, 25th APRIL, at 7.30 p.m.**
**LYONS' CABARET "IT" GIRLS**
*(by kind permission of J. Lyons & Co., Ltd.)*

● **N.F.S.  DANCE  BAND.** ●

**ADMISSION  BY  TICKET.**

Civil Defence staff find time for relaxation: dance ticket
*(Bishopsgate Institute file 'Institute, 1941–7')*

Ephemera, the commonplace throwaways of everyday life — tickets, programmes, business cards, bills, advertising leaflets, postcards and the like, can add to our understanding of the war period. They may turn up anywhere among archives and correspondence, but some museums and some libraries have set out to collect them separately. The Museum of London has a large collection containing a great variety of material, from a child's uniforms book *We're All In It*: *Mummy/Daddy Puts on Uniform* (Raphael Tuck, *c*.1941) to a Borough of Hornsey certificate awarded for the successful completion of an anti-gas course, printed cards left in church pews telling worshippers what to do in the event of a raid, air raid shelter tickets, water board handouts urging economy at all times, and samples of Sanderson's special ARP blackout wallpaper.

Lastly, the evidential value of contemporary costume, including uniforms, and objects used in daily life — stirrup pumps, ARP badges, tin hats, gasmasks, make-up, blackout curtains and almost anything else — should not be overlooked. Good sources for these are museums, especially the Museum of London and the Imperial War Museum, but they have sometimes survived with other wartime material in libraries and record offices. The WRVS archive, for instance, preserves some of the thick tweed overcoats issued to their volunteers, as well as badges and other items of uniform.

# 4. The Changed Face of Wartime London

## MANNING THE HOME FRONT: CIVIL DEFENCE

### Air Raid Precautions

#### Coping with the raids

London was harder hit than any other British city, both in number of bomb attacks and number of casualties. 'Throughout the war it had 101 daylight and 253 night attacks by piloted aircraft. It was attacked at some time during the day or night, with the exception of only two twenty-four hour periods, for the whole of September, October and November 1940. London received 41% of the attacks by flying bombs, and 49% of those by rockets', states Terence O'Brien's detailed official history of Civil Defence provision in the *History of the Second World War UK Civil Series*.

Plentiful evidence of this process of destruction survives for the historian in the records of a wide range of national and local administrative records, and beyond. Each incident was different and could involve several agencies in dealing with the aftermath. Each of these agencies recorded the matter from its own perspective; these reports can often be dovetailed to produce a detailed picture of the event. Further information may come from maps, photographs, paintings, film, newspaper coverage, and the personal testimony of diaries, memoirs, letters and oral history recordings, of which there are many, for the experience made a lasting impression on those who suffered it.

Overall responsibility for Civil Defence and its coordination rested with the Ministry of Home Security. Its records are in the Public Record Office, among those of its parent Home Office; there is a clear outline of both Ministries' administrative histories, and those of other government departments, in part one of the PRO's *Guide*. Terence O'Brien's authoritative volume *Civil Defence*, referred to above, is indispensable.

All too soon after the ending of the First World War international events made it apparent that the 'war to end wars' had been no such thing. The British government started to make plans for the defence of the civilian population if the unthinkable should happen — another European war. London had been bombed in the 1914–18 war and it was obvious that any future conflict would bring increased danger from the air. Gas was particularly feared and guarded against, but fortunately never used. Bombing raids during the Spanish Civil War, especially the attacks on Guernica and Barcelona, had reinforced official anxiety about the potential scale of damage. A sub-committee of the Committee of Imperial Defence had been set up in 1924 to deal with Air Raid Precautions (ARP); it was transferred in 1935 to the Home Office. But it was not until the Air Raid Precautions Act of 1937 came into force that the subject made any real impact on the general public through local government planning, shelter-building programmes, blackout regulations and the issue of gas masks. Volunteers began training for all aspects of ARP work, guided by a stream of ARP Handbooks published by HMSO covering, among other subjects, ARP for animals. The Home Office monitored the efficacy of the ARP system during the Munich crisis and learnt from it. HO 45/17626, reporting on ARP in Hackney in 1939, provides a good example.

### London Region: Civil Defence

ARP volunteer numbers increased when war broke out, at which point the ARP Department was transformed into the Ministry of Home Security for the duration of the war. It retained such close links with its parent the Home Office that they always shared the same Minister, and its records are among the HO classes in the PRO. The new ministry operated CD through Regional Commissioners. The best known of the London ones were the distinguished career civil servants Sir Ernest Gowers and Sir Harold Scott, and Admiral Sir Edward Evans. The painting by Meredith Frampton in the IWM's collection mentioned earlier, depicts *Sir Ernest Gowers, Lt-Col. A.J. Child and K.A.L. Parker in the London Regional Civil Defence Control Room 1943*, amid maps, telephones and tea cups. The Commissioners were based at the Geological Museum in South Kensington. Files relating to the organisation of the London Region and the rest of the country are in the PRO in various Home Office classes. General registered ARP files are in HO 186, Bomb census maps in HO 193, Chief Engineer's Department registered files in HO 197, Bomb census papers in HO 198, Intelligence Branch registered files in HO 199, Tube Shelter Committee registered files in HO 200, Regional circulars in HO 204, Air raid shelter papers including material on the Bethnal Green disaster in HO 205, Regional circulars, and Shelter provision and engineering works in HO 206. Headquarters and regional files in HO 207 are full of detailed London material, especially the 'London borough' series, pieces 504–1032 which also contain LCC, MCC, and City papers. There are files on individual shelters as well as authority-wide reports, papers on the WVS in HO 207/164, 171, 205 and on CD training in HO 207/138, 176. London Region's own premises at the Geological Museum and shelter accommodation there are documented in HO 207/336–7. More generally, files of the War Cabinet CD committees in CAB 73 also have some London material. Churchill College, Cambridge has the papers of some senior civil servants involved with the War Cabinet and in planning and organising Civil Defence, such as Sir John Colville, Sir John Martin and Sir John Hodsall.

The London and Home Counties No.5 CD Region covered the Metropolitan Police District, the City, and the remainder of the counties of Hertfordshire, Essex, Surrey and Kent, in a series of nine, later reduced to eight, groups. Middlesex formed group 6 within it. Each grouping had a control centre, and every borough within the group had its own local control centre, reporting to group control, which liaised with headquarters. Friction among the boroughs, and between the boroughs and Whitehall, was not uncommon. 'War had not extinguished the amour-propre and independence of spirit of these authorities', wrote O'Brien, and local pride sometimes needed soothing. London Region's Town Clerks' Advisory Committee helped considerably in this, meeting regularly and providing a forum for consultation. Its papers are in HO 186/2443. Success in coping with the results of bombing raids depended on local officials carrying out several Ministries' devolved responsibilities smoothly.

### Local authority records

An examination of the role of the the London County Council in this field reveals the enormous range of administrative work involved. Within its area the LCC organised the rescue of trapped victims of air raids and the removal of casualties, the ambulance and fire services, heavy rescue and debris clearance, the evacuation of civilians, the maintainance of welfare and rest centres and emergency feeding. All this was in addition to its normal functions, such as running its hospitals, schools and colleges, sewage, and parks, all of which brought their own wartime problems. Its staff also manned the CD Region's group control centres. The enormous range of work is documented in the Council's committee and sub-committee minutes and papers for the war period, especially those of the ARP, CD and Evacuation Committees, and in departmental papers generally. Unpublished, detailed departmental histories, in SC/PPS/41, provide a valuable starting point. The Clerk's Department (Civil Defence) and Departments of Housing, Public Assistance, Architects, Engineers, Fire Brigade, Public Health and Welfare records are particularly fruitful, but others with less obviously relevant titles should not be overlooked. The same principle applies to the Middlesex CC records and those of other county authorities with responsibilities in the Greater London area. LCC and MCC records are in LMA, those of other counties are with their County Record Office.

The metropolitan boroughs were responsible for providing public shelters, organising the Wardens' service, first aid parties, and light rescue work, but central government departments supervised and inspected the provision, and as a result a great deal of local information is to be found among central government records. Papers on local training for CD work, for example, are to be found in PRO HO 207/138 and 176. Civil Defence was essential, but expensive. Expenditure by local authorities could be recouped from the Home Office; Middlesex CC's 'Registers of CD expenditure' in LMA MCC/CL/L/CD/3 give an area by area account of items of expenditure submitted to the Home Office for disbursement.

*The Wardens' service*

ARP wardens were the linch-pins of the local CD system. The boroughs were subdivided into ARP sectors, usually following established council ward boundaries, each of which had several wardens' posts. These occupied a variety of premises. In the outer suburbs they were frequently set up in ordinary houses, more centrally they gradually acquired purpose-built, reinforced shelters. Tenders and building costs for these survive in some borough collections. Hackney, for instance, has a file of tenders for the construction of three reinforced concrete Report Centres: the Town Hall, Selman Street and Rossendale Street in H/CC/1/209. Rossendale Street ARP Centre still stands, and was the subject of a very detailed survey by the Royal Commission on Historical Monuments as recently as 1993 — RCHMons folder 91157 — with plans, photographs and a full building report.

In October 1939 Mass-Observation conducted an enquiry, documented in M-O file 4A 'Propaganda and ARP recruiting' into why people had joined ARP. Two thousand volunteers in Fulham, which had one of the highest ARP memberships in London, were surveyed. Seventy-eight per cent of respondents said they had been been persuaded to join by newspaper or radio advertisements. Like other apparently idle CD workers wardens were the butt of public jokes and complaints during the phoney war, and regarded by some as interfering busybodies even in more dangerous times. The MOI tried to boost their image through information films such as *Night Watch,* COI 259 in the IWM's Film and Video Archive.

The boroughs organised the Wardens' posts, so it is among their collections that any surviving material will normally be found. Individual ARP personnel sometimes retained material after the war. Of this, some is still in private hands and some has since been deposited with the appropriate local authority or elsewhere, such as the IWM Department of Printed Books, whose Civil Defence Collection contains a large amount of London local authority material, including items such as shelter and wardens' post plans. The IWM Department of Documents, too, has examples, like the ARP log book for Wardens' Post 60, Park Royal Industrial Estate, 1939–40, in Misc. 1874, and other items.

The borough material varies from authority to authority, but many have ARP sector maps showing wardens' posts, first aid posts, shelters and fire hydrants. Kensington has a map of its 28 Group, in Redcliffe ward, plotting which houses and shops were unoccupied in 1944, with monthly summaries of unoccupied properties for earlier dates too. Recruitment literature and staff records can be valuable, particularly after compulsory registration for CD was brought in from 1941. Hackney Archives, for example, have the registration cards for Hackney and Stoke Newington MBs, some with the original applications giving names, address, age, employer and details of any exemptions in force. Westminster's register of part-time staff has enrolment forms with name, address and next-of-kin and also preserves correspondence chasing up workers who had failed to report for their rota with their excuses and explanations, as in Westminster Archive Centre's file CD 83.

Duty rotas, attendance registers, correspondence, rolls of honour and other material survives widely in many borough collections. ARP magazines were popular. Hendon wardens produced *The Good Neighbour*, in Barnet Archives L614.9, with local advertisements, factual information, jokes, cartoons, decorating and gardening hints and even a spoof ARP coat of arms in the issue for June 1940. Kensington wardens contributed to *The Wardens' Post*, and the *Kensington Burrow News* (Kensington LS 940.549.WW). The IWM Department of Documents has copies of Battersea's equivalent, *The Striver* (Misc. 685), its Department of Printed Books has others including Finsbury and Wembley. Any of this material may prove useful, but for many historians the meatiest slice of ARP records will probably be the array of borough control CD log books, incident diaries and occurrence registers kept all over London. They all record the same sort of factual information about incidents, but the format varies with the borough concerned.

*Logging the 'incident'*

Hackney, an area that suffered badly from bomb damage, has an extensive series of CD diaries. Kept by date in contemporary buff folders, they are typed sheets with columns ruled to record a full range of information: Time; Position of incident; Type of bomb; Parties despatched, and when; Extent of damage; Number of casualties; Roads blocked and existence of gas; Remarks. Some of these files contain photographs as well as reports of the air raid damage, for example H/A/30/299 has four photographs including the Adam and Eve Public House, Homerton, and 30 Gayhurst Road, showing a pile of rubble, and a small tree still standing in the front garden. Hackney Archives holds the private papers of a former ARP warden, T.E. Browne, of particular interest because they include his typed incident reports and some of the original handwritten forms on which they were based, in D/F/BRO/2, as well as his private diaries in D/F/BRO/1. The brief handwritten notes are expanded in more detail in the typescript version, and his diaries often provide further background about the incident, with personal comments and criticisms of the CD organisation and personnel. On 8 December 1940 he was called out to an incident at Cassland Road. 'I was annoyed at this because I had asked to be taken off the Sunday rota for the time being. But I thought it must have been really necessary and in spite of protests from Mum I went. As there was not traffic running I had to walk all the way through the barrages which was rather unnerving at times... It then appeared I was at the wrong incident (see my report for further details). Arrived home about 1.15 a.m...' The papers of another Hackney warden, A.V. Monk,

S E C R E T

This document is strictly confidential and must not be shown to any
unauthorised person.

---

LONDON CIVIL DEFENCE REGION
18th January, 1943,
Situation Report as at 1800 hours.

---

PART I.

No bombing occurred during the period but further details are now available
relating to the previous raid.

Reports of bombing have now been received from 22 local authorities.
The number of bombs dropped is stated to be 124 comprising 65 exploded H.E.
21 exploded fire pots and 38 UXB's. Various types of 1 kilo I.B. over nine
boroughs; some explosive, but no I.B.E.N. One UX P.M. reported has been
rendered safe.

Much damage was done by A.A. shells which burst on impact, the number
of which so far reported is 47. In addition 8 A.A.U.X. & 2 U.P.U.X. were
reported.

The Listening Apparatus has been sent to the incident at Henstride Place,
Marylebone, where persons are still believed to be trapped. Work will
continue throughout the night.

No serious damage occurred to the Public Utility services and full details
of damage so far reported is given below.

Food situation unaffected and public morale good.

RAILWAYS.

L.N.E.R. Lisson Grove Goods Yard. Shunting discontinued owing to presence
of UXB.

Wellington Road Tunnel immediately beneath Lords Cricket Ground,
Bomb formerly reported as exploded, later identified as UXB which has now been
removed by B.D.S. and all lines now working.

Forest Gate Stn. A.A. Shell on lines between Station and Balmoral
Road Bridge. One rail and sleepers damaged.

ROADS.

Lower Road, Bermondsey - now fully open
Southwark Bridge Road, Southwark - single line traffic.
Old Kent Road, Camberwell - closed between Canal Bridge and Commercial Road.
U.X.Bs in Category B.
Rye Lane, Camberwell - closed between Peckham High Street and
Moncrief Street - debris.
Woolwich Road, Greenwich - by Anchor and Hope Lane - open.
Peckham High Street - closed between Hardcastle Street and Mellon Road
U.X.Bs.
Barking Road, West Ham closed at junction of Bartle Avenue and Green Street
and junction of Castle Street owing to U.X.B.

WATER

One 12" dia. main damaged in Greenwich Park, Greenwich.
Fourteen 4" dia. mains broken in various localities.
Damage to surface of Streatham Reservoir is thought to be slight.

Gas.

One 24" dia. main damaged in Southwark Bridge Road.
One 14" dia. main damaged in Romford Street, West Ham.
One 10" dia. main damaged in Green Lane, Woolwich.
Four U.X.Bs in and near South Metropolitan Gas Works, Old Kent Road,
in Category B. No interference with production
at present.

/Over

---

A Civil Defence situation report includes notes on infrastructural damage
*(LMA LCC/CE/WAR/4/9)*

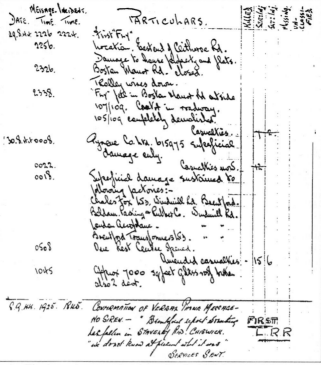

The 'secret weapon' arrives: the first V2 is recorded in
Middlesex County Council's logbook of air raid incidents
*(LMA MCC/CD/WAR/1/2)*

– 4 –

No. 5 Region (London)

WESTMINSTER:    Exhibition Road was closed owing to a burst water main at 2030.

CHELSEA:    Kings Road is blocked owing to damage to L.C.C. sewers.

FULHAM:    Minor bombing is reported.

PADDINGTON:    H.E. fell in Bayswater Road and Edgware Road, the former road is blocked.

MARYLEBONE:    A fire was caused at Lodge Road.

ST. PANCRAS:
STOKE NEWINGTON:
HAMPSTEAD :    Minor bombing is reported.

ISLINGTON:    Fires were caused at Market Road, Brewery Road, Bride Street, where a 42" gas main was fractured, and at the Caledonian Cattle Market. H.E. fell in Wheelwright Street.

CITY:    Serious fires were caused at Golden Lane, Barbican, and another fire was started in India Street. At 0308 H.E. fell in Smithfield Market, Smithfield Street is blocked.

SHOREDITCH:    At 0443 H.E. fell on the Wenlock Brewery, causing an explosion of the ammonia plant. City Road Chest Hospital was also hit but no details are yet available.

Part of the Home Security Intelligence summary report for 11 September 1940
*(PRO HO 203/4)*

including official material, are with the IWM Department of Documents, Misc. 1020, as are similar deposits from Southwark and Islington wardens. Westminster Archives Centre has the borough's Group Situation Reports for the whole of the war in CD 17. Typed on flimsy paper they vary greatly in length from thin strips saying 'nil' to far longer compilations. A typical entry reads: '19.12.42 Suspected UXB in Victoria Embankment Gardens fallen 10 May 1941, being investigated'. Kensington LS has a contemporary typed card index to ARP incidents, giving the date, time, post that dealt with it, description of damage and action taken. The borough's Report Centre Log Sheets (940.544 AIR R62742) are detailed original report forms written out at the incident, with a note of casualties and action needed. For instance, the incident form for the flying bomb attack on St Mary Abbot's Hospital, on 17 June 1944, lists the fatalities by category — nurses; children; male — and names the patients transferred to St George's Hospital giving their medical diagnoses.

Further out in the suburbs, Hendon Control kept an ARP Damage Log Book throughout the bombing, now in Barnet Archives MS 9215/1. It contained columns with the date, a running number, warden's post area, time, place, type of bomb, casualties, services despatched, damage to services and utilities, whether roads blocked, property damage, how many homeless, and 'remarks' such 'Aircraft crashed rear garden 55 Flower Lane, one RAF casualty' (31/8/44). Parts of Hendon were still rural: '14–15 October 1940 Daltons and Bury Farm Edgewarebury Lane 6 H.ES 1 INC. 2 horses killed 1 hiefer [sic] injured'.

The chain of official incident reports fed from the ARP posts to their borough controls, and then on to group control. Group control records are found among LCC and MCC records in London Metropolitan Archives in the form of daily log books, damage logs and situation reports of which the following is an example from LCC/CD/WAR/4/7: '9 March 1941 Situation at 6.00hrs. Pt.1 This was the worst raid since early January but was not on the scale of many last year. London was at the alert from 1948 to 0003. All groups and 55 local authorities were affected but the main weight of the attack fell on the centre of London... The worst single incident occurred at the Café de Paris, where so far 34 dead and 80 casualties taken to hospital have been reported.' Middlesex group has comparable material in MCC/CD/WAR/1. MCC/CD/WAR/1/2 is the Logbook of Air Raid Incidents, 1939–45, for Brentford and Chiswick. There are the usual columns for date, message time, incident time, particulars, and remarks. The entry for September 8 1944 records what turned out to be the first V2 hit: 'Confirmation of verbal phone message — no siren. Brentford report something has fallen in Staveley Road, Chiswick — we do not know at present what it was'. Services were sent, then 'Brentford think that explosion was caused by "Fly" — this is not definite — large blast area'. 'Report no sound of approach — deep & wide crater approx. 18 feet deep by about 30 ft. diameter — 8 houses demolished, others seriously damaged. Area of blast damage not as great as in "Fly" incidents.'

Finally, the whole picture is summarised in the Ministry of Home Security's Daily Intelligence Reports, in PRO HO 203. They comprise a two-part form, headed 'Secret', summarising the home situation in general and then region by region. A typical entry from HO 203/4 reads 'No. 728 1 Sept. 1940. London. STEPNEY. Between 21.43 and 22.10 hours both HE and IB were dropped, a few of them before the Red Warning was given. The Mile End Road was blocked in 3 places and gas mains were damaged. STEPNEY GREEN. Underground station was exposed by a crater. 3 persons, so far as is known at present, were killed and 15 admitted to hospital. 157 other people received slight injuries'. These reports are factual records, rarely containing any comment on public morale or reactions to incidents. Such information emerges, however, from Mass-Observation reports which record a wealth of detail about public reaction to the raids. M-O file 364 'Metropolitan Air Raids', for example, analysed thirty detailed reports from full-time investigators in August 1940. People were getting used to taking shelter, but some still refused to go. 'There is a great deal of latent antagonism against ARP personnel...' Mass-Observation sent its reporters out after raids throughout the war. M-O file 575, for instance, concerns reactions to a sudden bombing in Hendon in February 1941, after a lull. File TC/23/9/N, on air raids in London, contains lengthy 'Notes on the behaviour of the inhabitants of Ridgmount Gardens and Gordon Mansions WC1 during the heavy raid on the night of April 16 1941', by RF, 17/4/41. M-O 2121 is a survey of attitudes to pilotless planes in 1944 including direct quotations — 'Wicked I call it. It seems uncanny too — nobody up in them — I don't like it at all'; 2207 is about South London in February 1945 after many V2 attacks. Some people were terrified, others fatalistic. Most Londoners noticed only what happened in areas very close to home. One old lady told the observer, 'The rockets, dearie? I can't say I've ever noticed them.' P.M.F. Bishop, at Guy's Hospital, noticed them but shrugged them off: 'At last the Germans had invented a missile against which no precautions whatsoever could be taken. This was a great relief to everyone: there was to be no more of the ducking and diving under tables that had characterised the flying bomb era' (*Guy's Hospital Gazette* n.s. 59 (1945) p.179).

### Bomb censuses

The Ministry of Home Security's Research Department compiled bomb censuses to assess damage caused by types of explosive and to improve protection for the public. The papers are in PRO HO 198, including, for example, /18 on damage to Region 5 as a result of piloted aircraft January to April 1943 and /79 about flying bombs, 12/13–18 June 1944. The original data on which this was based sometimes survives in local authority collections. Finchley, for instance, kept an occurrence analysis book, 1940–5, now in Barnet Archives MS 9215/8, in the form of an exercise book listing on the left page: date, occurrence number, sector number, position of occurrence and ongoing totals, while the right page carried columns for HE, IB, PG, N/PG, OB, XAA, UXAA, UXB, PM, UXPM, MISC.

### Bomb damage maps

Maps of varying types are useful for pinpointing bomb sites and damage. Most boroughs maintained one for their area, sticking in map pins of different colours to indicate the kind of bomb that had fallen. Barnet's copy, for example, pins still intact, is kept with their archives. A wider area is covered by the set of bomb damage maps in the LMA collection. There are 150 sheets of them, shaded in a palette of seven colours from black — total destruction — to yellow — minor damage — with different sized rings marking V1 and V2 damage. The scale is 1:25,000. Similar maps are held for Middlesex, and the Guildhall Library has equivalents for the City.

### Personal experiences

Some wardens published their experiences later; there are examples in the bibliography. Unpublished ones survive, too. Hackney Archives' T.E. Browne's diaries, D/F/BRO/1–7, mentioned above, flesh out his formal incident reports, giving insights into the way the system operated from day to day. In 1944 an ARP messenger, W.E. Hall, kept a diary of 'The New Blitz. Written 3 weeks after it began...', in Hackney AD M4472. A lively teenager, he decorated the cover of his folder with a sketch of a messenger with his feet up, smoking and reading the paper. He encountered action on 30 June: '12.30 hours. After having lunch

SECRET

SECRET

MINISTRY OF HOME SECURITY

RESEARCH AND EXPERIMENTS DEPARTMENT

Incident at Gurney Street 6th June 1942

At 21.30 hours on 6th June 1942, an explosion occurred among tenement dwellings in Gurney Street, Southwark, and caused casualties and damage. The explosion was traced to a "G" mine which had fallen in May 1941.

Casualties.

　　　　　　18 dead
　　　　　　62 seriously injured
　　　　　　72 slightly injured

Damage.

The damage is indicated on the attached map, and illustrated in the photographs.

"A" damage　(red)　　4　- houses completely demolished
"B"　　"　　(blue)　 4　- houses beyond repair
"C"　　"　(yellow)　20　- houses severely damaged but repairable
"D"　　"　(green)　　　- houses inhabitable but requiring repairs to remedy serious inconveniences (not completely to be differentiated from previous damage).

The maximum distances for the various grades of damage were:-

　　A = 50 ft.　　B = 80 ft.　　C = 170 ft.　　D　360 ft.
while glass was broken up to 670 ft.

The equivalent radii for the various grades of damage, i.e. allowing for that in different directions were:-

　　A = 37 ft.　　B = 55 ft.　　C = 111 ft.　　D　226 ft.

In previously reported incidents due to "G" mines the following are the ranges of equivalent radii

　　A = 38-107 ft. B = 105-146 ft. C = 197-314 ft.

It will be seen therefore that the amount of damage is much less

Home Security researchers investigate the damage done by a late-exploding bomb
*(PRO HO 207/26)*

I was walking along the Strand with a pal when we heard the noise of a Flying Bomb. It went almost over our heads and then "cut out". We waited for the crash. It came, the column of dust and smoke seemed to be in the Regent St Region. So I went over to it. Eventually I found it, it had landed at the Regent Palace Hotel...' He reported to the Incident Officer and was given the job of roping off the street. Further diaries and memoirs by London ARP personnel are in the IWM's Document collections; these include the Revd. J.G.Markham's memoir of his time as an ARP post warden at his parish in Walworth, in 91/5/1. IWM also holds two extensive collections of full and informative personal letters written by Mea Allan and John Hughes, war correspondents who worked through the 1940–41Blitz.

ARP report centre and post staff also feature among the interviewees in oral history collections, such as Naomi Wolff's interview on NSA 609/03/01 C1, talking about her work as an air raid warden in Hammersmith. The Museum of London's collection of tapes made in connection with the *Making of Modern London* television programmes includes one in which the victim of an air raid remembers the incident, and a contemporary recording on NSA T8186/03 TR1 C3 allows a London woman to tell her bomb story.

## *Air raid shelters*

The anticipated danger from air attack, though it proved over-pessimistic, necessitated easy public access to secure shelters. Public shelters, especially those in the tube stations, have lodged indelibly in the collective memory, but in fact they were used by only a minority of Londoners. In the early days of the Blitz it was calculated that about one in seven people used the public shelters, and that number soon dropped. Many more sheltered fairly safely at home or at work. There is detailed information about all aspects of sheltering in London in Terence O'Brien's *Civil Defence*. PRO CAB 102/31 contains some of the notes on shelters used in O'Brien's published book, and can provide extra information.

### *Home shelters*

Londoners with gardens were supplied with 'Anderson' shelters of metal, half-buried in the soil, and proof against most damage short of a direct hit. Later in the war 'Morrison' shelters, strong metal cages big enough to take a large mattress, became available for indoor use. There were other solutions too. The Museum of London's ephemera collection has an advertisement dating from the earliest days of the war offering to convert garages into shelters by installing a tubular structure inside, padded all round with sandbags. The illustration is headed 'Gar-raid [sic] shelters, 42 Station Parade, Willesden Green NW2'. Paul Vaughan's father converted a spare room in their suburban semi with sandbags and strengthened walls — 'With bunk beds installed for all the family it would look like nothing so much as a dug-out in a quiet sector of the line around 1917...' (*Something in Linoleum*, (1994) p. 56). People quickly evolved a routine. When the siren sounded they seized children, pets and a waiting bag of necessities — thermos, snack, book, cards, knitting — and hurried to the basement, Anderson or Morrison shelter until the all clear sounded. Published and unpublished letters, memoirs, diaries, photographs and oral history tapes are the chief sources of information about this kind of sheltering.

### *Work shelters*

Institutions with more than fifty employees were legally responsible for providing them, and any customers or other visitors, with shelters, usually in converted basements. Department stores, business firms, government departments, shops and hotels equipped 'refuges' sometimes of considerable comfort. A visitor from the London and North Eastern Railway was very impressed by the Westminster Bank headquarters' advance arrangements in June 1938: 'You must, I am sure, have the best equipped shelters in London or elsewhere. We, unfortunately, have a tremendous area to cover and will have to forego all luxuries' (NatWest Group Archives 06854, Lothbury Office, files of ARP department). Banks had a head start in the provision of basement shelters, already having secure strong room accommodation on their premises, though they had to be careful in allowing too ready access to it for security reasons. Holborn Council tried to insist that thirty-three staff from the offices above a Westminster Bank branch should share the bank's shelter. 'As a principle — NO', wrote the manager firmly across the letter, now kept in Westminster Bank folder 'ARP suggestions 1938' in the NatWest Group Archives.

Factories had their own shelters. In Poplar, the match manufacturer Bryant and May's shelters could accommodate 500. Some institutional 'refuges' were extremely large, and would admit the general public as well as their own staff. Freemasons' Hall, near Covent Garden, had room for 1500 in comparative comfort. Like other shelters, it had its share of eccentrics, like the flamboyantly dressed Chinese man described by the Grand Secretary in a letter of September 1939: 'I cannot even describe his hat, but his only criticism of our arrangements is that we have no cocktail bar! There is a lady ARP warden who has been attached to us here (I am trying to get her transferred) and the Chinaman announced that he did not think she was a normal being, and that opinion was shared by others...' (Freemasons' Hall library, folder 'War and Freemasonry').

Clergy offered their church crypts as shelters, with the Archbishop of Canterbury setting an example at Lambeth Palace. Its crypt could take 'some 200 people — who rush in when the siren sounds like frightened sheep, but they are marvellously quiet and good humoured, and try to sleep fitfully', wrote Archbishop Lang (Lambeth Palace Library. Lang Papers Notebook transcripts 223 Notebook A f.265). The six vaults beneath St Martin-in-the-Fields in Trafalgar Square, for 600 people, made an excellent shelter. Some were less successful. The crypt shelter at Christ Church, Cubitt Town on the Isle of Dogs, quickly became notorious. It was investigated by the Ministry of Health. Their inspector wrote a memo: 'I visited the crypt of Christ Church, Cubitt Town with Dr Miller, the Deputy MOH, on Wednesday May 28th. This shelter is not a public shelter and for some considerable time the Town Clerk has exercised all his powers to close it, even appealing to the Bishop of London. The former vicar encouraged the people to use the shelter and when informed by the Council that it was not safe, his reply was that "the prayers offered up each evening by the shelterers and their friends all over the world were sufficient protection" ... The shelter itself is filthy and full of the most revolting bedding which is supported on old wood... There is only one entrance, a trap door in the porch of the church and the crypt is reached by a rickety ladder which is in complete darkness. Altogether the shelter is most unsuitable both from a medical and a security point of view and should in my humble opinion be closed as soon as possible'. The file contains a copy of the letter sent to the vicar requiring him to prevent access to the crypt, in PRO MH 76/590. The use of church crypts as shelters is further documented in PRO HO 207/422.

Even natural caves were used as shelters. The owners of Chislehurst caves opened them for this use early in the war, and they were later taken over by the local authority. Bromley Council minutes and papers dealing with this are with Bromley Central Library. They proved a popular refuge for thousands of Londoners through the war. A similar use of Blackheath caves is documented in PRO HO 207/977.

## Public sheltering

'Public' sheltering is well-documented at national and local level, and through the records of the London Passenger Transport Board and of the voluntary bodies. Londoners without garden space for Anderson shelters, and with no access to safe basement areas in their houses or blocks of flats — and this mainly meant those from the poorer areas — had little alternative other than to use public shelters as a matter of routine. They would be joined there by passers-by caught in an alert.

## Public shelters: national records

Shelter construction and provision became the responsibility of 'O' division of the Ministry of Home Security, operating through the Ministry of Works. Among the most useful PRO classes are the Intelligence branch files in HO 199, the Tube shelter committee files in HO 200, the Daily and weekly war room reports in HO 202, 'O' division papers in HO 205, Techical advisers' files in HO 206, CD Regional files, especially the Shelter progress reports at HO 207/365–83 and the Borough series, HO 207/504–1032) and files on ARP and CD matters in WORK 28. The Borough series in HO 207/504–1032 is very detailed. HO 207/653, for instance, concerns the adaptation of the disused British Museum tube station as a shelter, /662 reports on Arsenal Football stadium. The Ministry of Health dealt with the regulation of the shelters, especially the public health aspects. Its classes on Special wartime functions, at HLG 7, and on Emergency Medical services, in MH 76, contain a great deal on London shelters. Both Ministries worked through local government, so considerable information about borough arrangements may occur in both national and local government records. Home Office files at HO 45 contain useful material, HO 45/18548, for example, has details of approved designs for trench shelters.

When planning shelters, the authorities had expected short but devastating daylight raids. They had not expected people to spend whole nights sheltering, so little attention had been given to supplying proper sanitation, sleeping arrangements or food. The Blitz, continuing night after night, made these omissions very evident. Conditions in some public shelters, like the notorious Tilbury shelter, a railway goods yard in Stepney taking 14–16,000 people nightly in the Blitz, were disgusting.

People felt safest deep underground, and the easiest way to get there was to use the underground railway system, the 'tube'. The government's initial reluctance to permit the use of the stations as shelters is well known, and documented in HO 186/149 for instance, but it was overcome early in the Blitz by determined Londoners who simply bought a ticket and occupied platform space for the night. Backing down, the authorities co-operated with the London Passenger Transport Board to organise a proper system. Shelter wardens, sanitation, bunks, bedding stores, first aid centres, canteens, cleaning and even occasional entertainment were provided, though many of these improvements had to wait until the Blitz ended.

Generally speaking, public shelters performed well, preserving thousands of lives in the course of the war. There were some disasters, usually the result of direct hits, like the Bank station hit in January 1941 and Bullivants' shelter on the Isle of Dogs, hit in March 1941. One of the worst death tolls, however, was not directly caused by enemy action. One hundred and seventy-three people were crushed to death as they hurried down the dimly-lit stairs at Bethnal Green underground shelter on 3 March 1943. A woman tripped and the others fell on top of her. The accident was investigated by the Dunne enquiry, whose published report,

Cmd 6583, concluded that its cause was a loss of self-control by members of the public in a particularly unfortunate time and place. The published report is itself very detailed, but papers relating to it in PRO HO 205 and HO 206, reveal even more about the conduct of public shelters and the events of that night. HO 205/228, for example, includes statements from eye witnesses. HO 205/231 contains correspondence about the rumours, mainly anti-semitic, that quickly surrounded the incident. Tower Hamlets Local History Library and Archives holds the minutes and correspondence of the Bethnal Green Shelter Accident Fund, 1944–54, set up to help the victims' families, at BG 1028–32. Reginald Baker was an eyewitness; his taped recollections of the incident are in the IWM Sound Archive, on 6498/7.

*Public shelters: Ministry of Home Security and Ministry of Health records*

From January 1941 a new London Regional Commissioner, Charles Key, was put in charge of shelter arrangements on behalf of both the responsible Ministries. Ministry of Health files are particularly informative about shelters, especially Emergency Medical Services, MH 76, which includes files of borough reports. Ministry inspectors co-operated with the borough Medical Officers of Health to ensure sanitation, ventilation, heating, equipment and order in the shelters These reports and files have information on relations with the different local authorities and about individual shelters. Kensington's file, MH 76/586, for instance, contains detailed, handwritten forms giving accounts of lighting, water supply, any clothes-drying facilities, how many lavatories were available, and who emptied them, the 'social type' of the shelter — mostly 'working class' here — the proportion of women and children, of aged and infirm, how many bunks, their estimated capacity and actual occupancy, and whether a ticket system operated. The results of a census taken at Notting Hill Gate tube station on 21 November 1940 were relayed to the Ministry. The census gives details of the shelterers that night by age and sex, where they were from, whether they had used that shelter regularly since September, or since October, their reasons for not using surface or other shelters near home — 'Do not feel safe'; 'nervous case'; 'too noisy' they replied — the reasons why children had not been evacuated earlier, and whether parents would now be willing to consider it.

Kensington's file is a thick one, and the Ministry was impressed by the borough's efforts. The file for Poplar, MH 76/590, is far thinner. It reveals that in 1941 the borough's Medical Officer of Health was on long-term sick leave so the Ministry had to deal with his deputy. He was reluctant to put first aid posts into shelters, saying it would be 'well-nigh impossible to obtain doctors and nurses', and objected anyway to inspecting shelters which he thought a job for sanitary inspectors not medical officers. Bethnal Green, MH 76/580, had very bad conditions in its tube and railway arch shelters. A confidential handwritten report from a Ministry official mentions that the borough's MOH is 'rather lazy, but quite good to deal with and gets a move on when he decides to do anything. Does not seem to worry about consulting his committee'. All these files have a great deal of detailed material on borough matters, including disputes over pay rates and conditions of employment of first aid staff.

Liaison between the Ministries of Home Security and Health and the London Passenger Transport Board over tube shelters was necessarily very close, and some of the material is duplicated in each collection. MH 76/553 deals with financial arrangements with the LPTB over tube shelters, /557 is general correspondence with the Board. As might be expected, London Transport's archive has preserved more of the related technical plans and reports, and, for example, details of their 'food trains' that brought refreshments to the tube

Progress Report.

**Boroughs of Poplar and Lewisham.**

I have visited all types of shelters in both boroughs. On most occasions I was accompanied by the M.O.H. of the borough and on one by the Deputy Chief Warden.

**Poplar.**

The M.O.H. is away ill and his deputy, Dr. Mitchell, has not visited many shelters. The policy in Poplar is to concentrate on the smaller shelters and make them more attractive.

**Ventilation.**

In most of them this is very deficient.

**Overcrowding.**

The large basement shelters are grossly overcrowded, the trench shelters almost empty.

**Medical Aid Posts.**

Nil. The D.M.O.H. will now consider introducing these and has arranged to meet the local Doctors to start a group system.

There are no nurses available but I have advised the M.O.H. that a circular will shortly be issued.

**Special Difficulties.**

There is no person officially in charge of the shelters and the Chief Warden complains that the number of Inspectors is so high that one of his staff is almost constantly employed accompanying them.

**Lewisham.**

The general remarks also apply to this borough. The trench shelters are so damp that two of them, intended

/to.

to accommodate 400 each are entirely empty and . in.. ded to accommodate 3,000 only had 400 people in it.

There are now no shelters with over 500 occupants but the M.O.H. proposes to open a Medical Aid Post in a particularly bad one with 400 people in it.

There have been several cases of diphtheria and I have urged immunisation of the children in the shelters.

(Signed) D.M. LLEWELLIN

15.11.40.

A Ministry of Health inspector reports on local air raid shelters
*(PRO MH 76/590)*

shelterers. LPTB also adapted parts of the underground network for use as munitions factories and government departments. The Photograph Library at the London Transport Museum has a large collection illustrating all aspects of the operation of their many underground shelters.

### Public shelters: health concerns

Public health questions were of serious concern to the Ministry of Health. Two of their chief worries were the spread of respiratory disease in the crowded conditions, and of vermin infestation. MH 76/538 deals with vermin in London Region tube shelters, especially bed bugs, brought in with insanitary bedding. Mosquitos infested certain stations, breeding out of season in the fetid conditions. MH 76/546 contains the long-running story of attempts to eliminate them with the help of malaria experts.

Sanitation caused problems. At first most shelters only had minimal lavatory provision, usually buckets behind canvas screens. They soon overflowed and smelled. Shelter photographs from the Bill Brandt set show scenes of overflowing latrines and lavatory pails, with staff mopping the messy floor. Boroughs providing better facilities attracted shelterers from outside their own area. MH 76/586 reveals that in October 1940 the Emergency Committee on Kensington Public Shelters complained that people from the ill-provided tube shelters in the next borough, Paddington, were coming to Notting Hill Gate 'to use the better amenities. There is often a queue 50 yards long, practically on the edge of the platform. Although 12 of the chemical closets were emptied at 11pm yesterday, the whole of the lavatory accommodation was full and in fact overflowing by 7am today...'

When shelter conditions became severe during the continuing Blitz, the government appointed a small committee, chaired by Lord Horder, to look into the problem. They found that overcrowding was the chief difficulty, recommended cleansing routines, the provision of proper sanitary and first aid facilities, and instituted regular inspections and the appointment of shelter marshals in the larger shelters to help communications. The Committee's reports were published in late 1940 as Cmd 6234 and Cmd 6245.

Insights into the Horder Committee's workings emerge from the papers of two Ministry advisers, J.R. Hutchinson and W.H. Bradley, in the collection of the Contemporary Medical Archives Centre at the Wellcome Institute in PP/JRH. These doctors were concerned with the prevention of respiratory tract infections including investigating the efficacy — or otherwise — of protective masks. PP/JRH/B.103 contains some of their findings. The 'ridicule factor' restricted the use of hygienic masks according to Dr Bradley, who recalled jeers like 'What — yer frightened of being gassed?' and 'E's a snob — afraid of the smell'. Harrods advertised a 'fashionable yashmak' for the smarter shelterer, but it did not catch on. Technical detail on shelter bacteriology, with results of swab tests, is contained in a general file on the Epidemiology in Shelters Sub-committee in CMAC PP/JRH/B.107, and further reports on the use of germ masks in shelters are in PRO MH 76/547.

### Public shelters: local authority records

Local authorities built and ran public shelters in their area at the direction of the Ministries of Home Security and Health. Council minutes and committee papers contain information about all aspects of shelter provision and administration. By October 1939, for instance, Acton MBC discovered that its rudimentary trench shelters, dug at the time of the Munich crisis, were flooding badly. Its Emergency ARP Committee authorised the purchase of three electric pumps at £150 each because 'Water had accumulated to a depth varying from 3'6" to 2' in the public shelters at the Wesley Playing Fields, North Acton Playing Fields and the Green, East Acton' (20 October). Borough records usually have lists of public shelters in their area, at different stages through the war. Kensington's, for example, are subdivided by type — basement, trench, surface and mews shelters. Plans are sometimes extant. Shelters in the City gained a reputation for being particularly safe, and people travelled from other parts of London to sleep there. This placed an additional burden on the Corporation's Cleansing Department, soon noted by Common Council's ARP Committee minutes in December 1940 (CLRO C20). Other local authority records which may yield material on shelters are ARP records, because the ARP supplied shelter wardens, financial records of the catering arrangements, and welfare files as some boroughs appointed shelter welfare officers. In some cases, these officers set up shelter welfare committees including representatives of voluntary organisations. In addition, many of the large shelters organised their own informal committees, producing shelter minutes like *The Swiss Cottager*, and the *Warren Mag* which survive in borough collections. The LCC ran shelter evening classes, 464 of them by February 1941. The most popular subjects were current events, travel talks, community singing, first aid, needlework, and knitting.

*Public shelters: work of the voluntary bodies*

Voluntary organisations, such as the WVS, the Red Cross and the Salvation Army, became involved in several kinds of welfare work in the air raid shelters. The first priority was food. In the first days of the Blitz food provision was haphazard, later the Ministry of Food set up a Shelter Feeding Branch to coordinate the work. The Salvation Army was

Magazine compiled by and for tube shelterers
*(Camden Local Studies and Archives Centre)*

among several voluntary groups invited to undertake an experiment in supplying this need. A typed memorandum in the SA Heritage Centre's box 'Army Work', folder 'Wartime. General', describes the experiment. They were allocated seven shelters of varying types, mostly in South London but also including the arches at Liverpool Street Station, and later the notorious Tilbury shelter. 'The condition of these places and the morale of the people is, to say the least, not good', they reported in October 1940. The experiment worked well, the greatest demand everywhere came between 6–9 pm, when many men came straight from work and needed more than just a snack. So they provided meat pies and the like. In the mornings, from 4.45–8 am, the demand was mainly for tea and biscuits. The memo gives figures for tea/cake/meat pie/biscuit and small cake consumption at the various shelters and notes that 90% of the shelterers used the canteens.

The success of the voluntary experiment led many London boroughs to take over this provision, sometimes using commercial firms to provide the catering for them, sometimes organising their own. The Bill Brandt photographs at the MOL and the IWM include shots of shelterers queueing for food. 8806 shows a food counter at a North London shelter selling sausage rolls, buns and tea; 8811 is a West End basement shelter canteen with two women in charge, one is washing up in a bowl of dirty water. Commercial cafés also geared themselves to the new demand; a photograph in George Rodger's *The Blitz* (1990) shows the Woodstock Street Snack Bar and Continental Buffet just off Oxford Street and next door to an air raid shelter, offering an 'Air Raid Breakfast' for 1/8d.

Voluntary welfare groups began to provide amusements and advice services in the shelters. Initially, the Ministry of Home Security was wary of allowing organised entertainment in case it encouraged even more people to use the shelters, but they bowed to the inevitable and set up a Central Advisory Committee on Entertainment and Instruction, later the Welfare Advisory Conference, for the London area with representatives from national and local government. A full-time CD Regional Welfare Officer for London was appointed in 1941 from the WVS. Information about the WVS' shelter work can be found among its own archives, but also in PRO HO 207/388. Among the diversions offered in some shelters were library collections, discussion groups, children's storytelling, play centres and youth clubs.

*Public shelters: Mass-Observation*

Mass-Observation's ubiquitous observers made detailed notes in the shelters. Folder 5/A of the M-O's London Survey contains a report on all-night shelterers in the underground on 17 September 1940. The observer began work at Piccadilly underground station, moving on to other stations by train. At Piccadilly at 8 pm 'Only about 2% were already attempting to sleep in a sitting or doubled-position. Of the others some 46% were reading (mostly evening papers), some 14% eating (apples seemed favourites) and some 20% of the women knitting'. This file also contains handwritten or typewritten responses to questionnaires on topics like the effects of air raids on leisure activity, reading habits, and sleep patterns. Some give the addresses of respondents. In spite of continuing official endeavours, conditions in tube shelters remained unpleasant. M-O 2121, the V1 survey, contains a report from an M-O observer in the summer of 1944: 'I was coming home at 11 o'clock last night and my God, the tube! How people can stand it all night I can't conceive; I felt quite sick and faint with it just standing waiting for my train. It was packed with people. You could cut the air with a knife'. The writer is described in M-O shorthand as F 30 B, that is female, aged 30 and of social class B.

*Public shelters: discipline*

ARP shelter marshals, or shelter wardens, were responsible for keeping order. They were identified by a white armband with black lettering and a tin hat with the initials 'SM'. Many were part-time, though some larger shelters had paid full-timers. Among the IWM Sound Archive collection are some marshals' memories. Mrs Rennie, on IWM 2335/D/B, recalls her work as a part-time warden in an unnamed East End shelter, and her horror at first seeing the crowd staggering and fighting its way in. The state of the shelter was deplorable — 'it hit you in the face', with inadequate sanitation and water streaming down the walls. She recalls the difficulty of getting children to settle for sleep while adults were still moving about. Mrs Rennie used to bribe them with sweets, bought with a levy of 1 d per adult, offering a sweet for the first one ready for bed. The wardens operated under Defence Regulation 23AB which empowered them to give instructions to shelterers, and eject trouble-makers. Dolly Rolph, on IWM 2336/D/C was a deputy warden in shelters in the Bethnal Green area. She describes discipline problems. Some of the shelterers brought a piano in and began to have noisy singsongs after the pubs closed, keeping others awake. Failing to persuade them to be more considerate, she had to ask the local council to bring in regulations to restrict noise. They were 'lively times', she says.

*Public shelters: visual representations*

Among the best known visual representations of air raid shelters are the photographs taken by Bill Brandt and a colleague in the late autumn of the Blitz. They visited shelters of all types, from the 'Hungerford Club' at the Embankment, particularly used by down and outs, to peaceful, comfortable West End department store 'refuges' and all the variations in between. The photographs show people passing the time in many ways — reading, knitting, talking, joining in singsongs and, of course, trying to sleep. Other useful sources are the great number of MOI photographs, usually taken to publicise new amenities, such as first aid centres — the one at Notting Hill Gate was a showpiece — or to show shelterers being entertained by big stars such as George Formby. Newsreels also liked to feature such scenes. Tube station shelters are covered very thoroughly in the London Transport Museum photograph collection. Drawings and paintings of shelter life can convey a vivid impression of the feel of the time. Henry Moore's famous series of drawings of huddled figures sleeping on tube platforms are perhaps the best known, but the IWM paintings collection has examples by several other artists including Edward Ardizzone and John Farleigh.

*Public shelters: personal recollections*

Like evacuation, sheltering made a great impression on the individual memory and there are plenty of published and unpublished memoirs, diaries and oral history tapes recalling the experience. Some were written soon after the event, others many years later. The IWM collection contains numerous examples, including a description of the organisation, routine and conditions in a shelter during an air raid in 1943 or 1944 in Misc. 167 (2546) and a six year old's letter to his grandfather, written in a Blackfriars shelter in 1940, describing the sights and sounds around him, in 88/49/1. Anthony Heap enjoyed the regular shelter entertainment. 'Went round to the weekly BMA shelter concert in the evening, co-shelterer Collins and the two curates from St Pancras Church being the star turns. A lively affair', he wrote on 16 January 1941 (LMA ACC 2243/15/1). Interviewees talk about shelters, among many other topics, in the *Making of Modern London* television programme tapes held at the Museum of London.

## *Firefighting*

It was clear to the Home Office that fire would be one of the great hazards of enemy attack and that extra resources would be needed to cope with it, especially in London. The London Fire Brigade, controlled by the LCC, already had a long history since its origins in the 1830s. Middlesex had twenty-six local authority fire brigades, which became part of the London Region under emergency wartime organisation. To supplement the personnel of all these brigades, volunteers were recruited for the Auxiliary Fire Service from early 1938. They were organised on a local basis, by borough. After some months of the phoney war, during which complaints about comparative terms of service, pay and accommodation in the two services had surfaced, the LFB and the AFS in London were amalgamated. However, when the Blitz started it became apparent that still more efficient national co-ordination of the service was vital, so in 1941 the government set up the National Fire Service. In Greater London this meant the London Fire Brigade merging with suburban fire services, like Hornsey, and Tottenham, to become the London Region of the National Fire Service.

### *National records*

The chief national sources for this topic lie among the Home Office records in the PRO, particularly with the London Region Fire Service papers in HO 209 and the reports of bomb damage in HO 197. Terence O'Brien's *Civil Defence* volume in the *History of the Second World War* series contains detailed information about fire services, especially in London. Drafts and notes for this section of the volume are preserved in CAB 102/294 and may provide extra information. Records of the Fire Brigades Union, at the Modern Records Centre of the University of Warwick, can add a further dimension to the picture.

The London Fire and Civil Defence Authority (LFCDA) retains some committee papers of the Fire Brigade for the early part of the war, and has a card index of members of the NFS and the AFS. Their museum also has some wartime records and memorabilia, and their separate photographic library has material from this period. But for the daily record of wartime fire-fighting, the bulk of the information will come from the London Fire Brigade records in LMA.

### *The London Fire Brigade records*

There are four main kinds of record: LFB fire reports, daily fire returns from the LFB and Engineers' Dept., records of the Regional Fire Control Room, and London Region situation reports. LCC/FB/WAR/2/49, for instance, is a bound volume of air raid fire reports covering just one very bad day, 11 May 1941 in 'B' district, which covered a wide area of central London including the West End, the Barbican, Fleet Street, Camden Town, Kentish Town and Holloway. It consists of typed forms giving details of the time the Brigade was called, by whom, to what address, the apparent cause of the fire, how many appliances were needed, and whether there were any casualties. These reports were incorporated into returns for the whole London area, like LCC/FB/WAR/3/8, 'Returns of fires and other occurrences due to enemy action attended by or reported to the Fire Service'. These reports cover twenty-four hour periods up to midnight, and were classified 'secret'. Their length varies, the one for the same bad night of 10–11 May 1941 occupies seventy-

Damage to local businesses recorded in the Fire Brigade's air raid fire reports
*(LMA FB/WAR/2/49)*

four typed pages, others might only report one brief incident. They are arranged by fire service area and give the time of the call, the address, name of the occupier, type of business, the supposed cause of the fire, such as IB, or EB, damage caused, and any other particulars. On Saturday 10 May 1941, for example, the brigade was called to the British Museum: '23.52 Museum St WC1. British Museum (Office of Works) I.B. A range of buildings of 2 and 3 floors & basement covering an area of 900x600 feet (used as exhibition rooms and galleries); about one-sixth of buildings and contents severely damaged by fire and part of roof off, rest of buildings and contents damaged by heat, smoke and water'. Casualties are noted, and named if they were LFB personnel. This data was then sent to the Home Office where it was used to prepare the broader area reports found in HO 209. LCC Fire Brigade and Main Drainage Committee Papers can also be informative. Those covering 1941–2, such as LCC/MIN 6211 for instance, have reports on the damage to Soho Fire Station where the officer in charge had lost his living quarters and possessions and negotiations were under way with the valuer on 11 October 1940, as well as containing a report on the supply of emergency fireboats dated 22 January 1941. Other items include arrangements for a Christmas broadcast from Whitechapel Fire Station, a negligence claim brought by a woman who tripped over loose sandbags outside a fire post, gallantry awards, invalidity claims, complaints and misconduct cases, and inventories of equipment. Stray items sometimes surface in other collections, The IWM Department of Documents, for example, has two manuscript logbooks kept at a fire station near the City from May–September 1940 in Misc.4 (48), and the papers of an auxiliary fireman, R.F. Coster, with his drill book, training notes and other items associated with his service. A monument recording the names of London firefighters who lost their lives in the war stands in Sermon Lane, near St Paul's cathedral.

Some large commercial firms and other institutions had their own fire-fighting teams. The Palace of Westminster was one, and here security was an important extra consideration as the firemen needed access to all parts of both Houses of Parliament. House of Lords RO file FW/8 gives the names of ARP firemen submitted for vetting to Scotland Yard in 1942–4, while FW/4 contains correspondence, rejections, and refusals relating to firemen at the Palace, 1942–4. Applications were invited from NFS firemen recently discharged on health grounds. Many attended for interview, others wrote that they were still too sick to take up work again, or that they had found other employment. Personal information emerges: 'I am afraid in my present condition I shall be unable to accept any position for some considerable time. Thanks to the perfect food in the National Fire Service I now have a Duodenal Ulcer...'

*Personal memories*

The bibliography contains memoirs from several wartime firefighters, and unpublished ones may be found in some collections. The Department of Documents at the IWM has several accounts or diaries by serving firemen, including a description of firefighting through the Blitz by F. Hurd, who was killed in a raid at the end of December 1940; their Sound Archive also has tapes of wartime firefighters, such as Maurice Richardson on 2340/B/B and Margaret Jacobs on 5342/1. John Horner was a fireman at the Hampstead Fire Station from 1933; on tape C609/13/01 C1 in the National Sound Archive's Labour oral history project series he criticises the station's old-style organisation which only changed with the formation of the AFS, and describes his Blitz service and his work as General Secretary of the Fire Brigades Union. Kensington LS has 'South Ken Station' an illustrated memoir written by John Ivey in 1977, remembering his AFS days at LAFS 8-X sub station from 1939. In the Blitz his group was sent all over London, and his description of the ensuing confusion over lines of command illustrates why the government needed to nationalise the system. Ivey was a journalist. Many other professionals also chose to volunteer for the fire service, writers and artists being particularly well represented. There were so many artists in the service that regular exhibitions of their work were staged. Their paintings illustrate fire station life in periods of quiet as well as of action, and include portraits of firefighters and other station personnel. William Sansom's *Jim Braidy, The Story of Britain's Firemen* (1943) reproduces some examples.

*Films*

The LFB passed over all the film of its wartime activities to the IWM Film and Video Archive for preservation, and the collection is accessible through the IWM. Some understanding of the dangers faced by wartime firemen is conveyed by Fire Brigade film footage such as LFB 53 which shows the terrible fire on the City and Southwark on the night of 29–30 December 1940. One hundred thousand incendiaries, an experimental and extremely destructive German weapon, were dropped over four and a half hours. One thousand five hundred appliances, were involved, sixteen firemen were killed and over 250 people injured. Part of the film was shot by the Army Film Unit from the roof of St Paul's cathedral. It also shows the control room at work, firemen receiving medical attention, despatch riders taking messages, and finally the smoking ruins the next morning. Before the bombing started, firemen had suffered the widespread opprobrium attached to ARP personnel, apparently hanging about doing nothing and getting well paid for it. The terrible conditions and danger they faced during the Blitz turned them into popular heroes, assisted by the feature films *Fires*

*Were Started* (1943), a dramatised documentary using some real firefighters, and *The Bells Go Down* (1943), with actors, including the popular comedian Tommy Trinder.

*Fires Were Started* caused the Ministry of Information considerable anxiety. As first shot it was too long and had to be severely cut. The Ministry feared that the public would not differentiate between the old volunteer days of the AFS depicted in the film, and the new era of National Fire Service professionalism. Details of the lengthy negotiations between the Ministry and the director will be found in PRO INF 1/212 F256/376/2. Albert Levy worked through the Blitz and was one of the real firemen used in the film. He recorded his memories for the IWM Sound Archive, on tape 11345/2, where he described his training, the early days of the war, and his Blitz experiences including the devastating Rum Quay fire. *Fires Were Started* was made in Wapping during the lull following the Blitz. The firemen found it relieved the monotony, especially as the film unit encouraged them to make free use of the Artichoke pub on expenses.

### Roof spotters and firewatchers

The damage to the City during the great incendiary raid in late 1940 was aggravated by the nature of the business premises there. Larger firms had already organised firewatchers, roof spotters who noted where incendiaries fell and sent colleagues to take some immediate action while the fire brigade was on its way. Small shops, offices and warehouses, of which there were many in the City, were not similarly protected. City property was scarce and expensive; inner courtyards were glassed over for extra space, and quite commonly contained inflammable material. All this meant the incendiaries took hold and wreaked havoc before the firemen could get to them. New regulations were brought in by the Ministry of Home Security on 15 January 1941, obliging local authorities, government departments and others — like the Palace of Westminster — to 'make adequate arrangements for detecting and combating fires' in designated business and industrial districts. Men between sixteen and sixty who lived in the designated areas had to register for possible fire prevention duty. If they worked in the City of London but lived elsewhere, the City's needs took precedence. PRO HO 207/68, for instance, concerns the registration of Civil Servants working in the City for fireguard duties. The new firewatchers were trained by the Fire Brigade, the AFS, or the wardens' service and then joined regular rotas for the work. Documentary evidence survives even in unexpected places. The Jewish Museum, for example, has two 'blue notebooks on wartime fire fighting' in Box 2 WW2 15–1994/10, 11. Their author is unknown, but he or she kept lecture notes on nozzles, sprays, how to deal with incendiary bombs, and how to use breathing apparatus.

The Midland Bank archive's folder 'Blitz stories and war damage', 255/21, contains a brief typescript history of the Guildhall Fire Guards. Two hundred Head Office staff of all grades had joined this unit, recruited by the City Remembrancer early in 1941. Ten squads were formed. They went on duty from 5 pm–9 am every 10th night, for forty-five months. Their Log Book is in the CLRO where Misc. Ms. 229.4 lists the teams on duty every day and notes incidents: 'Friday 14 March 1941. 11.2 pm. Two bombs in the South and a fire in the West. Generally considerable amount of gunfire all around and planes passing over'.

At St Paul's Cathedral the firewatching team attracted a specialist team of architects and surveyors. The architect A.S.G. Butler's letters to his mother are in the Cathedral Library. 'I have in my "gang" C. Farey who is the greatest living architectural draughtsman, a rich and very jolly architect of 60 called Phipps and Edgar Frith, sculptor, who I took in with me, also a quantity surveyor. Some do 2 nights a week but I find one quite enough...',

*3009.*

C O N F I D E N T I A L.                              1.7 FEB 1942

                                        February 17th, 1942.
To the Chairman and Members of the
  A.R.P. Emergency Committee.
-------------------------------------

Mr. Chairman, Madam and Gentlemen,

        F I R E   G U A R D   O R G A N I S A T I O N.

        COMPULSORY ENROLMENT OF PERSONNEL
        FOR BUSINESS PREMISES AND STREET
                  FIRE PARTIES.

BUSINESS PREMISES.

        Although business premises in the Borough are fairly well
covered by the Fire Guard Organisation, the defects experienced
owing to non-raiding are that some of the personnel do not report
dor duty, or, if they do report, are apt to go home when they feel
that the Fire Guard Inspector is not likely to call round.

STREET FIRE PARTIES.

        The general position in the Borough is that enrolments have
been made in 21 out of 37 Wardens' Post Areas.  The other 16 Areas
are being organised as quickly as Reporting Posts can be set-up.

        Of the 21 Post Areas dealt with, working on the basis of
30 houses for every team of three, 6,000 fire watchers are required:
the number enrolled and reporting for duty, however, is 2,000.
1,500 have applied for exemption on medical grounds on Form F.F.2.
and the remainder have either not reported or are engaged on other
Civil Defence duties.

        Briefly, the defects are:-

    (a)  We have no record as to the people who should have
         registered under the Civil Defence Duties (Compulsory
         Enrolment)Order, 1941, and have not done so.  We know
         that there are hundreds of these cases from what
         householders say.

    (b)  Many men, when instructed to report for street fire duty,
         neither acknowledge the receipt of the letter nor report
         for duty.

    (c)  Even when people do report for duty, they learn, after
         a few weeks, that a friend of their's is not doing duty,
         and they drop out.

    (d)  Certain of those who are on Rotas of Duty do not carry-
         out their obligations, but go to bed normally.

    (e)  Although training is given through the Wardens' Service
         and special demonstrations are staged by the Instructors,
         it is not compulsory to attend the training.

        This position of fire watching may be due to a large extent to
lack of air raids: but the picture, though depressing, must be
faced, and it is felt that the scheme as existing will not provide
the fire watching as envisaged.

                I have the honour to be,
                Mr. Chairman, Madam and Gentlemen,
                     Your obedient Servant,

                     C. S. BAINBRIDGE.

                     A.R.P.Controller.

Firewatchers got lazy when there were no air raids. St Pancras Council attempts to remedy the problem.
*(Camden Local Studies and Archives Centre. St Pancras Borough Council ARP Committee Minutes)*

he wrote in September 1939. These distinguished firewatchers entertained each other when off duty with lectures — Gerald Cobb on Wren churches, and on heraldry; W.N. Medlicott on economic warfare, J.D.M. Harvey on 'Aluminium'. A publicity drive to recruit more firewatchers for the cathedral in 1944 yielded an interesting collection of photographs for press issue, showing teams of firewatchers hearing a lecture on the steps to the Listening Gallery, or practising first aid in front of funerary monuments. The IWM Sound Archive's tape 2334/D/A records C.A. Linge, the Clerk of Works at St Paul's, describing firewatching duties there in wartime. Other famous London landmarks were equally concerned about fire risk. A letter in the Westminster Abbey muniments (ARP Correspondence. 61254) documents the abbey's worries about the danger to its roofs and the unfitness of its firefighters, stressing to the Civil Defence authorities in 1940 the need for young, agile men, rather than the middle-aged and elderly ones mainly available.

Across the road, staff at the Palace of Westminster were also obliged to take their turn as firewatchers. This applied to members of both Houses as well as employees. Two boxes at the House of Lords Record Office, numbered FW/1–16, contain Firewatching papers. They include FW/12, a firewatching scheme for the palace in 1941–4, listing the coverage post by post, duties, and pay — 3/- a night from 1941, 4/6d if on duty over 12 hours. FW/14 contains a sick register for 1942 with details of sick leave with pay, and contribution lists for the Christmas dinner fund, in FW/15, reveal what peers and MPs donated towards firewatchers' Christmas dinners year by year. Chips Channon's standard donation was 10/-. Channon and Harold Nicolson both mention these firewatching duties in their published diaries. Nicolson records on 15 January 1941, 'I have had a bad night in Committee Room 9 [the firewatchers' dormitory]. There are two stokers in the room who spit and snore all the time, and I hear Big Ben booming hour after hour, while the paraffin lamp makes little round circles through its eye-holes on the ceiling'. Later in the war, on 28 June 1944, he discussed postwar politics as 'Up on the Victoria Tower I stood on guard with Hinchingbrooke gazing out towards the Surrey hills. It was a comparatively quiet night and I managed to get some sleep upon my pallet'.

Firms' firewatching records survive here and there. LMA has a ledger from Whiffen & Son, the manufacturing chemists, labelled Fire Watchers: record of payments, in B/WHF/213. Ruled into columns, it gives the names of volunteers for firewatching, their dates of duty and payments made directly by the firm, which reclaimed the allowances from the Ministry of Labour, and later from the Ministry of Supply. No institution was exempt from firewatching duties. Even the Children of Mary at the Convent of the Good Shepherd in Finchley took their turn, as their Air Raid Diary in Barnet Archives MS 16526, shows. 'June 10 1941. No raids T. God but tonight is my night on duty for Fire Watching and my what a night, let me explain. This Fire Watching started about 3 weeks ago by order of the government all buildings must be guarded in case of fire caused by incendiary bombs Mother has picked 30 children and we all do watching for 1 night a month, on that night we are left with a nice flask of tea and some biscuits!' Notices and a rota for the Hendon and Edgware Fire Guard 1941–5 are also in Barnet's collection, in MS 19199. Mass-Observation reporters sometimes sent in ephemera like firewatching rotas, notices about fire precautions and similar items with their diaries. M-O TC23/9/0 includes similar material from a block of flats in Ridgmount Gardens, WC 1. The IWM Sound Archive has an interview with Wilfred Littleboy, a London firewatcher, on 485/6. Firewatching was uncomfortable, boring and unpopular, but the records demonstrate that it proved its worth by preventing fires taking hold.

## Rescue work

Once Fighter Command had signalled 'raiders passed', police sounded the 'all-clear' and the emergency services could draw breath and assess what further action was necessary. The CD Regional files in PRO HO 207 are full of information about this work, and more is available at local level. Every effort was made to clear building debris as quickly as possible, but this was difficult, dangerous work. Sometimes survivors and bodies were trapped for days. Military help might be needed to defuse unexploded bombs, and troops were sometimes used to help clear wreckage. Gas, electricity and water supplies might need restoration, sewage pipes require repair. Often essential links in the transport network had to be rapidly restored — roads, bridges, tunnels and railway lines. Goods were salvaged if at all possible. An incident enquiry point would be set up in the nearest usable building, or in the street, where local WVS volunteers could pass on news of survivors and of the dead to families and friends. Later, compensation claims had to be compiled. And there was an urgent need to rehouse, reclothe and feed all the Londoners made homeless by the massive damage to housing stock.

### Damaged buildings: rescue and debris

Heavy rescue squads had to shift tons of dusty rubble to search for survivors and bodies, while salvaging anything useful and disposing of the debris. This was another responsibility of the Ministry of Home Security, working through the local authorities. PRO classes HO 186, ARP registered files, and HO 207, CD headquarters and regional files, illustrate this work, for instance in HO 186/1273 and HO 186/2059, HO 207/19, 99, 166, 186 and 218. In London's case the LCC and the MCC were the authorities most closely involved, using their architectural, surveying and engineering staff to carry out the work. District surveyors acted as controlling officers in charge of rescue and demolition work, their staff manned the rescue department's control centres and later the War Debris Service, which cleared away the mess. Many papers of the LCC Architect's Department have detailed information arranged by area, as in AR/WAR/1/1–5 — orders to contractors to carry out urgent emergency work, AR/WAR/1/11 — pay rates for rescue personnel, 1939–44, and AR/WAR/1/16, concerning staffing for war debris and disposal work, 1941–2. AR/WAR/3 is a useful miscellaneous group, typical contents of which include /1, from Paddington heavy rescue service, detailing war damaged premises; /12, a file of incident report forms 1940–1; and /15, daily returns of incidents February–September 1944. Some files contain maps of bomb damage, as in /17, which relates to flying bomb and rocket damage in Stepney. Troops were occasionally used to help clear debris, but government policy was to avoid their regular use for civilian work, Labour ministers arguing strongly for the employment of unionised labour as a point of principle. Local authorities frequently had long-standing links with small local building firms, and continued to use them.

The LCC Engineer's Department was responsible for clearing roads and dealing with other transport problems. Debris from the bomb sites went to Hackney Marshes by lorry and by barge, raising the surface level of the marshes by several feet and, incidentally, helping to prevent flooding of the River Lea. LMA LCC/CE/WAR/5/9, covering 1944–8, is the Chief Engineer's Department's daily journal, a day-to-day record of keeping roads and railway bridges clear, and of dealing with complaints, claims by boroughs, and dumping problems. Records of the Building Research Establishment contain reports on specific damaged buildings — LMA ACC 4002/006 refers to Selfridges, for example, /008 to Four Mills Wharf in Poplar, /013 to Marylebone Town Hall.

The City of London ran its own rescue service. An ARP Emergency Committee report presented to Common Council on 19 December 1940, CLRO C20, recorded that Rescue Service training had paid off: 'The behaviour of the Rescue Parties in carrying out their work has been favourably commented upon by those who have had the misfortune to suffer as a result of enemy action'. 'The amount of debris concerned has been very large, and much difficulty has been experienced in its transport and disposal by reason of the absence in the City of sites or open spaces suitable for the dumping of materials which have therefore to be removed by land or river transport.'

Rescue work was hard and unpleasant, and the workers needed frequent breaks from the plaster dust and debris. Barnet Archives' collection contains detailed contemporary evidence in a folder of handwritten meals statements and orders for rescue parties from the Central Fire Station and AFS, 20 March–24 April 1940. Handwritten forms give a statement of meals for the week, the number of shifts worked, the amount due, vouchers issued, and totals, with clumps of daily vouchers attached to the summary. Westminster's file CD 68.23, Mobile Canteen, records the row resulting from an official attempt to make rescue workers pay for refreshments while engaged on this dangerous and unpleasant job.

### Reminiscences

Unpublished personal memories and other sources for heavy rescue work can be found in some collections, including the IWM Department of Documents, such as Bernard Regan's vivid diaries describing his work on the Isle of Dogs in 1940–1 in IWM 88/10/1, and W. Stead's notebooks and papers concerning his service at Salter's Hill Rescue Depot, West Norwood at IWM 94/10/1. The IWM Sound Archive also has recordings of interviews with men who worked on these heavy rescue squads. Conditions were tough. Another IWM interviewee, Eleanor Hudson, on 6085/2, drove a mobile canteen in Notting Hill at the time of the flying bombs. She describes arriving at the bombed-out Troy Court flats, giving half cups of tea to men choked by the fog of dust, and the reaction of an American soldier, in shock after retrieving bodies, who begged to help with the washing up to reclaim some feeling of normality.

Once initial clearance had been done the demolition of unsafe buildings was often subcontracted by the LCC to teams of builders from local firms. Life in one of these demolition squads, covering a three month period in 1941, was minutely chronicled for Mass-Observation, in TC15 Demolition in London. It describes the operation of the business, the men, their attitudes to work, to each other and to the government, their values, interests and conversations. One of this gang was black, another Irish. In St Pancras, many of the workers were Maltese, as the WVS report for that borough noted in November 1940. Records of the National Federation of Building Trade Employers, and the National Joint Council for the Building Industry shed further light on wartime conditions. They are held by the Modern Records Centre of the University of Warwick, in MSS.187.

## Disposing of the dead

Air raid victims needed to be dealt with rapidly, for reasons of morale and of hygiene. The Ministry of Health oversaw the arrangements for their burial, details of the emergency arrangements for the London CD Region are in PRO HLG 7/762. The Ministry worked, as usual, through the local authorities. It had planned ahead, in the light of pessimistic government forecasts of casualty levels. Westminster Council Minutes, for example, record the purchase of 3,000 shrouds costing £562.10.0. in June 1939; the Corporation of London set up an extra mortuary at the City of London Brewery, to take 1136 bodies. Other boroughs made comparable preparations. Mercifully the estimates proved wrong, the greater problems were homelessness, and rescuing people from collapsed buildings. Nevertheless, there were many fatalities — 30,000 altogether in London — and the dead had to be accounted for and buried.

## Local authority records

The bodies of those killed in air raids were retrieved as soon as possible by those who found them — whether ARP wardens, police, or rescue squads — cleaned up, labelled, and taken to a designated mortuary in special vans. The City used cleansing vehicles, and recruited Billingsgate porters for the job. Correspondence about this, with sample mortuary forms and labels, survives in the CLRO in Folder CD2.2, Deaths due to war operations. Boroughs were encouraged to cooperate with one another to ensure coordination and give help in emergencies. The same folder contains letters concerning such cooperation between the City and Stepney over civilian fatalities.The IWM Sound Archive has an interview with a mortuary worker, Miles Mordaunt, on tape 2338/2, who trained a diverse group of drivers for this job.

When the tagged body arrived at the mortuary, a detailed form was filled in with the help of the delivering driver. Identification could be difficult, and victims were not always local. It helped if they wore a metal identification disk. Many people took the precaution of having one engraved at a 'while-you-wait' kiosk, and wore it in case the worst happened. Hendon's register of Deaths due to War Operations, Barnet Archives MS 9215/5, is a ring binder of two-part forms arranged by victim's surname. The first part was filled in on the arrival of the body, with an assessment of cause of death, the date of death, or of finding the body, the name if known, sex, and probable age. The second part of the form gave more details after a closer examination, and bears the signature of a relative or friend claiming the body for burial. Details given cover the name, address, occupation, marital status, age, sex, cause of death, the signature of the person identifying the body and his or her relationship to the deceased. If the body was buried by the authorities, details of the place and time are given. The back of the form contains an inventory of clothing and effects found with the body, such as 'blue dressing gown; wedding ring; bunch of keys; comb; 7/- in silver and 8d in copper'. Finchley kept a Deceased Persons' register, Barnet Archives MS 9215/10. It lists seventy-eight people, almost all killed in 1940–1, giving the date of the raid, the incident number, full names and the address, with a week by week summary and running total. And Kensington Local Studies Library has a register of Civilian War Deaths with full names, addresses, places of burial and other detail, in alphabetical order, in 940.5467 AR/A. Other boroughs kept comparable records.

## Funeral and cemetery records

Funeral directors' records and those of coroners do not usually differentiate between deaths due to war operations and the rest, but inevitably some wartime ledgers contain examples of air raid casualties. LMA has the journal of Spicers, the undertakers in B/SPC/3. Their handwritten ledger gives the date of the order, the name and address, age, date of death, date and place of the funeral, whether the grave was private, if so its number. If applicable, it also lists the hospital involved, and any inquest held. The measurements of the coffin, its type and fittings, how many cars as well as the hearse, and the charges made are listed. A recording by Ivor Leverton, an undertaker and member of the AFS is in the IWM's Sound Archive, on 5336/1. Cemetery records can also be informative, LMA has the records of the City of London and Tower Hamlets Cemetery Co., Camden Local Studies and Archives Centre has those of the London Cemetery Co., which ran Highgate Cemetery. Some of these cemeteries have group memorials to local air raid victims, Abney Park cemetery in Hackney has an example. Full lists of civilian dead for the whole country were split into local authority sections and published separately after the war by the Imperial War Graves Commission. Local collections have a printed copy for their own area.

## The ambulance service

Ambulances took the seriously injured to hospital, driving through blacked-out, bomb-damaged streets, often while the raid still continued. Provided and maintained by the LCC, the London Ambulance Service came under the operating control of the London CD Region, but its surviving records are in LMA LCC/PH/WAR/3. One hundred and twelve auxiliary ambulance stations were set up and auxiliary volunteers enrolled as drivers and other helpers. Middlesex had an auxiliary CD ambulance force, using commercial vehicles and cars. The Friends' Ambulance Unit, run by the Quakers, was also active in this work, and a popular choice with pacifist volunteers prepared to do non-military war work. E.M. Delafield's description of the LCC ambulance station under the Savoy in the early days of the war, fictionalised in her *Provincial Lady in Wartime* (Macmillan, 1940) conveys an authentic flavour. Rose Macaulay, whose driving skills always appalled her friends, was another volunteer driver. She recounted some of her experiences in *Letters to a Sister*. Mass-Observation's diarist no. 5427, a well-to-do widow, volunteered for ambulance driving, later changing to mobile canteens, and wrote regularly about her work in central London. Extracts from her diaries appear in Dorothy Sheridan's *Women at War.* Some oral history tapes in the IWM Sound Archive record the experiences of ambulance workers, such as Nancy Spender, on IWM 2339/B/A, and stretcher bearers like Albert Prior in West Ham, on 5347/2. The IWM Department of Documents also has written material, such as Miss N O'Conner's memoir covering ambulance driving and instructing in South London in 87/14/1 and a West Ham CD stretcher bearers' log book for January–June 1941 survives in the IWM Documents collection, giving details of casualties and first aid treatment. The Museum of London's ephemera collection contains items like the Certificate of Merit awarded to Gladys Oliver McClelland for a year's safe driving of a CD ambulance, 1942–3, in Box A3.

## First aid posts

Local authorities provided first aid posts throughout their areas to deal with minor injuries and leave hospitals free to concentrate on more serious cases. Some first aid posts were attached to hospital buildings or wardens' posts, others used suitable premises elsewhere. The Corporation of London records include file CD2.1, Air Raid Casualties treated at First Aid Posts, containing a 'Record of First Aid Treatment of Casualties due to Enemy Action', and completed Ministry of Pensions forms. They are grouped by originating first aid post — 'Mobile'; 'Gt St Helens', 'Chartered Insurance Institute' — and so on. Each casualty treatment has a running number, and the name, age, address, nature of injury and action taken is noted, as in: 'Mobile FAP, City of London 8/3/45. 32 Mears, Doris. 19. 54 Bushberry Rd Homerton. Shock. Home — kept on FAP 4 hours'. The form usually mentions if casualties were ARP or AFS personnel.

Photographs of first aid posts in action are numerous, especially of those in underground shelters. One of Bill Brandt's shelter photographs shows an East End underground station First Aid Post on 12 November 1940, with a doctor examining a woman's eye as a nurse writes notes in the background (8731 in the Museum of London's collection). The London Passenger Transport Board supplied seventy-nine tube shelters with well-equipped medical posts, the London Transport photograph library has a large collection of illustrations of them.

## *Helping the homeless*

Advance planning had envisaged provision for the bombed-out being made through Public Assistance, a poor law system not noted for its sympathetic approach or for flexibility. The Blitz soon revealed the inadequacy of this plan both practically and in terms of morale. People needed somewhere to eat and sleep while they reorganised their lives, and access to advice about the bureaucratic ramifications. Responsibility for the homeless was soon transferred to the Ministry of Health, working through local authorities, and improvements were rapidly made. Papers of the Blitz Committee on the evacuation and care of the homeless are in PRO MH 79/487. Schools and church halls were converted into comfortable rest centres, and officials from different departments were moved into information posts where the homeless could sort out most of their immediate problems under the same roof.

### *Rest Centres*

At national level, much of the documentation is in PRO classes HLG 7, Special wartime functions, and MH 76, Emergency medical services. For instance, HLG 7/357 relates to the LCC Rest Centres and MH 76/488 to payments and expenses incurred by them; MH 76/495 relates to their use for returning evacuees at the end of the war; HLG 7/518 to administrative and information posts within rest centres and HLG 7/519 to cooperation between London and neighbouring counties in this matter. Centres and their information posts were staffed by local authority employees, with additional help from WVS volunteers, a service documented in its own branch narrative histories and in PRO HO 207, and from the Charity Organisation Society, whose records — closed for sixty years — are in LMA A/FWA, and also the London Council of Social Service, who records are in LMA ACC 1888.

The LCC ran its Rest Centres from County Hall, through its Public Assistance Department. The county was divided into ten districts, each with its own Area Control Office. Initially the LCC equipped ninety-eight centres, designated first- or second-line, but another 500 third-line centres were added from May 1940, managed by the WVS, local clergy and other volunteers. Some people stayed at the centres for considerable periods. Rehousing was a major problem, for it took time to repair damaged buildings and to remove unexploded bombs — there are said to be at least a hundred still beneath the streets of London. Accommodation at the rest centres was free, so some inhabitants were reluctant to move out and start paying rent again. Borough rehousing officers had a difficult task, and some boroughs were conspicuously more efficient than others. Stepney was notoriously disorganised, with results described later in this section

Surviving records for LCC rest centres are in LMA LCC/WE/RC. They include Area Control Office records — log books, returns of food and goods supplied, staff information, reports and correspondence, and rest centre records — log books, admission and discharge registers, official forms concerning food supply, laundry, inventories, correspondence and plans. Boxes 11–18 are files for various rest centres, box 43 contains logbooks for centres in Lewisham, Kensington, Battersea, Hampstead and many more. Middlesex's comparable material is among its wartime public assistance records in MCC/WE/PA/2. For example, /93, covers emergency rest centres 1941–3, /96 has details on furniture in rest centres, and there are files on individual centres like /131–2 the Empire Pool, Wembley, including daily numbers books. Further information occurs in personal memoirs, such as Miss H Helliar's account of rest centre work in IWM Department of Documents, in 92/49/1, and the menus and 'ready reckoners' used by Mr W Taylor as a Welfare Adviser to the Rest Centre Service, to calculate varying food ration entitlements, in IWM Misc 147 (2312). Visual representations of rest centres can be found in many Ministry of Information photographs. Rest centres also feature in Mass-Observation reports. An observer visited Paddington Rest Centre on 13 May 1941, soon after a bad raid. He saw people eating their tea, quiet and subdued.The raid had happened on a Saturday night/Sunday morning, when the billeting office only ran a skeleton staff and no doctor could be found. 'The Superintendent said his first care was to give the people a cup of tea, and then send them to bed. What he wanted to avoid at all costs was to keep them hanging about — "that's what tells on morale" he said with a laugh' (TC 23/9, Air raids 1940–1).

## Billeting and rehousing

Hard-pressed local authority staff needed voluntary help to cope with aspects of this emergency welfare work. One of the most active voluntary services was the WVS, which successfully tapped the energies of an army of women, mainly middle-class, to tackle any task the Home Office gave them.They organised evacuee groups, arranged clothing exchanges and the distribution of overseas clothing and food gifts, ran emergency canteens, set up incident enquiry points, organised salvage drives and car pools, and worked in rest centres. They worked in close liaison with borough rehousing and billeting officers to prepare accommodation for those who had lost their homes. The 'narrative reports' sent monthly by their branches to headquarters contain detailed accounts of the work they undertook, with copious local information. In October 1940, the Camberwell branch wrote 'Work on billeting the homeless has continued ceaselessly. The Sanitary Inspectors were driven round and helped to inspect the commandeered houses... The blacking out of the houses still continues to be done by the WVS. Much extra work has been entailed as out of 170 houses commandeered and got ready, 40 have been bombed'. The borough of St Pancras asked for WVS help with billeting during the Blitz as they had already coped well with the placement of foreign refugees, '...but our new task was made exceedingly difficult by the Borough's complete failure to realise the magnitude of the problem, and to requisition houses and hotels on a sufficient scale. One day we had 824 homeless persons and about 30 billets'. They protested, forcing the Council to take over two big hotels. 'After we had done the billeting for about a month the Borough decided, without giving any reason, to take it over.' The reports are in the WRVS Archive, County of London files L–Z, St Pancras.

The Blitz took a heavy toll on housing stock, especially in the crowded East End. Some local authorities were better than others at organising repairs, rehousing and billeting. By December 1940 the Ministry of Works decided to set up a special repair service, using 'flying squads' of men who could be sent anywhere in the country as the need arose. The Army released some experienced building workers to join this scheme. Some authorities, like the LCC, coped efficiently without outside help, others had to call upon the Ministry of Works to a great extent. Stepney was so bad in this as in other regards, that the Ministries of Health and Home Security acted to deprive it of some of its powers in December 1940 and the Ministry of Health installed its own rehousing officer there. This *cause célèbre* is documented in PRO HO 207/1026, but the file is closed for seventy-five years. PRO classes MH 79, the '100,000 series files', and HLG 7, Special wartime functions, have some material on rehousing, for instance MH 79/ 503 on winter shelter in London in 1944, with a statistical digest of houses damaged, and HLG 7/561 on the rehousing of London homeless in Southend towards the end of the war.

The involvement of many of these groups of volunteers for welfare work is documented not only in their own archives, but is also reflected in national and local authority records. Ministry of Home Security records deal at length with the WVS — HLG 7/334 is general correspondence; HO 207/164 is about their 'Housewives' Service' for example — and Hackney Archives has a folder of correspondence relating to the local operation of the WVS' 'Good Neighbours' scheme, through which the county of Shropshire 'adopted' Hackney, donating household goods to restock bombed homes, in H/CC/2/20. The National Sound Archive has a copy of a contemporary recording in which a grateful London refugee thanks the WVS, on T 8186/04 TR1 C4.

*Emergency feeding and laundry*

Water, gas and electricity services were commonly disrupted by air raids, leaving hundreds of people without access to cooking and washing facilities. The WVS trained teams to set up emergency cooking stoves, assembled from debris taken from ruined buildings nearby, to provide hot food for the inhabitants of a damaged street. More elaborate provision was made through the Ministry of Food's Queen's Messenger convoys, kept on standby to go at once to affected areas. Each convoy had six mobile canteens, with water carriers and supply lorries, and was designed to be self-sufficient. They were staffed by the WVS, Salvation Army, Red Cross, YMCA and other volunteers, and could produce hot meals for 3,000 people in a few hours. These canteen services were coordinated on behalf of the Ministry of Food by the local authorities, which had invited the voluntary bodies to join the London Division Food Office Canteen Pool. MCC Welfare files are informative about this, for instance LMA MCC/WE/PA/2/143 is a file of air raid and emergency feeding reports for North Finchley, /145 covering Hornsey, and so on. /152 details the Council's correspondence with the WVS. Photographic records of this service are plentiful as they were a popular subject for Ministry of Information propaganda purposes. Agency photographs in the IWM collection, for example, show a Queen's Messenger canteen parked in Norbury in July 1944, amid severe flying-bomb damage (HU 49498–9). The residents sit on the grass, drinking from mugs and smoking, cheerfully. Regular mobile canteens also served the air raid shelters where people who had sheltered all night could have breakfast before going straight to work. And if damage to local buildings had been bad, ARP staff, police, firemen, rescue and demolition workers required food and drink on site, sometimes for several days, while they dealt with the problem.

Mobile laundries and baths, often sponsored by soap firms, were similarly organised by volunteers who would collect washing from bombed areas and return it, still wet, later that day. The IWM has a photograph of the service in action, 'Blitz laundry' (HU 36150). It is dated 26 April 1944 and shows women queueing with bundles of washing at a van marked 'National Emergency Washing Service', financed by Lever Brothers. Lifebuoy soap sponsored the mobile emergency baths unit pictured in ZZZ 8938C, which shows the unit with canvas tents, emblazoned 'Lifebuoy emergency service', parked in a bomb-damaged area.

Many volunteers recorded their memories of this work in some form. The bibliography contains published examples, oral ones are to be found in the IWM's Sound Archive, such as those of Mrs Tingley, on 5360/1, and Muriel Cowell, on IWM 11834/1, and the IWM Documents collection has unpublished written examples like the log books of the YMCA mobile canteen in Wimbledon compiled by Miss R.C. Desch, 89/19/1.

## Requisitioned property

Among the many provisions of the Civil Defence Act 1939 was a clause allowing the government and local authorities to requisition property for wartime purposes in return for compensation. The resulting records can be useful for information about individual buildings and for local history generally. LMA MCC/CD/WAR/2 has correspondence files on this matter, /3 containing schedules of requisitioned property, by area — /1 is Acton — giving details of furniture storage, cleansing, debris clearance, rateable value, the occupant, the owner, date of the Council taking it over, the agreement, and the date of vacating. MCC/CL/L/CD/2 relates to the utilisation of county and other property for CD purposes, /13 concerns mine-watching posts at Kew and Chiswick bridges, for instance.

## War damage claims

Until the summer of 1940 the government refused to consider plans for dealing with claims for war damage before hostilities had ceased, because of the cost. But the Blitz made it clear that people of limited means, at least, must be allowed compensation at once so that they could replace furniture and clothing. This led to the War Damage Act of 1941, which permitted insurance on all types of property to certain limits, for everyone. Property owners made contributions through the Inland Revenue, which used its own valuers for assessments, but there was no direct link between how much they had paid in and how much they were awarded. The Assistance Board processed the claims, now in PRO AST 1, and made advance payments for damage claims, final settlement of which could take many years through the War Damage Commission, which had four offices for London. War Damage Commission files in PRO IR 36 and 37 provide detailed information and plans of buildings of all kinds for which damage claims had been submitted, such as the church of St Mary le Bow, IR 36/13, the Convent of the Holy Child Jesus, Cavendish Square, IR 37/47 and the Tate and Lyle Sugar Refinery, Silvertown, IR 37/271. County Council records also contain records on specific damaged properties, for example about the Central Middlesex Hospital in MCC/CL/L/CD/4/8 and about Chiswick Polytechnic in MCC/CL/L/CD/10. Damage claims are also documented in the archives of the institutions concerned. Westminster Abbey Muniments, for instance, have a file of war damage correspondence at 61587–605. The bureaucracy could be daunting for the individual claimant, but commercial publications stepped in to advise. The Museum of London's ephemera collection, ARP/CD box A2, preserves a booklet published by Hamish Hamilton in 1940; *After the Raid is Over*, by S.W. Pollard, solicitor. 'Do you know how you stand regarding compensation for personal injury, damage to property...?' asks the blurb.

## Invasion defence plans

Local authorities were required to imagine the worst, and to prepare contingency plans to use in the event of invasion. Middlesex County Council's CD Department, for example, asked its local authorities to submit such plans to be held centrally. They were to cope with possible enemy attack, with provisions for emergency feeding, sheltering the homeless,

WOMEN'S VOLUNTARY SERVICES.

Items of Interest for the week ending August 26th,1941.

1) London Region Salvage Drive. In addition to helping the
   local authorities in their individual drive, W.V.S.
   Headquarters have been asked to arrange the exhibit in
   Trafalgar Square for the fortnight September 13th - 27th
   and to organise speakers and special features during the
   first week.

2) Chevrons Club. W.V.S. have been asked to help the Chevrons
   Club to re-start their Service Hostel, formerly situated
   in St. George's Square.  On W.V.S. advice, the idea of
   taking over Lord Iveagh's house in St. James' Square has
   been dropped and Hopkinson House, Vauxhall Bridge Road,
   is now being considered.

3) Feeding the Dockers.  Continual discussions have taken
   place with the Ministry of Food, L.C.C., P.L.A., Ministry
   of Labour, and Admiralty, regarding the feeding of the
   dockers who threatened to come out on strike if they were
   not provided with a hot mid-day meal.   The matter is still
   under discussion but the probable solution will be for the
   West Ham Emergency Feeding Scheme eventually to provide this
   meal and in the meantime W.V.S. in conjunction with the Queen's
   Messengers will be used.

4) Ford Emergency Food vans.   There are to be about 50 of these
   vans stationed in the London Civil Defence area and negotiations
   are taking place with regard to the staffing of these by W.V.S.
   members.   Colonel Dudley of the Automobile Association has
   visited us to offer the services of the AA. to the members of the
   W.V.S. staffing these vans.

5) Provision of occupation for the physically handicapped.  The
   report of the first three months work in connection with these
   cases has been made to the L.C.C.

6) Cyclists.  A survey has been made of the members of the Centre
   staffs possessing bicycles and all those people who bicycle, so
   that the information may be available in case of breakdown of
   communications.

Wide-ranging activity from the WVS
*(PRO HO 207/164)*

stalling enemy advances and protecting civilians, and animals. The MCC plans are kept in LMA MCC/CL/CD/1, and they vary with the individual borough that produced them. MCC/CL/CD/1/2 contains the Borough of Brentford and Chiswick Invasion Defence Scheme 1942. It has two coloured maps of the borough showing ARP posts, rest centres and other emergency provisions. The borough is subdivided into five smaller units, and the plan explains there is plenty of scope to involve the public, because there was so much to be done and it was better to keep people occupied. The plan appends lists of personnel — Invasion Defence Wardens, WVS District Leaders, Home Guard, Ministry of Food officials and so on, with their names, addresses and phone numbers. Billeting and Rehousing Officers were included, though 'it is hoped that action will be taken to persuade people to stand firm and, if necessary, to compel them to keep off the roads'. There is a list of wardens' posts, and a volunteers' form attached, giving their names, addresses and the kind of work they were prepared to do.

## Strain on CD personnel

London CD workers were put under considerable strain, especially during the Blitz. Their need to escape from London for a period of rest and quiet was recognised by the authorities which attempted to coordinate the various schemes set up by well-wishers to send them away for short breaks. PRO HO 207/196 contains papers on 'Recuperative rest for CD personnel', and the IWM Department of Documents has a file relating to the use of Oxford colleges for this purpose, with administrative arrangements and case histories.

## OUT OF HARM'S WAY: EVACUATION

'Evacuation' is often remembered solely in terms of the great wartime exodus of London children to safer country areas in anticipation of the bombing. As the bibliography shows, many authors have written on that subject, frequently from personal experience, and it has been examined at length in television and radio programmes and in exhibitions like the one organised by the Imperial War Museum in 1996. But evacuation affected many other sectors of society as well. Expectant mothers, the frail elderly, the disabled and the chronically sick were also relocated if possible, and institutions of all kinds also moved out of London, at least temporarily. Objects, too, were evacuated for safe keeping — paintings, museum treasures, historical records and books. Extensive documentation survives about all these aspects of evacuation.

Fearing that war would bring immediate bombing and gas attacks, the government had made plans for the priority evacuation of mothers, children and the handicapped from vulnerable areas. In the case of London, which was regarded as the main target, these plans were made with the help of LCC officials. A million and a quarter people were to be moved out of the capital including the pupils and staff of entire schools, and into reception areas across the south, East Anglia and the Midlands. In practice, about 600,000 actually left in August/September 1939 and many of these had returned by the Christmas as the uneventful phoney war lulled parents into a sense of false security. There were later flurries of evacuation following the fall of France, at the onset of the Blitz in the autumn of 1940, and again with the coming of the flying bombs in 1944, but it was this initial exodus that posed the greatest logistical challenge and which has lodged so vividly in popular memory. Evacuation was never compulsory, but it served as a safety valve throughout the war, allowing those who needed it to get away from the stress of London for a time.

Official sources relating to evacuation from London are in the Public Record Office and London Metropolitan Archives, though other repositories have useful additional material. The administrative history of the evacuation scheme is exhaustively covered in Richard Titmuss' *Problems of Social Policy* (1950), and, especially with reference to maternity provision, in *Studies in the Social Services* (1954) by Sheila Ferguson and Hilde Fitzgerald. Both form part of the *History of the Second World War UK Civil Series.*

### *National records*

The main sources in the PRO are to be found in the records of several departments. Policy decisions on evacuation are reflected in the records of the Cabinet Office, especially the War Cabinet Minutes in CAB 65, Memoranda in CAB 68, and the Committee of Civil Defence papers in CAB 73. Notes for the *UK Civil Series* histories are at CAB 102, and often produce information not used in the published version. CAB 102/669 and 677, for example, have extra material on the evacuation of Londoners in 1944. Home Office records including Registered files in HO 45, and Circulars in HO 158, may have useful material generally; so do HO 186 for ARP matters, HO 199 for the Intelligence branch, HO 202 for Daily reports, HO 204 for Regional circulars and the Regional Commissioners' files in HO 207, all of which come from the Ministry of Home Security. Ministry of Information records, notably the Social Survey reports in RG 23, the Registered files in RG 40 and correspondence in INF 1 are worth checking, too. Assistance Board papers, AST 11, can also be useful for the issue of allowances to evacuees under government schemes. But the ministries most closely involved with implementing evacuation schemes were those of Health and Education.

Evacuation plans were the responsibility of the Ministry of Health, which established a special division to deal with it. The work fell into three main phases: dispersal in 1939, fresh evacuation in 1944 because of the flying bombs, and the organised return of remaining evacuees in 1945 with the winding-up of the scheme. The most useful PRO classes are HLG 7, covering Special Wartime Functions — HLG 7/335, for instance, contains reports and complaints about LCC-organised evacuation parties 1941–2; HLG 7/336 relates to evacuees returning to London in 1944–5, Circulars in MH 10, Emergency Medical Service papers in MH 76, and the '100,000 series files' in HLG 68 and MH 79, any of which can yield occasional London finds. The Miscellaneous category in HLG 102 also has files on the evacuation scheme.

Young evacuees needed schooling, so the Ministry of Education was also heavily involved with the evacuation arrangements. Record classes ED 10 and ED11 have General files on elementary and secondary education. ED 10/309, for example, includes material on the financial position of elementary schools affected by evacuation. ED 134, Miscellaneous files, ED 137 concerning School Health Services and ED 138, a draft of the unpublished history of education in the war, are all potentially useful for London data.

Mass-Observation reports, some prepared on behalf of the government, include comments on evacuation and reactions to it. The Mass-Observation Archive's 'Evacuation' topic collection is a very valuable source for all aspects of the subject, including the evacuation and billeting of East Enders to other parts of London as the result of severe bomb damage. TC5/2/G, 'Preliminary impressions on evacuation from the East End 9.9.40', reports a conversation at a coffee stall. Observers ascribed an age and social class to each speaker, so this exchange is between two men in their thirties, one from social class C — 'Artisans and skilled workers' — the other from D — 'Unskilled': 'M35C "I've been bombed out, so we went to Richmond, but they've bloody well bombed there three times in the last 2 days. Had a wopper last night". M30D "What you go there for, then?" M35C "They sent us there. They send you any bloody place. This isn't dispersal, it's just shifting people round from one place to the next".' Box 1, file E in the same collection also contains a description by a young woman teacher of evacuating her pupils from Walthamstow to St Albans.

## Local authority records

The crucial role of the LCC in organising the evacuation of children is well covered by *We Think You Ought to Go*, edited by Richard Samways and based on the LCC's records. It outlines the main sources of relevant material, found in the records of the Council itself and its various committees, espcially in those of the Education Officer's department, the Clerk's and Children's departments, and the departments of Public Health and Welfare, giving many examples and illustrations of the records themselves. The coverage is huge, but a few examples will give an idea of the sort of information available.

Evacuation caused the LCC's Education Department an enormous amount of work and anxiety in the autumn of 1939. LCC/MIN 4984 gives the Education Officer's October report: 'Receiving authorities, confronted by social problems with which they were totally unfamiliar, have turned to the evacuating authority for advice and assistance...' (p. 5). 'My staff are having to cope with a postbag of 500 letters a day. These letters contain complaints by Londoners of unsuitable accommodation in the country; complaints by people in the country of the condition or behaviour of Londoners... allegations that certain parts of the reception area were unsafe owing to proximity to military formations, aerodromes, anti-aircraft guns (and, in one case, a circus of wild animals)...' (p. 6).

LCC/EO/WAR/1/194 concerns Operation Rivulet, the scheme that evacuated a fresh wave of children in 1944 when the flying bomb raids started; LCC/EO/WAR/2 deals with special categories of evacuees — /46 is Jewish school children, /50 bombed-out TB contacts, others deal with blind children, and diabetics. LCC/EO/WAR/3 concerns schools remaining in London /8 has weekly estimates of children in London December 1940–March 1942. School diaries and magazines can be useful sources, some examples are given in the Education section later in this guide. Also in LMA but not covered by *We Think You Ought to Go* are the Middlesex CC's records dealing with evacuation, mainly to be found in their Education Officer's and Welfare departments' holdings, like MCC/EO/WAR, the Education Officer's files including evacuation returns, and MCC/WE/PA/2/23, Evacuation arrangements, 1938–9. MCC/WE/PA/2/32 relates to the evacuees' return to London and /34 to the Wembley evacuation scheme.

London evacuees made a considerable impact on the reception areas and the subject was widely discussed at the time. The arrival of large numbers of mothers and children from inner city areas brought inevitable problems of adjustment for both sides. Manners, behaviour, habits and expectations differed. Some evacuees found country life very dull, some host communities thought the new arrivals a bad influence locally. Yet in most places matters settled down. The most discontented elements rapidly drifted back to London, but many school communities settled in quite happily for the duration. County Record Offices for the reception areas usually have administrative records about their local authority's involvement in the evacuation process, including billeting and welfare work. Education records may contain material on school-sharing with evacuee groups, and local newspapers are a good source of comment and description 'HUNTINGDONSHIRE INVADED BY THOUSANDS OF LONDONERS' headlined the *Huntingdonshire Post* in September 1939; 'WIDE OPEN DOORS FOR SOUTHERN EVACUEES: 1600 WARMLY WELCOMED BY CITIZENS OF LEEDS', wrote the *Yorkshire Post* in July 1944, both with photographs, reports and human interest stories.

### A PATHETIC SIGHT.

In the afternoon the first train arrived at 4.20 and the children on this train were younger than the others and were more excited. Only here and there were children who showed any signs of tears, but these were soon wiped away, and as the party marched from the station groups of the youngsters started singing.

It was pathetic to see the little children bowed down by the weight of their pillow cases and haversacks which contained a change of clothing, gym shoes and a day's supply of food. Each child had three identity labels attached to their clothing. In one case a girl of about 13 was in charge of her brothers and sisters who numbered seven altogether, while there were six in another family.

Everything possible was done to see that no families were split up and although one or two children became detached from their parties they were soon found. At intervals an official would shout and ask for the owner of a pair of shoes or luggage that had been left lying on the grass. The children were so thrilled at being in the field that they danced around and raced about in it.

On Saturday morning more children were expected, but mothers with babies and expectant mothers arrived. These had luggage with them and it took longer to transfer them on the buses. On Saturday afternoon and Sunday morning more mothers and children arrived.

On Sunday afternoon two more trains were expected but at 4.20 p.m., when the first train was due to arrive, it was announced by Major Cook that evacuation from London had stopped and that helpers were asked to report to their posts when it was announced on the wireless that evacuation had begun again.

Evacuees arrive in the country
*(Huntingdonshire Post, 7 September 1939)*

### Reception areas: records

A substantial contingent of London evacuees was sent to Huntingdonshire, only sixty miles from home but still comparatively rural. Huntingdonshire Record Office holds some illuminating material on this influx, and may serve here as an example of the kind of information available in the reception areas. The Earl of Sandwich, whose house, Hinchingbrooke, lies just outside Huntingdon, was chairman of the County Council throughout the war. His papers include the file 'Evacuation' in Hinch 11/92, with a good cross section of typical correspondence and reports.

Prompted by the Munich crisis, the Home Office's ARP Department had organised a dummy run for evacuation procedures in September 1938. All had not gone smoothly; the receiving authorities were invited to submit frank comments. In a report dated 11 October the Clerk to the Council made a number of practical criticisms. How were they to cope with the planned arrival of 750 Londoners every half hour, locked in their carriages, in trains too long for the local platform, and process them onto the correct buses — with a prudent trip to the latrines beforehand — for the next leg of their journey? He also complained about lack of liaison between the various official and voluntary bodies concerned, and accurately foresaw some billeting problems. 'It is not in my mind that Londoners, even from the poorest districts, are of a different kind from the rest of the community. Rather it is that I feel that to herd people of different antecedents together and keep them together for a protracted period certain precautions calculated to make contact harmonious must be taken.' Above all, the local authorities must be given powers to compel billeting: 'On the last occasion we were given great responsibilities without any powers of compulsion at all'.

In the same file are letters and reports about school accommodation and the problems of sharing it. On 24 October the Rector of Brampton wrote: 'It is bad for our children and worse for the London children that so much time in the week should be unproductive, at the best the London children have only part of their time occupied, most of their time they are mooning about; voluntary efforts to occupy and amuse the children are a palliative and not a remedy'. Staff problems arose, too. The County Education Department reported to Lord Sandwich on 21 May 1940: 'There has been very considerable difficulty with a Mr Winsten who is one of the Tottenham teachers accompanying the evacuated children attending our Stibbington School'. The local headmaster had complained several times about Mr Winsten, because he had 'not received from him the support or loyalty which a HM has a right to expect of his assistants'.

Lady Sandwich was President of the local WVS in the early years of the war. The file Hinch 11/94 contains material about WVS involvement with welfare work for London evacuees. It includes details of local children's homes and information on the appointment of a woman psychologist as a child guidance officer to deal with difficult child evacuees. There are typed reports from local branches about their reception and billeting work, cleaning premises, and about their very popular clothing shop. A handwritten report on East Lodge, Leighton, by Mrs Herschel describes the setting up of this evacuation hostel for Jewish mothers and children in a farm house two miles from the nearest bus stop. 'One of our only distractions at East Lodge is a weekly visit to Huntingdon which is usually achieved by most mothers. On their return they all speak glowingly of their visits to the WVS canteen where they can at so little cost obtain a meal and meet other evacuees'. This material can be supplemented from the WRVS own archives, in Box R4/5: Huntingdonshire.

Huntingdonshire County Council's Public Assistance Committee Minutes and those of its Emergency Medical Sub-committee also yield some information about London evacuees. On 2 September 1942 the sub-committee's minutes record a report from the Child Guidance Officer: 'Evacuation to St Neots district. In April, the evacuation of about 150 children

# NEWMARKET RURAL DISTRICT COUNCIL.

TEL. 62 & 638.

THB/VDC.

RURAL DISTRICT COUNCIL OFFICES,

PARK LANE,

NEWMARKET.

6th December, 1941.

Dear Miss Brindle,

Evacuation – 4th December, 1941.

In regard to the evacuation of unaccompanied school children which took place last Thursday, the total number which arrived here was 112.

The nurse who accompanied the children brought a list of about thirty children who were unfit for billeting. This list was handed straight to the County Medical Officer of Health who was present. The Medical Officer apparently decided that the brothers and sisters of these children should also go to the cleansing station which brought the list up to thirty-nine.

Great difficulty was experienced through the lateness of the evacuation and the fact that there were no proper nominal lists. The children did not arrive at the dispersal station until 3'o clock, and it was impossible to get them all cleared before about 4.20 with the result that they did not arrive in the villages until it was getting dark. Considerable difficulty was thus caused in billeting them out.

I am to suggest that in future arrangements should be made (1) for the medical inspection to take place in London.
(2) for the children to come by an earlier train.
(3) for proper lists in triplicate to accompany the children giving their names, ages, and home addresses, also the London schools.

Even if the medical examination could not be arranged in London, the last two suggestions if carried out would save a great deal of time at this end.

Yours faithfully,

Clerk to the Council.

The Evacuation Officer,
Ministry of Health,
12, Queen Anne Terrace,
CAMBRIDGE.

A Suffolk local authority complains about an LCC evacuation group
*(PRO HLG 7/335)*

from London to the St Neots area presented a number of problems. These children consisted of two main groups — the little ones evacuated for the first time on reaching an age to leave home unaccompanied, and the "seasoned travellers" who had spent the war years in various reception areas with intervals of running wild in London. Practically all had experience of bombing. Both types were very hard to settle satisfactorily in billets'. The small ones had night terrors, anxiety, and bed wetting, but most did well with generous foster mothers. The older ones 'comprised a number of tough and difficult or unstable children, two of the latter, boys of 11 years old, threatened suicide, and in one case is said to have attempted to carry out his threat'. But he had now settled. Lack of hostels for them, as a respite for the foster parents, was a problem. 'Many foster parents are tired and some soured by apparent ingratitude on the part of the London parents — "When they took him home and never said a word of thanks, I said I wouldn't never have no more".' Some were pitiful cases. The billeting officer at St Neots had asked for immediate help for a child of six 'in a state of terror, screaming and trembling at every bomb alert. He had been bombed successively out of three houses in Poplar, his father and grandmother being killed'.

The elderly could cause problems, too. The Welfare Office, reporting on Bluntisham Old People's Hostel in January 1945, noted: '...one woman caused some commotion by disappearing just before Christmas, but was found to have made her way to some friends at Mitcham. She was an air raid casualty, and had always been a little strange in her manner'. Regional film archives usually have footage of evacuees in their area. The East Anglian Film Archive at the University of East Anglia has examples, including a newsreel interview with Huntingdon's billeting officer, newsworthy because she was the youngest in the country at the age of twenty.

## Other sources

The London borough authorities were not directly involved in evacuation procedures so their official records contain little of great relevance on the subject, though it could affect their work peripherally. However, borough collections usually have non-official records of evacuation from their area. Photographs, oral history tapes, published and unpublished memoirs, school histories and local newspaper coverage can provide useful information. Local residents who helped with WVS evacuation work may have deposited relevant papers with the borough collection. Kensington Local Studies Library, for instance, has a collection of WVS letters, memos and other papers in 940.5477 AR/A, and Lady Philippa Harvey's unpublished 'WVS: a record of 21 years service in the borough of Kensington' in 940.5475 WW. Records in the WRVS archive are informative about London evacuation, not only that of children, but also of 'unofficial' adult evacuees in need of refuge in the country. The WVS's Camberwell Centre sent needy cases to a WVS hostel in Gainsborough, Lincolnshire. Making arrangements, their centre organiser wrote in October 1940: 'We are so delighted with the way you helped us with the Morris family we wondered if you could possible help us with this case. Two old women, 78 and 73 the former a dwarf — "both able-bodied and of sound mentality". They are very game but thoroughly terrified and longing to get away. They want to keep their two rooms, but even so they can pay up to 25/- a week for everything between them. They can't be evacuated under the aged and infirm scheme as they go to a private shelter and not a public one! It seems quite mad but there it is'.

Specialist collections may also contain material relevant to evacuation from London. For example, the Contemporary Medical Archives Centre of the Wellcome Institute has the papers of the Health Visitors' Association, in SA/HVA. They include those of Rachel Brimley,

SA/HVA/G1/14, a Health Visitor professionally involved in the evacuation arrangements from Barnes in 1939. Evacuees were medically inspected before they left, to try to prevent the spread of infection. Mrs Brimley saved the official paperwork issued to her at the time by Surrey CC — notices, booklets, duplicated memos, instructions, sample stationery and a list of 'pink card' and 'blue card' expectant mothers with names, addresses and likely date of confinement. The spiritual as well as material welfare of evacuees concerned churchmen and the public. Lambeth Palace Library's Lang Papers, 88, reveal a flurry of correspondence from members of the public to the Archbishop, urging him to ensure that foster parents sent evacuee children to church and Sunday School while in their care, and citing many cases where this was not occurring.

Departing child evacuees provided a photogenic subject and the press, both national and local, liked to include pictures with their coverage of the event. Agency photographers were also active on behalf of the Ministry of Information, and most large collections like LMA, the IWM and Museum of London have numerous examples showing children mustering at their schools, waiting at railway stations, or sitting in trains. London Transport photographs show them on trams setting off for Waterloo, or on Green Line coaches en route to the country. Radio journalists recorded their descriptions of the great exodus, several of which survive in the BBC collections. The National Sound Archive and IWM Sound Archive have copies, such as S.J.de Lotbinière's commentary on the evacuation of London children, recorded at Waterloo Station on 1 September 1939.

## Personal memories

Evacuation made a tremendous impact on personal lives, so it is not surprising that so many people have written about their own experience of it. The bibliography contains many published examples; archives and libraries of all kinds contain unpublished diaries and memoirs. The IWM Department of Documents has a good collection of this sort of material. Mrs M. Dineen deposited a four volume manuscript diary concerning her time as an LCC helper with a group of Streatham schoolchilden evacuated to Eastbourne, and later to South Wales, 87/40/1; Miss H. Helliar was a teacher in Stoke Newington who took groups of children to Luton, and to Wiltshire, in 92/49/1. The collection also has many accounts by child evacuees, like that of Mrs J.A. Otley, in 92/9/1, whose school was evacuated to Buckinghamshire from north west London, and Mr T. Nunn, on evacuation to Glamorgan from Acton, in 91/5/1. Most were written later, but the collection also has a twelve year old Lilian Hansen's account of being evacuated, written in verse, in Misc.151 (2331).

Some former evacuees have recorded their memories on tape instead of writing them down. The oral history collections at the British Library National Sound Archive, Museum of London and IWM Sound Archive contain many examples, like Edward Butt, who talks about his memories of evacuation with his school from Plaistow to Chipping Norton, Oxon, on IWM 5225/8, and Jean Stogdon, on NSA C642/42/1–3 C1, who was evacuated from North London to North Wales. The Museum of London's collection of interviews for the television programme *The Making of Modern London* also contains evacuation interviews.

## Evacuation of institutions

As war approached, institutions made contingency plans to evacuate their staff from the London area so that their activities could continue as normally as possible. Country houses and other premises were earmarked in advance — the Royal Society of Arts moved to Buxted Park, Sussex, a house belonging to Basil Ionides, a member of its Council. The BBC dispersed its departmental activities to a variety of provincial towns — Children's Hour to Bristol, Music to Bedford — and prepared Wood Norton Hall in Worcestershire for use as a headquarters if Broadcasting House fell to the enemy. Universities, colleges, public and private schools made arrangements to take over country properties, or to share with similar institutions out of town. Their own archives should contain any surviving material on these moves.

Moving many government departments out to the provinces seemed a wise safety precaution, accordingly suitable premises were taken over and billets for their staff sought. PRO CAB 73 in the PRO has papers of the War Cabinet committees on Civil Defence, including government evacuation. Some indication of the problems thrown up are well illustrated by a report in the House of Lords RO, PO 313/8, dated 4 November 1939, about finding accommodation for Ministry of Labour staff to be evacuated to Southport. The twenty billeting officers had had a hard time. Some canny householders were holding out for tenants from the Midland Bank and ICI instead, who were thought to have more cash available. And there was 'an undercurrent of feeling that Civil Servants were all highly paid and were running away from London to save their own skins...'. The billeters tried to match staff to suitable households to avoid embarrassment: '...no officer has had to be declared unbilletable — though one or two have tried official patience to the limits. It is remarkable how true to form some of our colleagues run!'

Some businesses, too, chose to move out of London at the start of the war. The long phoney war period induced some of them to return to London fairly quickly. Most then preferred to stay put unless forced out again by bomb damage, especially when it became clear that provincial areas previously considered 'safe' were almost as risky as London.

Parliament itself made evacuation plans, though they never had to be implemented. Jennifer Tanfield's short book *In Parliament, 1939–45* makes a useful introduction to the subject, and surviving records are listed in Maurice Bond's *Guide to the Records of Parliament* (1971). Pre-war planning envisaged the removal of both Houses to 'another place', in reality Stratford-upon-Avon, to continue their business. Papers of the Parliament Office in the House of Lords RO contain exhaustive schedules of office supplies to be moved, right down to individual books, typewriter oil and adhesive tape, with travel and billeting arrangements for peers, Members of Parliament and staff. Box ARP/7 contains an envelope with personnel billeting cards for the Parliament Office, despatching, for instance, Sir H. Badeley to 'Clifford Manor, Clifford Chambers' where his host would be Lt.Col. Rees-Mogg. He was to make his own travel arrangements with Mr Goodman. Staff rather lower in the pecking order were told 'At end of train journey get into bus labelled Bus No.2 H/L and take a seat about the middle of the bus'. PO313/11 and 12 contain secret memos and notes for the guidance of those responsible for evacuating government departments and Parliament. In fact the evacuation plans were never tested. The Blitz and the extension of the bombing to other cities, especially Coventry, made it clear that nowhere was likely to be completely safe. Members preferred to be in London, so Parliament continued to meet at Westminster, occasionally at Church House — PO 313/25 lists the alterations required to accommodate the Lords there — and in various parts of the Palace.

Museums, art galleries, archives and libraries had to plan the safe evacuation of their greatest treasures as well as the continuation of their normal work as far as possible. Their own records should contain details of preparations made and carried out, and PRO EB 3/18 has information from the Museums and Galleries Standing Commission about this operation. WORK 17 and 19 also deal with the preparations and AR 1 relates to the Wallace Collection in particular. In 1935 the Office of Works had convened a meeting to consider what all these institutions should do to cope with a modern war. They had agreed that each should make its own arrangements with a country house to which stock could be evacuated when necessary. The experience of the National Portrait Gallery, described in Sir Henry Hake's 'National Portrait Gallery History, 1939–43' in the Heinz Archive, makes a good example. Their country refuge was Mentmore, Lord Rosebery's house in Buckinghamshire, where they were offered a group of outbuildings in which the gallery's carpenter built timber racks for storing paintings. Gallery staff drew up a priority list of sixty items to be evacuated immediately if war broke out, and the Office of Works built a strongroom, known as 'the dugout', in the basement of the London building to take 600 framed canvases. In the winter of 1938–9 the Gallery experimented with packing methods, and tested packing materials. When the Home Office decided that the time had come, on 23 August 1939, the Gallery's stock was sent down to Mentmore, to be guarded by four attendants who lived in, on fortnightly shifts. The collection contains an album of photographs showing them on duty, and tending their chickens and vegetable patch in their spare time. They were not immune from the war, however: 'Life at the refuge has not been altogether uneventful. Six bombs were dropped in the Park in the late summer of 1940 and two landmines exploded about a mile away during the night of Nov 17/18 1940' (p. 4). In London, the Gallery's building sustained some minor damage, but work carried on, including the new task of advising the Board of Trade on export valuations, and on damage claims for privately-owned works of art lost or damaged by enemy action. By March 1942, it was possible to reopen the Gallery, on a limited basis, for exhibitions of Forces' art and similar shows. Other museums and galleries shared comparable experiences. Most of the British Museum stock was sent for safe storage. Some went out of London to a quarry at Westwood, near Bath, and other provincial stores, but some remained very close to home. A Ministry of Health scientist visited the Aldwych-Holborn tube shelter in June 1941 looking for insect infestation, his report is in PRO MH/76/546. 'No 2 platform is occupied by the British Museum where many treasures are stored. Beneath the platform there is a large expanse of water about 2 feet deep and 400 yards long. The caretakers who sleep here have bunks which are screened with mosquito netting, a most extraordinary sight, situated in the heart of London and nearly 100 feet underground'. Westminster Abbey spread its treasures widely, as a 'schedule of war removals 1939–42' among its muniments shows. The organ case went to the Bishop of Southwell, in Nottinghamshire; wax royal effigies to Piccadilly underground station and their robes to the Victoria and Albert Museum. Some busts and statues joined the NPG collection at Mentmore, while the muniments were sent to the National Library of Wales. The Public Record Office's own arrangements are thoroughly documented in its own files PRO 1, 18, 43, 45 and 46. Some of its holdings found temporary refuge in repositories as varied as Shepton Mallet Prison and Belvoir Castle.

Some great institutions later published separate accounts of their wartime activities, or included the period in more general histories of the gallery, museum or library. Some remained unpublished, like Hake's 'National Portrait Gallery history' mentioned above, or the 'War History of the Imperial War Museum, 1933–47', available in its Department of Printed Books.

## TROOPS ARE EVERYWHERE: THE ARMED FORCES IN LONDON

The emphasis of this guide is upon events in London during the war, so the activities of the various London regiments serving elsewhere are not covered here. Their regimental histories and battalion war diaries will provide a lead for those who wish to work on them. J.M. Brereton's *Guide to the Regiments and Corps of the British Army* (Bodley Head, 1985) is a useful starting point. The focus of this section is therefore upon forces involved in the defence of London, including the Home Guard, bomb disposal and clearance squads, British and Allied troops on leave and enemy records for the London offensive.

### British troops: regular forces

The main defence of London was an aerial one by the RAF, with fighter planes, anti-aircraft fire and barrage balloons. Ground defence, if invasion came, would consist of concentric rings protecting the suburbs stage by stage, with crack troops deployed to defend the centre in a last stand. Tank traps, in the form of large concrete bollards, were erected to slow the invader's progress through major thoroughfares. A number of PRO classes contain Air Ministry and War Office records on the defence of London and the South East in general.

### The RAF

PRO AIR 2, Air Ministry registered files, contain official reports of air attacks on Britain. Casualty figures, both British and German are in AIR 8, AIR 16 and AIR 22. RAF Fighter Command, with its headquarters at Stanmore, had operational control of the Army's Anti-Aircraft Command, of RAF Balloon Command and of the Observer Corps. AIR 16 contains its intelligence summaries, AIR 16/166–73 covers crashed German aircraft, with more in AIR 22/266–7 and AIR 40/45 and 1166. The work of RAF Hornchurch, a key station in the defence of Greater London, is recorded in the controllers' logs, squadron combats, daily casualty lists, pilots' operational sorties and intelligence diaries in AIR 16/853–863. Its operations record books are in AIR 28/384–5. Balloon Command's operations record books are at AIR 24/131–54, providing a daily report of activities; other files are in AIR 13 such as AIR 13/66 on the Thames Estuary and Harwich balloon barrage, 1939–40. Barrage balloons, a defence against low-flying aircraft, had an eight-man crew, and were anchored to lorries. The log book of Bromley Royal Observer Corps is in AIR 16/998–1002 and 1004. AIR 22/266–7 covers the location of enemy aircraft brought down in the U.K. during 1940–1. Photographs, maps and descriptions of RAF stations are in AIR 10/ 4038–9 and AIR 20/7585–6, WORK 44 also contains some. AIR 4 preserves some sample pilots' log books. Historical studies of many aspects of wartime air defences, including balloons, are in AIR 41.

RAF Bomber Command was based beyond the London area, at High Wycombe in Buckinghamshire. Coastal Command HQ was at Northwood, Middlesex. Both played important parts in the defence of London. Their records are in AIR 14 and 15 respectively, with operational books in AIR 24 and AIR 28. The RAF Museum at Hendon has Air Ministry daily summaries and summary reports of enemy action, squadron histories and reminiscences from those who served in the London area in wartime and some station site plans.

SUMMARY R.E.A. No. 46    6th January 1941.
Page No.1.

25.  R.A.F. STATION.
5/Jan.
HONINGTON.  At 1330 hours a low-flying enemy aircraft dropped
10 H.E. bombs of which 9 fell on the aerodrome surface, causing
craters and some damage to windows and doors and to the oil installation.
One aircraftsman was killed and another wounded, it is thought by
machine-gun fire.

26.  MAJOR DAMAGE.
(i) Night 4/5 Jan.
SWANSEA.  Details of the raid now show that many incendiaries
and 12 H.E. bombs were dropped, causing twelve fires and fairly extensive damage to utility services, business premises, shops and
houses in the centre of the town.   Very little damage was done to
objectives of a military character, and casualties were confined to
9, of which 5 were detained in hospital.

(ii) 5/Jan.
WITHAM (Essex.)   10 H.E. bombs were dropped at 1400 hours, and
5 fell on the factory of CRITTALLS LTD.   The Power House and the
main machine shop windows were badly damaged, but as far as is known
the shell production plant is unaffected.   No casualties were incurred as employees were in the shelters following a warning from the
roof spotter.   Work will probably be held up for one week.
Slight damage was also done to the railway track near the
Station and to the EAST ANGLIAN Power Transformer.

(iii) Night 5/6 Jan.
CRAYFORD (Kent).  At approximately 1900 hours bombs fell on
THE THAMES AMMUNITION Works, causing outbreaks of fire at two buildings,
probably shell-filling sheds.   Shells and, it is believed, a magazine
exploded, but owing to the buildings at this point being widely
separated, the fires did not spread and were reported to have been
extinguished by 2155 hours.

LONDON.  At 1900 hours bombs and flares began to fall in the
Eastern outskirts and raiding continued over many districts of the
Capital until 2322 hours, when all activity ceased.   Very few fires
were reported, and much of the damage appears to have been of a minor
character, although parachute mines caused local devastation.   Several
of these weapons which did not explode constitute a danger to factories
and communications, and have caused much evacuation.
Among the major incidents were the following:-

Hammersmith.  An H.E. bomb fell on the railway at 1920 hours
completely blocking the line.
Willesden.  2 unexploded mines fell within 450 yds. of the
Metropolitan Railway, the L.M.S. main line and two important
factories, and have caused the closing of the Edgware Road
and large scale evacuation.
Hayes, Middlesex.  A small fire was caused by incendiary
bombs at the I.C.I. Factory, but only slight damage was
incurred.   There is believed to be an unexploded bomb near
the premises.
Stoke Newington.  A parachute mine exploded in St. Matthias'
Square, causing devastation in the Square and surrounding roads.
The Church house was demolished and utility mains were damaged.
There were 28 casualties of which one was fatal.
Barnet Rural.  H.E. bombs fell on the AMALGAMATED STUDIOS,
BOREHAM WOOD, causing considerable damage to the building which
is occupied by the Ministry of Health.

/ Lambeth.

**Part of an RAF Summary Report of Enemy Action**
*(Crown Copyright RAF Museum Hendon)*

*The Army*

Headquarters papers of Home Forces Command are in PRO WO 199; those for Southern Command HQ include useful London material such as WO 199/425–30 on bomb disposal; WO 199/624 on the defence of the Thames, WO 199/917 on the use of Indian troops in London, WO 199/1202 about defence scheme 'Cinderella', and WO 199/1399 for London district maps relating to operation 'Overlord'. Anti-aircraft defence papers are in WO 199/1594–1613. The war diaries of the Home Forces in WO 166 are also very informative, covering the activities of anti-aircraft — 'Ackack' — and bomb disposal units as shown in WO 166/2901 and WO 166/3993. Histories and battalion diaries for the appropriate regiments, for example the Royal Engineers can also yield London information. The National Army Museum, the Imperial War Museum and the regimental museums will also be able to help.

*Film sources*

Army and RAF units sometimes recorded their work on film, including bomb disposal and clearance work in London. The IWM Film and Video Archive has many examples. RAF film in their collection includes silent footage of suburban damage in North London after a V1 attack in ACB 195; Army film includes footage of Indian troops clearing wreckage at Sloane Square tube station after the direct hit in November 1940 in AYY 57.

*Personal memories*

Troops who served in London have also left written or recorded memories of the period. The IWM Sound Archive has a tape of Len Jeacock, 5339/1, a sapper with the Royal Engineers in London from 1940–1, talking about bomb disposal and Frank Higgins, 9539/2, remembering guarding the Cabinet War Rooms while serving with the Military Police; the IWM Department of Documents has numerous diaries and memoirs covering service life in London. Lieut. F.S. Balch recalls work with a bomb disposal unit, in 91/43/1. Capt. H.W. Beckingham served with 35 Bomb Disposal Unit RE in Wanstead, defusing bombs all over North London, in 90/29/1. Mrs G.H. Breaux, in 89/19/1 writes about service as a WAAF balloon operator in Hackney, Flt. Officer B.C. Bullard, in 86/46/1, of her cypher work for the Special Operations Executive in Baker Street, at the Air Ministry in Bush House, at Transport Command in Harrow 1943 and at RAF Hendon. Miss V. Chenery, in 88/3/1, trained as a wireless telegraphist with the WRNS in North London, Private A.B. Savidge, in 91/16/1, served with the Royal Electrical and Mechanical Engineers in London in 1944 and describes V1 attacks including the one that hit Cambridge Barracks, Woolwich. Miss O.C. Rollason, in 93/30/1, deposited the humorous sketches she drew while training and working as a medical orderly with a Royal Army Medical Corps unit in Chislehurst.

## Home Guard

Invasion fears in May 1940 led the government to set up a new 'citizen's army' to supplement national defences at a local level. The Local Defence Volunteers, or LDV, were soon renamed the Home Guard, and from August 1940 were affiliated to county regiments of the army. Volunteers were eager and plentiful, but initially frustrated by a lack of equipment, training and proper organisation. Full details will be found in S.P. Mackenzie's *The Home Guard* (1995) which is very informative about the organisation in London as well as nationally. When the invasion scare had passed the Home Guard were used for duties such as aircraft spotting, operating searchlights, or guarding bomb sites and important buildings. Its national records, many dealing with London, are in PRO groups PREM (Prime Minister's Office), WO (War Office), HO (Ministry of Home Security, and Home Office), and examples also survive in local collections, as will be described later.

Among the 'operational' papers of the Prime Minister's Office in PREM 3, reflecting the Prime Minister's role as Minister of Defence, is material on setting up and running the Home Guard. Reports of the HG Inspectorate and its successor Directorate, are at WO 165/92–3. HG war diaries, among other diaries of Home Forces, are in WO 166 and HG papers, including information about London units are in WO 199, especially in WO 199/341–402, 1847–90, and 3301–2. Home Office registered files can also be productive. HO 45/25009, for instance, relates to the vetting of Home Guard applicants, including aliens. Home Security ARP files and Intelligence Branch files, HO 186 and HO 199, predictably cover the Home Guard among other topics. HO 186/651 is the papers of a 1941 HG exercise codenamed 'Thruster' testing liaison with CD in the London area. HO 207, the CD Regional files, also has HG information where it overlaps with other CD work, as in HO 207/172 which reports on the special problems caused by volunteers' dual enrolment in the Home Guard and Civil Defence in the London area. A final list of Home Guard officers was issued at the time the force was stood down in 1944, the files are in WO 199/3210–17. The Imperial War Museum has a copy, and area sections are usually available in local history collections; Guildhall Library, for example, has listings for the County of London, Essex and some other battalions, at L75.5. Personal records are kept by the Army Medal Office.

Records of the many, and sometimes idiosyncratic, London units may be found in several repositories. Middlesex had thirty-three Home Guard battalions, including a flotilla on the Thames. Many of their records have been deposited in LMA ACC 1101, including several relating to firms' own units, such as the Paper Cap Manufacturing Co Ltd Home Guard Unit (Bedfont), and the Tipsey Aircraft Co Home Guard Unit, as well as more conventionally organised groups. The documents — nominal rolls, registers and miscellaneous papers — contain personal information about the volunteers, giving the name and address of the employer, any past military service, National Insurance number, next of kin and the relationship, whether the volunteer had a car or cycle, telephone number, age, religion, and reasons for resignation, like 'pressure of business'. The LCC had its own County Hall Home Guard unit, documented in LCC/HG/01–84. Among its papers, in LCC/HG/3, is an interesting folder on the 48th London Battalion's women auxiliaries, thirty-five of whom are listed with their office addresses at County Hall. Olive Dallimore, of the Typing Branch, was keen to arrange weapons training for the women, but met with resistance. The Group Commander was personally sympathetic and seems to have condoned some introductory classes, but the file contains a handwritten memo dated 16 September 1942 stating 'Weapons training — women — cases continue to be reported where instruction is being given... This practice is strictly forbidden and will cease forthwith'. Instead Miss Dallimore and her colleagues were enrolled at Westminster Technical Institute for a course in 'good plain cooking', with special emphasis on making suet pudding for seventy men. By January 1943 the Group Commander was writing to the College to apologise for low attendance at the cookery classes. Catering or secretarial duties were the usual lot of women Home Guard members. Kensington's collection includes a report on the Women's Home Guard No 3 South Kensington Unit, in 940.5411 W, revealing that in 1943 they 'provided in rota an Orderly Room Clerk; Asst Quarter Master Sergeant; Platoon Clerks; and other members keep the Company records'. However, 'the Unit has the use of a .22 range each Monday'.

London Home Guard units were unusual in their variety and eccentricity. Many large organisations started their own, as the Palace of Westminster did. The squad's records are in the House of Lords RO in HG/1–12. One of its responsibilities was to man the gun at the Westminster underground station entrance to the Palace, members also laid anti-tank traps at the end of Westminster Bridge. A ledger, HG/1, lists the name, rank, date of birth, date of enrolment, casualties, previous service, with next of kin's address. HG/2 gives appointments and promotions. HG/8 concerns the bombing of the Palace of Westminster on 26 September 1940 when a bomb fell close to the Richard Coeur de Lion statue, breaking all the West Front windows and blowing sandbags and glass fragments into the Home Guard refuge where seven of the picket were sitting or sleeping, including Lord Lawrence, Lord Teviot and the librarian, Mr Kitto — 'all casualties though not really serious. All had to have first aid attention for cuts and shock ... they were all very lucky to have escaped as lightly as they did'. The section leader was Mr E.C. Delmege, a first class messenger, from the House of Commons. 'Everyone gives him the highest praise for the way in which he dealt with the situation, and although he had some nasty cuts in the face he got first aid for the rest immediately'. HG/1 reveals that Edwin Charles Delmege, born 19.11.1889, lived in Whitstable and had served twenty-one years with the Royal Dragoons.

London Passenger Transport Board staff formed Home Guard units all over London, and some of their records survive in the LT archive. Files typically contain papers on training arrangements, rotas, and letters from bus and train drivers requesting exemption from HG duty because of shift difficulties. The LT Museum's photograph library has pictures of LT Home Guard on duty in London, training at country camps, and marching in Victory parades. The Post Office had eight London Home Guard battalions, and the BBC Written Archives retain the papers of the 5th Battalion 'E' (BBC) Company Home Guard from 1942–5. Some groups produced their own periodical. The PRO has a run of the Southern Region's railway Home Guard magazine in ZPER 96. References to Home Guard activities occur occasionally in the records of other organisations involved in some way with their activities. The Shoreditch branch of the WVS, for instance, provided twenty-four cooks for Home Guard exercises in November 1942, according to the WRVS Narrative reports London, L–Z 1942. Muriel Quinn, sub-librarian of the University of London, whose diary is in the University's archives in UL 3/3, complained that Senate House's Home Guard, based in the Art Deco splendour of the Chancellor's Hall, kept trespassing upstairs in the library. One of its members was Sidney Bernstein, among whose papers at the Imperial War Museum Department of Documents is a file of memos, circulars and letters relating to his duties with the Ministry of Information's unit and eventual discharge due to pressure of work.

The IWM Department of Documents has other examples of London Home Guard diaries and papers. Mr G.W. King of Sanderstead, a shorthand writer at the Law Courts, kept a manuscript diary of his training and service with the Home Guard to show to his serviceman son. Captain H.F. Reeve kept his letters, orders, reports and training details from the 3rd Platoon of the 55th County of London (Metropolitan Electricity Supply Co) Battalion, Home Guard, based at Southall. Second Lieutenant G.D. Simons kept similar material about his service with 30th County of London (Tooting) Battalion in 94/2/1.

Photographs of Home Guard units survive in many collections, sometimes with other items like armbands, uniforms, proficiency and discharge certificates and badges. The Museum of London and many other museums have examples, as does the IWM.

## On leave in London

Troops of all nationalities, stationed all over the country, flocked to London on leave or passed through it en route to other postings. The temptations were obvious. Various organisations opened hostels, clubs and canteens in an attempt to keep the servicemen and women out of trouble. The Salvation Army's Red Shield organisation provided clubs and hostels for servicemen and women, the West London Synagogue started a club for Jewish service personnel, the YMCA, YWCA and church groups provided refreshments and staged entertainments. St Barnabas, Dulwich, hosted an ENSA concert party in February 1940, written up in the parish magazine: 'To spend a jolly evening in our warm and brightly lighted Parish Hall is both cheering and a welcome relief from roaming the dark and lonely streets of Dulwich...' (LMA P73 BAN 489). Services clubs for officers or for other ranks catered for members of the Forces in London. The records of the United Services Club are at the National Army Museum, the RAF Museum at Hendon holds those of the Royal Aero Club and those of the Sailors' Home and Red Ensign Club are at the National Maritime Museum. There was a Welsh Services Club in London, its records are at the National Library of Wales, and there were international clubs like the Inter-Allied Services Club in Earls Court. *On Leave in London*, a free fortnightly 'what's on' listing, was published by the London Regional Committee for Education among HM Forces. It listed theatres, films, exhibitions, talks and concerts and other useful information such as the times of the last underground trains.

## Allied troops

The arrival of Dominion and then of Allied troops brought colourful variety to the capital's streets, attracting comment at first. 'Walking up the Mall and round the Park I felt that this was less a war than a fancy-dress parade — soldiers and sailors and airmen, English and Scots, Anzac and Canadian, all crossing and recrossing like the convolutions of some gigantic minuet, which impression was enhanced by their stylized salutations', recorded 2nd Lieutenant T.E.B. Howarth in early March 1940. His diary is now in the IWM Department of Documents, at 84/7/1. On 19 May 1940 Charles Ritchie noted 'A group of Dutch soldiers in the street in German-looking uniforms gives one a turn' (*The Siren Years*, p. 53). Overseas troops were a popular novelty with the female population. 'Grass widows in black with diamond clips or pearls are finding the conversation of Polish officers refreshingly different from that of English husbands', observed Ritchie in October 1941 (p. 122). The overseas contingents had their own clubs and bars — the Polish Hearth, Netherlands House, the York Minster in Soho, haunt of the Free French, but the troops became familiar figures in pubs and restaurants all over the West End. 'London is full of young Canadian soldiers', wrote Joyce Grenfell to her mother in January 1940, 'We see them in groups at Lyons where all the waitresses vie with each other to serve them' (*Darling Ma.* Hodder, 1988). The Café de Paris was full of Canadian servicemen and nurses when it was bombed in March 1941.

The arrival of American troops in 1942 greatly increased the overseas presence. Their Rainbow Club, in Piccadilly Circus, became a mecca for girls from all over London. Inevitable complaints arose about the decline of public morals. The Public Morality Council, whose records are in LMA A/PMC/41, received a denunciation of the Hamilton House Hotel, 140 Piccadilly, 'concerning young woman going to the hotel with soldiers

# ON LEAVE IN LONDON

## 94

Published fortnightly by THE LONDON REGIONAL COMMITTEE FOR EDUCATION AMONG H.M. FORCES, 21 Bloomsbury Street, London, W.C.1. Subscriptions (post free) 13/- per annum, 7/- half-yearly, 4/- quarterly; single copies 7d., individual members of H.M. Forces etc. at a reduced rate of

3d. post free. The closing date for the next issue is the 13th January and thereafter every second Thursday. There is no charge for inclusion in this compilation, but the London Regional Committee reserves the right of selecting from the material submitted. — *Hon. Editor.*

**Number Ninety-Four**    FOR DISPLAY    *from 20th to 27th January, 1945*
*The next issue will appear on 27th January.*

DEAR FORCES,

If you care for Shakespeare, you will like Henry V, if you don't you may, after seeing it, be left wondering why. Eric J. Batson, A.L.A., the lively young temporary Senior Assistant of St. Pancras Public Libraries, contributes the following report on this exceptional film :—

"There seem to be two very distinct methods of presenting Shakespeare. Simply (and most effectively) as on many occasions at the Westminster before the war, or with fanfare and pageantry as by Sir Henry Irving and company at the old Lyceum, on one occasion by Mr. Ivor Novello at Drury Lane, and now by Mr. Laurence Olivier in the Chronicle Film of Henry V. As many of us enjoy the second method, just as we like double-feature programmes in the cinema, I'd be willing to wager money in the ratio that has never been done better than in the present instance.

Mr. Olivier and his colleagues had the brilliant idea of filming the first act or two of Shakespeare's play as it might have been staged at the Globe Theatre in Will's own day, with the audience laughing and talking in the wrong places and 'taking the mike' out of some of the characters they didn't like quite so much. (Just as I think they were afraid some of us might do if we weren't used to taking Shakespeare seriously as if he had a lesson to teach us or not plenty of fun of his own kind in his characters, Falstaff, Pistol, and the others—the first played, in a few moments dying appearance, by Mr. George Robey, and the second by Mr. Robert Newton.) This excellent idea is a little overdone, but at a cue from the noble and just Mr. Gielgud who takes the extracts out of Henry's heads, for at least 100 minutes we share in imagination the same unforgettable experiences of war and bravery that the Soldier of Agincourt had in common with the Man of Arnhem. And in the midst of all, virile and inspiring, is the Henry of Laurence Olivier—not the typical king of mediaeval times as we imagine him from our history books, but Shakespeare's Henry, the Englishman in arms fighting that the world may have peace again, and that he and Katherine (played so charmingly by Renee Asherson) may look forward with other lovers to the day that 'Shall change all griefs and quarrels into love'."

I would mention in conclusion that the colours which in many scenes have been conceived as a pattern, are exquisite, and the idea of leaving the artists' and technicians' names till the film's end has my heartiest approval.

THE EDITOR.

## CHURCH SERVICES IN LONDON

3rd Sunday after Epiphany. For details see *The Times* on Saturday.

St. Paul's Cathedral, Ludgate Hill, E.C.4. (*Blackfriars, Mansion House, St. Paul's Stations*): M.P. 10.30; Evening 3.15.
Westminster Abbey, Parliament Square, S.W.1. (*Westminster Underground Station*): M.P. 10.30; Evening 3.
Southwark Cathedral, London Bridge, S.E.1. (*London Bridge Station*): M.P. 11; Evening 6.

The Royal and Military Chapels all have Services in the morning, and most of the Parish Churches at 11 and 6.30.
St. Columba's (Church of Scotland), at Imperial Institute, off Exhibition Road, S.W. (*South Kensington Station*): 11 and 6.30.
St. Martin-in-the-Fields, Trafalgar Square: 11.30, 3.30, 6.15.

357

## PLAYS RECOMMENDED

*Garrick Theatre* : Uncle Harry. A nightmarish murder play with a psychological interest. Outstanding performances by Michael Redgrave and Beatrix Lehmann.
*Aldwych Theatre* : To-morrow the World. A play about the post-war problem of Nazi Youth. David O'Brien, a boy of 14, gives a quite remarkable character-study of the Nazi child.
*Vaudeville Theatre* : No Medals. Witty comedy in the lives of the housewives of England in war-time. Fay Compton gives a delightful, humourous performance.
*Savoy Theatre* : The Last of Mrs. Cheyney. Revival of Lonsdale's well-known comedy. Jack Buchanan plays a 'straight' part—in a 'crook' play.
*St. Martin's Theatre* : The Magistrate. Pinero in one of his lighter moods. Victorian Farce.

*Supplement to 'On Leave in London' Reference List, No. 9:*

## MUNICIPAL LIBRARIES—II

*ST. MARYLEBONE PUBLIC LIBRARIES, Public Library, Marylebone Road, N.W.1. Nearest terminal station : Marylebone. Nearest Underground Station : Baker Street. Bus : 1, 23, 27, 27a, 18, 2, 13, 113, 30, 53, 53a, 74. Telephone : WELbeck 7766. Hours of opening : Winter, 9 a.m. to 8 p.m. Summer, 9 a.m. to 8 p.m.
*WESTMINSTER CITY LIBRARIES, St. Martin's Street, W.C.2. Nearest Underground Stations : Leicester Square and Trafalgar Square. Telephone : TEMple Bar 0111 (Extension 32).
Buckingham Palace Road, S.W.1. Nearest Underground Station : Victoria. Bus : 11, 39, 46 (near Coach Station). Telephone : TEMple Bar 0111 (Extension 11).
Great Smith Street, S.W.1. Nearest Underground Station : Westminster. Bus : to Great Smith Street, nr. Westminster Abbey. Telephone : TEMple Bar 0111 (Extension 31).
South Audley Street, W.1. Nearest Underground Station : Green Park. Bus : to Mount Street, off Park Lane. Telephone : TEMple Bar 0111 (Extension 12).
*At the above libraries the hours of opening are : Winter, 10 a.m. to quarter of an hour before dim-out. Summer : 10 a.m. to 8 p.m.
*BISHOPSGATE INSTITUTE LIBRARY, 230, Bishopsgate, E.C.2. Nearest Terminal Station : Liverpool Street. Nearest Underground Station : Liverpool Street. Bus : 8, 8A, 6, 7, 9, 11, 22, 35, 50, 133. Trolley Bus : 557, 649. Telephone : BIShopsgate 2254. Hours of opening : Winter and Summer : 10 a.m. to 5 p.m. This library, which is adjacent to Liverpool Street Station, is similar to the public libraries but administered by a non-municipal board of governors.

*'On Leave in London' Reference List, No. 14:*

## U.S. ARMY CHURCH SERVICES IN LONDON (W.1)

Protestant :
*Sundays :*
08.30 hr.    Communion, St. Marks, N. Audley Street.
09.15 hr.    FUSAG. Church of Annunciation (back of Cumberland Hotel).
09.30 hr.    U.S. Army Service, Grosvenor Chapel, 24, S. Audley Street.

Catholic :
*Mondays, Wednesdays and Saturdays :*
18.00 hr.    1, Green Street.

Jewish :
*Fridays :*
18.45 hr.    Balfour Service Club, 41, Portland Place.

360

## NEW PLAYS

The *Chanticleer Theatre* is producing the Restoration Comedy, The Provok'd Wife by Sir John Vanbrugh this month. *Wyndham's Theatre* re-opens with Daphne du Maurier's new play, The Years Between. Clive Brook is playing a leading part in this.

## DRAWING SECRETS.

Since lots of you have an idea they would like to draw, but sooner or later realise that no matter how much native talent for drawing they may have, they need expert guidance, an inexpensive booklet of instruction by a successful daily newspaper cartoonist should be just the thing.

*Drawing Secrets* (Simpkin Marshall, 3/6) is by Jack Greenall cartoonist and creator of a *Daily Mirror* character 'Useless Eustace.' It makes forty-four pages and has an attractive pictorial cover.

Entertainment ideas for troops on leave
*(Bishopsgate Institute file 'Institute, 1941–7')*

and stopping the night... the Charwomen have often mentioned the disgraceful goings on there'. Mass-Observation investigated reports that Allied troops were taking young women to pubs around Victoria and Covent Garden to buy them strong drink and seduce them. Thorough investigation led the observers to conclude, in M-O File Report 1835 of 11.6.43, that 'If anything the boot would seem to be on the other foot' — the women were waiting in the pubs, hoping to have an exciting evening at the expense of American and Canadian soldiers. 'I'm drunk, she's drunk, you're drunk. God if my husband could see me now', said a WAAF, swaying about in a Canadian's arms. Everyone was struck by the sheer numbers of the American troops. 'The West End of London had more American troops than ever; there was a queue of them outside the Windmill Theatre with a solitary member of the RAF at the rear', wrote Henry St John, whose diary is in Ealing Local History Library, in February 1944.

Records relating to Dominion and Allied troops in the U.K. in general and London in particular are kept in most cases by the national archives of the countries concerned. Netherlands records, for example, are housed in the Ministerie van Defensie central archives, listed in Somers and Pier's *Archievengids van de Tweede Wereldoorlog* (1994). National listings for other countries and the Dominions should be consulted as appropriate. In some cases the PRO has useful information. WO 315, for instance, comprises papers of the Army Records Centre, Polish section, with Polish war service records. FO 892/7 is a report on Free French forces in Britain.

Some personal testimony can be found among the collections of the IWM's Department of Documents. Mrs L. Boyde, in 89/4/1, served as a Voluntaire clerk with the Free French in London. Her letters describe her duties, and her flirtations. Mrs J.R. Demey's memoirs include some time as a WAAF attached to the Belgian Air Force in London in 1944, in 88/2/1. The collection even has items collected by a GI on leave in London in 1943 and 1944 — leave passes, theatre ticket, ration coupon and other ephemera, in Misc. 1187.

## *Enemy documents*

After a mission over England Luftwaffe pilots were debriefed and then compiled a quick report on the sortie. A fuller report was made later. These reports can be contradictory, and sometimes claim successful hits that were not in fact achieved. Some of this material was destroyed in the war, or lost in the confusion of the post war period. Some was seized by the British and American authorities for examination, though most collections have now been returned to the Bundesarchiv Militararchiv in Freiburg. Most of the London raids were mounted by Luftflottenkommando 3 — High Command of the 3rd Air Fleet — from Northern France, but Luftflottenkommando 2, based in the Low Countries, was also active. The surviving records are in Freiburg. The Department of Documents in the IWM has two Luftwaffe Flying Log Books kept by a wireless operator, 1938–41, including entries for London raids, in Ger. Misc. 19 (156). The LMA collection contains a copy of a German map of London made in 1941, based on the 1933 Ordnance Survey map, with significant features marked for pilots as targets for aerial bombardment, in SC/PM/XX/02/109, FW 5866. Further information about the map, a prime source for London topography of the period because it was updated by reconnaissance photography, will be found in Christopher Board's article in the *London Topographical Record,* XXVII (1995). As mentioned elsewhere, some German film of raids on London is available, such as IWM GWY 333/2, a night raid on the docks, GW 502, aerial attacks on London, and GW 202.2, showing night raids.

## POLYGLOT STRANGERS: OVERSEAS VISITORS

Londoners have always been accustomed to overseas visitors. From the earliest times foreigners came to the city as traders, as diplomats and later as sightseers, students and journalists. Some groups stayed, became assimilated and thoroughly anglicised, others retained their language and cultural identity in a London context, like the inhabitants of Soho, and of 'Little Italy' in Clerkenwell, who suffered for it when Italy entered the war in 1940. Over ten per cent of the capital's population was composed of immigrant groups by the 1930s, and students from the colonies and Dominions were familiar figures. But the exigencies of war brought thousands more visitors from abroad and Londoners were acutely aware of the change. London had never seemed more of an international crossroads than at this time.

## *Refugees*

The arrival of increasing numbers of refugees from Germany, Austria and Czechoslovakia during the 1930s had started the process, with 55,000 of them settling permanently in London. From the spring of 1940 they were joined by civilians escaping to England ahead of the advancing German invasion troops. Crowds watched them arriving at the main line stations, on their way to the nine LCC reception centres around the city. Here they were registered, medically examined, bathed and fed before being passed to the borough councils for billeting. These reception centres were all staffed by WVS volunteers who provided food and drink, looked after small children, and found interpreters. The borough councils set up clearing stations to receive parties sent on from the Reception Centres. They were given identity cards, ration books and gas masks before being billeted. Charles Ritchie, the Canadian diplomat, described the new arrivals in his diary, *The Siren Years*, on 19 May 1940: '...tough-looking Norwegian seamen with shocks of coarse blond hair, dressed in blue serge suits, lunching at Garland's Hotel — Dutch peasant girls in native costume like coloured photographs in the Geographic magazine — walking down Cockspur Street carrying their worldly possessions tied up in bundles'. Records of this influx survive in a wide range of repositories.

### *National records*

Several government departments were involved with the refugee problem, so various classes at the PRO have useful records. The Assistance Board made grants to refugees as well as to the bombed-out homeless, see AST 11; the Ministry of Education dealt with the education of refugee children, see ED 11 and ED 128; the Ministry of Health had responsibility for refugees, see MH 57, MH 76 and MH 79. MH 76/516, for example, concerns appointments to the Central Committee for War Refugees from Holland, Belgium and France; MH 76/521 deals with the reception of refugees from the Channel Islands and MH 76/525 covers those from Gibraltar. MH 79/565 is a folder about medical arrangements for war refugees, particularly wounded civilians, of all nationalities arriving in Britain.

Home Office papers contain naturalization records in HO 334 and the records of the Czechoslovak Refugee Trust in HO 294. Treasury files have Czechoslovak Financial Claims Office files in T 210. Some Foreign Office files, such as FO 940, Control Office: Travel, yield information about individual refugees as well as policy matters. The British Council established several 'National Houses' for refugees and Allied troops in London, the surviving records are in BW 108 and include those for the Polish, Yugoslav and Dutch homes. Those for Netherlands House, in Charles Street, W1, in BW 108/2, for instance, contain papers on its constitution, committee, alterations to the premises, subscription rates, guest lists for the opening in August 1943, and letters from well-wishers, as well as applications for the post of Director. The interview panel thought they had found a strong candidate except for 'the unfortunate impression created on two members of this committee by his wife...'.

*Public reactions*

Public reaction to the arrival of refugees was monitored by Mass-Observation at various points in the war. In May 1940 the authorities decided to billet Dutch and Belgian refugees in the Cricklewood and Wembley area. Air Raid wardens distributed forms to houses willing to take them in. The government paid 35/- per couple per week or 21/- a head, and the refugees were expected to help with some domestic work. One hundred and twenty householders agreed. Mass-Observation, in M-O file 143, recorded surprised reactions that a high risk area like Cricklewood had been chosen, near the Smith factories and Hendon aerodrome, 'one of the most exposed parts of London' and a likely target. 'On the whole Cricklewood people are very sorry for the refugees', but there was some resentment. Why should the locals look after other people's children when their own had been evacuated? The government was accused of spending money on refugees and stinting the English over shelters and food. Rumours spread about German uniforms worn under other clothes. Memories surfaced of bad experiences with Spanish refugees in the 1930s and Belgians in the First World War. When observers returned to Cricklewood in June 1940 for a follow-up report, in M-O file 174, they found that opinion about the refugees was still fairly evenly divided.

North London refugees                                    HJ    26/5/40

Cricklewood -- Saturday 25th.

Cricklewood is an evacuation area, but the authorities have decided to billet Dutch and Belgian refugees in every house where there is room available. This step seems to be surprising as Cricklewood is one of the most exposed parts of London and one of the most legitimate military objectives, with the Smith factories nearby and the Hendon aerodrome. Airraid wardens went round to every house, leaving forms to whoever wished to take any refugees. The government pay was 35/- per couple and 21/- a head. The refugees were also expected to help in domestic work. 120 houses agreed to take some, out of six streets covered by the wardens. This will probably mean that about 250 refugees would be billeted in the vicinity of Coles Green Road.

In this neighbourhood the arrival of the refugees was preceded by several rumours and stories, Cricklewood being full of foreigners. Spy rumours went round about the German uniforms found underneath the clothing of some refugees.    On the other hand, pathetic stories were told of the dreadful sufferings of the Belgian and Dutch. One

Mass-Observation reports on attitudes to refugees in Cricklewood
*(M-O Report 143)*

## The voluntary bodies

Among the Family Welfare Association papers in LMA is a minute book of the British War Refugees' Fund, 1940–2, in A/FWA/C/J8/1. Monthly reports of the WVS's St Pancras branch, in the WRVS archives, trace the rising tide of refugee arrivals through the summer of 1940. In May they visited and classified about 1350 billets in advance and dealt with 150 arrivals. Helpers met trains at St Pancras station. Belgians, Dutch, Poles, Maltese and Czechs came in ever greater numbers. Some had very large families and it was difficult to billet them together. By August there were 517 refugees in the borough. The WVS ran English classes, clubs, and craft classes for them. In November the branch reported: 'The main problem facing the Refugee Department in November has been housing. The Maltese refugees, once they are off billetting, tend to move from furnished to unfurnished rooms. These moves necessarily involve help with furniture'. 'The clothing department is now dealing mainly with Czech, Polish and Maltese cases — either invalids, merchant sailors on shore sick leave or families where the earnings are insufficient to meet essential needs.' The YWCA was another voluntary organisation greatly concerned with refugee welfare; their records are at the Modern Records Centre of the University of Warwick, MSS.243.

Ordinary Londoners also made an effort to help the refugees settle in. The parish magazine of St Barnabas, Dulwich, in LMA P73 BAN 489, recorded in September 1940 that a tea party had been given for them in the parish hall in July, with over a hundred attending. Now the parish needed volunteers to help with English classes and a club. 'Can you spare an hour a week to come and talk to them?' The vicar appealed for books, pencils, and sewing materials to help prepare for a sale of work.

## Local authority records

Local authority records, mostly emanating from welfare departments, contain material on their dealings with the refugee problem though personal information may still be closed to general enquirers. At county council level, for example, Middlesex CC refugee records occur mainly in MCC/CD/WAR/3/33, about the War refugees' service, and MCC/WE/PA/2/38 on War refugees, /42 on the refugee scheme 1940–2 and the Jewish Hospital, /46 on Belgian nationals, /47 on Channel Island refugees; /57 on Gibraltarians and /64 on billeting in general. MCC/WE/PA/2/51 contains typescript weekly and monthly war refugees' assessment returns, giving the number of assessments made and a note of decisions to cease paying billeting allowances to certain refugees. The weekly return for 12 September 1942 for Hendon notes 'Nil. (10 assessments totalling £7.12.0 per week have been cancelled owing to Belgian refugees now being required to pay economic rents for accommodation in requisitioned houses'. Borough collections occasionally contain records about refugees. Kensington Local Studies Library, for instance, has some lists of war refugees made in the autumn of 1940 by the Kensington War Refugees' Committee. 940.5315 AR/A is a handwritten 'List of Overseas War Refugees' gives the address of billet, refugee number, date of birth, nationality — mostly Belgian — and occasional brief comments such as 'obtained work; keeping herself; army; moved to Marylebone; gone to Canada; left for Lisbon' in a 'remarks' column.

## Personal memories

Personal testimony from refugees occurs in many published and unpublished diaries and memoirs, among them Ilse Meyer's reminiscences about her experiences in Hampstead before and during the war, kept at Camden Local Studies and Archives Centre, and Dr H. Enoch's journal, a copy of which is in the IWM's Department of Documents. He was a German Jewish refugee initially interned but later released and working in wartime London. Other diarists occasionally comment on refugees, like Anthony Heap, who noted a novel sight on 22 March 1941 — football in Russell Square: 'It was being played by a swarm of young refugee urchins, all kicking up the deuce of a row and ruining the place. A thing British children would of course never be allowed to do in this land "fit for foreigners to live in". Is this an uncharitable thought? Perhaps it is, but not unreasonably so' (LMA ACC 2243/15/1).

The IWM Sound Archive contains hundreds of refugee interviews, such as the tape of Gunther Wittenberg, 11930/2, who arrived as a schoolchild in 1939 and spent some of the war in London. The National Sound Archive's 'Living memory of the Jewish community' series contains interviews with several people who arrived as refugees just before the war, such as Mrs Friedel Kochman, C410/099 C1, who describes her experiences living in one room, very short of money, in London during the war, and her first impressions of the English and the Jewish community. Jack Habel, on C410/033 C1, arrived in London from Berlin in 1939 and stayed at a Salvation Army hostel. As his English was good, he was given the job of meeting new arrivals and helping them to settle in. Hanus Weisl, on C410/022 C1, arrived as a child from Czechoslovakia, sponsored by a Quaker organisation. He remembers staying in a Paddington boarding house with a 'generally unhappy atmosphere', and later moving with his parents to a refugee hostel in Kingston.

### Enemy Aliens

Enemy aliens resident in Britain were interned by the War Office at the start of the war, but from August 1940 this became the responsibility of the Home Office. HO classes 213, 214 and 215 contain files on individuals and internment camps. Enemy aliens were arrested by the police, so Metropolitan Police classes such as MEPO 3–5 are also useful here. As is well known, the initial sweep of aliens rounded up refugees from Nazi Germany as well as its sympathisers, and the entry of Italy into the war in June 1940 occasioned the internment of many unfortunate long-established London Italians who had not taken British nationality. Mass-Observation studied the anti-Italian riots in Soho in M-O file 184. Three observers visited the area the evening after Italy came into the war. They concluded that press stories of 'riots' were exaggerated. Police kept the crowds under control, very little damage was done, only a small number of people felt violently about it. 'There was no mass movement or surging tide of racial feeling in Soho'. Some cafes put signs out to say they were Swiss. All the Italian cafés in Old Compton Road [sic] were empty of customers. The Home Office asked for WVS help in dealing with the practicalities of internment. The WVS Regional Reports box 'London Region 1938–80' contains Region 5's (Metropolitan London) report for June 1940, recording that, at very short notice and in conditions of great secrecy, the WVS had been asked to help with the internment of class B women aliens. They organised a hundred volunteers for a Sunday, fifty to staff Fulham Institute, which was used as a clearing house, and fifty to escort the women to Liverpool on their way to the Isle of Man, providing nappies, baby food and other essentials for dealing with small children and mothers. Attached is a 'Report on work undertaken by the WVS in connection with the arrest of women enemy aliens and their children on 27 May 1940'. The London section gives a vivid description of the difficulties of the journey. The IWM Sound Archive has many interviews with enemy aliens among its refugee coverage.

Report from

MASS-OBSERVATION.

on

ANTI-ITALIAN RICTS IN
SOHO

Obs: arrives at the corner of Old Compton Street and
Dean Street. about 8 o'clock. Many groups of people were standing
about. English, Italians, French and many Jews of those nationality one could not be sure. There was much excited talk and
everyone seemed to be expecting something to happen. Several
policemen mingled with the crowds, stood at corners and in door-
ways.

The Italian restaurant situated at the actual corner
of these two streets was full of customers. As Obs; stood about,
a woman seized her by the hand "They're rounding them up" she
said with excitement and an air of great satisfaction. She was
eager to talk, a capable middle-aged working-class woman who
knew her own mind.

"They've raided the Station Club near St.Martin's
Lane" she continued. "Fifty police went in." Another, slightly
older working-class woman was with her.

"After they've cleared out the Italians, they'll clear
out the Jews" she said "You'll see - and a good job too. I ask you,
why should these foreigners be here, why should they be employed
at lower rates, and so many English out of work. It isn't right
now, it is ?

The other woman laughed - both women were extremely
good humoured. There was nothing vindictive in their satisfaction.

"We're going to choose the cafe we'd like" she said -
"We're going to go round and have a look at 'em all to-night".
"My, aren't they frightened, look at that man over there ! he's
green " said the first woman as an elderly, stout, jewish-looking
Italian came out of the corner restaurant. The other woman added
"You should have seen one of 'em a bitago. Knawing his finger
nails 'e was. Real frightened 'e was - they're not good fighters,
these Italians. Won't make it any worse for us, them coming in -
don't you worry about that."

"No, my dear" said the first woman. "make no mistake
about that, we're going to win this war, after that it's going
to be England for the English. There'll be none of this" -
indicating Soho with a wave of her hand."All these cafe'll be
owned by the English. And why shouldn't they be ? I ask you -
why not ?

A third woman (middle-class) who had joined the group,
said, in gentle remonstration "You know who talks like that,
don't you?" "England for the English" That's what Hitler says.
I don't know what you mean and you're right, but you want to be
careful. Don't say things like that in the street."

"She's right" said the elder women "They twist what
you say these days, don't they?

A Mass-Observation reporter notes reactions to Italy's entry into the war, 11 June 1940
*(M-O Report 184)*

## Diplomats

Diplomats from friendly and neutral states stayed on in London throughout the war, sending detailed analyses of all aspects of life and the war effort in Britain back to their home governments. Such despatches are now in the national archives of the countries concerned. Some ambassadors and diplomatic staff later published memoirs, letters and diaries from their time in London; several are listed in the bibliography. The Canadian Charles Ritchie's *The Siren Years* (1974) is full of insights. On 29 January 1941 he wrote: 'I am ashamed of the despatches we sent to Ottawa. They give an officalese picture of England at war without conveying any sense of the cross-currents. Above all they leave out any pictures of the social changes stirring just under the surface. Mr Massey does not want the Government at home to glimpse these abysses lest they should be disturbed in their belief that they are fighting for the survival of political democracy, liberal ideas and human individualism side by side with the traditional England' (p. 86). Visiting politicians often recorded their impressions of England at war. The Australian Prime Minister, Robert Menzies, arrived in London in February 1941. He stayed at the Dorchester, in the suite recently vacated by the American envoy Wendell Willkie. Menzies' diary, published as *Dark and Hurrying Days* (1993), describes his view of London: 11 March 1941 'London is dull and grey. There is a tough and determined spirit, but the colour and gaiety have gone. In squares like Berkeley Square, houses ruined, windows boarded up. The shops everywhere with windows reduced to peep holes. The luncheons reduced to oysters and one course (fish or meat or chicken or eggs or cheese)' (p. 87). He visited air raid shelters, on one occasion addressing shelterers in Bermondsey, and on 25 April he toured more: 'At dusk, visit Air Raid Shelters in the Tubes at King's Cross and Old Street. Indescribably pathetic. Malodorous, or rather stuffy. Bunks of wire arranged in tiers of 2 or 3 along the platforms and in the recesses. Canteen arranged... They are drab, dreary and look infinitely sad — standing in the queues for their places, for which they have tickets' (p. 118). The outsider's view is also to be found in several collections of letters and journals in the IWM Department of Documents, written by foreign nationals (mostly American) living, working or visiting London during the war.

## Governments in exile

With the German advance across Europe in the summer of 1940 politicians from several countries took refuge in London to set up governments in exile. The Free French, the Netherlands, Belgium, Poland, Norway, Luxembourg and later Czechoslovakia, Yugoslavia and Greece operated in this way, and dissident German Social Democrats were also active. Though their records (where they survive) are naturally chiefly concerned with resistance at home, the Allied war effort and their national politics, they do shed light on London life as experienced by their ministers, civil servants, other staff and troops. The Foreign Office co-ordinated dealings with these Allied governments in London, and the FO classes in the PRO contain material of potential interest. Among them are embassy and consular files, such as FO 536 for Yugoslavia; FO 561 for France, FO 606 Belgium, and correspondence files for the FO's dealings with the London-based governments — FO 688 Poland, FO 817 Czechoslovakia. A special department was set up to deal with negotiations with the Free French, documented in FO 892.

After the war most of the exiled governments took their records back to their own national archive collections. Dutch records for this period, for example (listed in Somers and Pier's *Archievengids van de Tweede Wereldoorlog* (1994) are in the collections of the Algemeen Rijksarchief, the Ministerie van Oorlog, Rijksinstituut voor Oorlogsdocumentatie and the Koninklijk Huisarchief, depending on provenance. Free French material is in the Archives Nationales in Paris, or the Archives du Ministere des Affaires Etrangères, listed in B. Blanc and others, *La Seconde Guerre Mondiale: Guide des Sources Conservées en France* (1994). Private papers, published and unpublished, of the main figures involved and their staff frequently contain background material on life in London.

The Polish government in exile stayed on in London after the war and took care to preserve its archives for posterity. Milewski's *Guide to the Archives of the Polish Institute and Sikorski Museum* v.1 (1985) explains the background and lists their holdings, which cover government departmental papers of many kinds and an abundance of personal papers, some of which refer to life in London. Dorothy Annesley, KOL 211, for instance, was an ambulance unit volunteer who joined the Polish Red Cross and ran a Polish Army Hostel in London in 1943. KOL 15 concerns the activities of Polish Radio in London, and generally in the UK, and there are the papers of the London branch of the Scottish-Polish Friendship Society in KOL 267. The Polish Library has books, newspapers, photographs and other material about aspects of Polish life in wartime London, including the Polish Catholic Mission and the Polish Hearth Club as well as the government in exile. Another London collection of Polish archival material is held by the Polish Underground Movement (1939–45) Study Trust in Ealing. Their collection relates mainly to Poland, but contains some items of London interest, like the personal papers of Lt-Col. Konrad Bogacki, a signals officer, with material on signal communications between occupied Poland and London, Polish Radio in London and the wartime organisation of the BBC.

The British Library National Sound Archive has tapes made from the Polish Institute's recordings of wartime Polish Radio broadcasts, dealing with Polish affairs and the government in exile in London, on C499.

All the governments in exile broadcast to their home countries with the help of the BBC, whose written and recorded archives contain relevant material about this cooperation and the resulting programmes. The governments all ran news agencies and periodicals dedicated to their cause — the Belgians' INBEL bureau issued *La Belgique Independante* and *Onafhankelijk Belgie*; the Free French *La lettre de la France combattante* (later *Tricolore*), *La Marseillaise, La France Libre* and others. Occasionally these publications contain pieces on London life. *La France Libre* 7 (38) 1943, for example, carries an article by Jean Oberlé, 'Images Anglaises' which is an amusing survey of London pubs.

The United States government was anxious to monitor events in occupied Europe. The *Introductory Guide to American Documentation of the European Resistance Movements in World War II* by D.W. Ellwood and J.E. Miller (Turin: Univ. Inst. of European Studies, 1975) includes items relating to exiled governments in London.

Some evidence of public concern for beleaguered foreign communities in their midst occurs in sources as unexpected as the LCC Parks Committee minutes in LMA LCC/MIN and departmental papers in LCC/PK/GEN, which contain correspondence and arrangements about holding circuses, concerts and other events on behalf of such bodies as the Yugoslav Relief Society, the Hungarian War Effort Committee and others.

# IMAGES ANGLAISES

IL y a beaucoup de gens qui cherchent l'Angleterre dans un tas de choses: le Parlement de Westminster, les matches de football à Wembley, la relève de la Garde à Buckingham Palace ou la procession du Lord-Maire à travers la Cité. Il y en a d'autres, comme moi, qui la cherchent—et la trouvent—tout simplement dans les *pubs.*

Ce n'est pas uniquement par amour de la boisson, bien entendu, quoique, avant tout, on aille au *pub* pour boire et quoique, au premier coup d'œil, tous ces gens, plantés sur leurs jambes, devant le comptoir, comme le cheval devant l'abreuvoir, n'aient pas d'autre alternative que de commander bière ou whisky, à la barmaid, ou au barman, qui les interroge du regard. Non, c'est parce que le *pub*, c'est ce qu'il y a de plus anglais, véritablement anglais, en Angleterre, et c'est aussi ce qu'il y a de plus sympathique, de plus gentil. D'ailleurs quand un ami anglais veut vous montrer sa confiance, il vous dit, presque en confidence: «Je vais vous emmener dans un *nice pub.*»

Il faut absolument éliminer la notion du « café ». L'apéritif, la banquette en moleskine, la belote, la « verse pour un », doivent disparaître de votre mémoire, malgré vingt ans de souvenirs. On retrouvera ça (espérons-le) en rentrant en France. Il faut aussi éviter de critiquer, et de protester contre les heures d'ouverture et de fermeture, incompréhensibles et regrettables. On est en Angleterre, et le *pub* c'est l'Angleterre.

Le mot, ou plutôt l'abréviation, déjà est intime, presque amical. Et puis il est, dirai-je, universel, unanime, presque sacré. Le lord comme le *cockney* l'emploient, en vrai Anglais, sachant que c'est du vrai anglais. Et l'emploient avec une nuance de sympathie, alors qu'en France, la châtelaine ne parlera jamais du « bistrot », si ce n'est avec mépris. Non, *pub* est très gentil. On ne peut tout de même pas dire *public-house!* Les vieux habitués appellent leur *pub* « *the local* », mais c'est par pure familiarité.

Le *pub*, c'est l'Angleterre, parce que c'est l'Angleterre comme elle est vraiment, bonne enfant, simple, aimant boire, familière même (malgré qu'on parle rarement à son voisin de tabouret ou de comptoir) et puis presque enfantine, se distrayant à des jeux simples: fléchettes, dominos, et ce *shoveha'penny*, si mystérieux pour les «continentaux», et qui, depuis tant de générations, groupe les Anglais autour de la petite planche sur laquelle ils font glisser un sou, en le cognant du plat de la main. Les temps modernes ont amené d'Amérique ces machines à sous, électriques, compliquées, qui ne riment à rien, et qui détonnent dans l'atmosphère familiale du *pub*, où elles annoncent la mort d'un tas de vieux trucs qu'on aimait bien.

Car, dans cette petite pièce où brûle un feu de charbon, où l'acajou du comptoir reluit comme un banc d'église, où les pintes d'étain brillent doucement, où le vieil habitué parle à mi-voix au patron, tandis qu'une femme de ménage, en chapeau, sa journée finie, rêve vaguement sur son verre de bière, où le choc léger des fléchettes sur la petite cible de bois accompagne le crissement de la craie sur l'ardoise, on se croirait vraiment chez soi, et bien des gens s'y trouvent mieux que chez eux, dans la fumée des pipes et la procession interminable des verres de bière. Des objets

London pubs are a culture shock for French visitors
*(La France Libre, volume 7, number 38, 1943, p. 120)*

# 5. The Pursuit of Normal Life

The government was acutely aware of the need to foster good morale among a population facing sudden death or injury as well as discomfort and personal inconvenience for an indefinite period. Londoners suffered the lion's share of these problems, so the authorities paid particular attention to monitoring their reactions to all aspects of the war. The results were studied and used to inform propaganda campaigns and policy decisions on a wide variety of subjects.

Historians wishing to investigate the fluctuations of public morale at this period will find the chief sources lie in the PRO, among the records of the Home Office and the Ministries of Home Security and of Information. The Mass-Observation archive also contains invaluable data on this subject generally, and its observers were also used for a short period to monitor civilian morale on behalf of the government. Contemporary diaries and correspondence, whether personal, commercial or official, can also cast light on the ebb and flow of morale in incidental comments and anecdotes. Such material may occur in almost any collection, but can be difficult to pin down without a lengthy search.

## National records

Liaison between the Ministry of Home Security and the Ministry of Information was close, and resulted in some overlap among the records. The Ministry of Information both collected intelligence for other departments and co-ordinated its public dissemination. Staffed by a motley collection of academics, writers and artists as well as some career civil servants seconded from other departments, it operated out of the University of London's Senate House building. Its activities are described in Ian McLaine's *Ministry of Morale: Home Front Morale and the Ministry of Information* (1979). Its slightly surreal atmosphere features in a large number of autobiographies, memoirs and novels, among them George Orwell's *1984* (Secker, 1949), Evelyn Waugh's *Put Out More Flags* (Chapman Hall, 1942) and Graham Greene's *Ministry of Fear* (Heinemann, 1943).

The Ministry of Information's Home Intelligence Unit played a twofold role in monitoring the state of civilian morale. Its regular Home Intelligence Reports appeared daily from May to September 1940, and in the flying bomb summer of 1944, and weekly at other times, HO 203. Material for them was collected from a wide set of informants, including Mass-Observation, the Social Survey, BBC listener research, postal censors, cinema and bookshop managers, and the voluntary services. Among the Sidney Bernstein Collection at the IWM Department of Documents are letters from London cinema managers to the Ministry of Information, commenting generally on audience morale, on audience and staff behaviour during air raids, and on the reception given to MOI films. The letters include a frank one from the young manager of a cinema in East Ham in early September 1940 describing local reactions to high explosive bombs, sheltering, transport problems and the MOI: 'I don't think many of us trust the Ministry of Information

Bulletins. The same old voice on the news talks about aircraft "believed" to have been destroyed and "a few" casualties. Hundreds of people have access to accurate information which soon spreads. I know how many people were killed in East Ham on Friday night, so when I see bulletins in the local paper lying about it, I can only treat the rest of the MOI bulletins as bunk' (SBC box 5, Theatre Managers' Reports).

---

3rd September, 1940.  Reference..................

4│1

To :-  Mr. N. Bentley - Home Intelligence.
From:- Mr. Sidney Bernstein.

          I attach hereto excerpts from a letter from a
cinema manager in East Ham.

          The writer is a young man of 28 - level-headed
and intelligent, well trained to observe public reaction
and by no means a jittery or alarmist person.

Encl.

COPY

          After nine months of complacent waiting followed by
three months of setbacks and disasters, the man in the street is just
about grasping the fact that we're in a hell of a mess.

          This week has turned us into a very frightened and
a very desperate crowd of people.  East Hammers had not had the
opportunity of hearing high explosive bombs until Friday.  Short of
sleep as they were, it has properly put the fear of God into them, and
as far as cinemas are concerned "night-time business has been killed
stone dead.

          Men on my staff that were in the last war show their misery
in the present situation more openly than the rest, and their nerves
have been "opened up" again.  Stranded in the theatre all night with
half a dozen of them it was very pathetic.  They must keep talking and
yarning while we wait for the "All Clear" because they 'can't sleep
themselves and they are unconsciously too selfish to let anybody else
sleep.  These old sweats are very defeatist in their views and keep
rubbing in the terrible future they think we have in store for us.

---

Further views of a cinema manager on the state of public morale in early
September 1940, with covering note from Sidney Bernstein
*(IWM Sidney Bernstein Collection, Box 5)*

The Home Intelligence Unit's second function was to run the Social Survey, which conducted market surveys on behalf of other departments to investigate the effects of various practical problems on the population, such as food rationing, and shortages of consumer goods. Its reports and papers are in RG 23. In 1941, for example, it conducted research on foundation garments for the Board of Trade; in 1942 it looked at the salvage drive for the Ministry of Supply. RG 23/9a, for instance, comprises 'A summary of studies on the subject of food made by the Wartime Social Survey between February 1942 and October 1943', under the title 'Food during the war, by Gertrude Wagner'. This had examined attitudes to rationing, changes in food habits, knowledge of nutrition, regional differences, and eating away from home. 'The only significant differences so far found in the London region are a greater use of British Restaurants and the greatest number in favour of extension of food rationing'. These investigations did not focus on London in particular, but much of the research was done there and they can prove fruitful sources.

Home Intelligence Division files in HO 262 contain reports on public opinion and morale. Typical examples are HO 262/12, from late 1940, which includes a folder marked 'Home morale: report on decline of public confidence'. A gloomy memo from a Home Security civil servant notes 'a wave of depression is passing over the country which conceivably might lead to the strengthening of the party which desires negotiated peace, and, short of that, may attenuate the war effort'. After citing a list of potential causes, including the weather, he advocates that the government should 'administer encouragement as a tonic'. Among the resulting morale-boosting suggestions from the Ministry of Information's Duty Room were the ideas of relaying wireless to the air raid shelters, and of urging railway companies to play cheerful music over their station loudspeakers.

The coming of the flying bombs in 1944 revived the government's difficulties regarding public acknowledgment of the effects of bombing. Publishing the correct details might assist the enemy as well as sapping morale at home. But failing to do so encouraged the spreading of damaging and inaccurate rumours. HO 262/15 contains a buff folder labelled 'Morale of Civilian Population at Home. Flying Bombs and V2 rockets'. In it the director of Bourne & Hollingsworth, the Oxford Street department store, complains of 'a rumour in the provinces that Bourne & Hollingsworths is "flat to the ground". If this is the sort of story that is going about as a result of the lack of information being given to the public, I feel you should know about it' (June 22 1944). The Ministry offered to arrange for verbal denials. '... No denial can be published. Apart from anything else, this would spread the rumour and we should then be committed to doing the same for every commercial enterprise in London.' Other correspondents also bemoaned the widespread rumours of the day. Mr Hawker, from Staffordshire, wrote 'one or two damned fools that have come up here from there [London] are painting vivid stories of the bombing. Thus upsetting my parents and family. "There's hardly a street without houses down" is one of the foolish statements made'. The Ministry replied mildly that it was only natural that people leaving London should exaggerate their experiences — 'At the same time one has to realise that they have, many of them, been through a very severe strain and it may help them to talk about their troubles'. This file also reflects the resentment of Londoners who felt that their sufferings from the V1s were being played down for censorship reasons, although they deserved acknowledgement and sympathy. It also contains an assertion from the Metropolitan Police Commissioner (7 July 1944) that in three weeks of touring South London, where most of the bombs were falling 'Wherever I have been, I have found the morale remarkably high... Police morale is astonishingly good...'

HO 199, the Registered Files of the Home Intelligence Branch, also yield valuable material on London morale. Reports investigated the situation after raids — HO 199/104 deals with Harrow, Edmonton and Willesden on 23 August 1940, /112 with Lambeth on 16 January 1941 — and sometimes contain graphic detail on local conditions. HO 199/438 reports on the notorious unofficial air raid shelter in the crypt of Christ Church, Cubitt Town, in February 1941: 'Christchurch crypt has been described as a very black spot of bad conditions, but we were pleasantly surprised to find a sense of pride in their shelter among people who use it...'

## Mass-Observation records

The other main source of morale surveys and comments is Mass-Observation. The organisation was founded in 1937 by Tom Harrisson and Charles Madge to apply anthropological techniques of enquiry to social research in Britain. The resulting material is a rich source for social historians, covering an enormous range of subject-matter. Dorothy Sheridan's *Mass-Observation Archive: Guide for Researchers* (1992) indicates the full range of sources in the collection; several anthologies compiled from its material have also been published, such as *Speak for Yourself* (1984) and *Wartime Women* (1990). Although Mass-Observation operated throughout the country its report research was frequently done in London and many Londoners sent in diaries and questionnaires.

Morale was sometimes specifically targeted by M-O reports, like file report 605 on General morale in London, 11 March 1941, but it also recurs as the background to many other reports, such as M-O 364 on Metropolitan air raids, M-O 2121, entitled 'V1: survey on pilotless planes', and even in M-O 804 about 'Dogs in London': 'The effects of air raids or food shortages on your dog may worry you just as much as the effect of these things on yourself...'. The reports were compiled by undercover investigators who recorded comments made to them, or overheard by them, about the topic under consideration. The voice of the Londoner comes through with great clarity in many cases. 'I tell you what put the wind up me. When that bleeding plane came low-diving — just before the bang', said a young man at the height of the V1 raids, quoted in M-O 2121.

The Imperial War Museum's Department of Printed Books has microfiche or duplicate copies of many Mass-Observation reports, and some additional material from Mary Burns of the Wartime Social Survey, at Rare Book 31 (41) 5.01, most of which relates to her work in London, especially Paddington and St Pancras.

Further M-O records useful for the study of morale are the topic collections, boxes of material grouped by subject, such as TC 23, Air raids 1940–1, subdivided by place name. Box TC 23/9/H, for example, includes notes made on 13 September 1940 after a bad raid on the Isle of Dogs. Two thirds of the population had been evacuated, 'Those that are left look worried and weary but are still fairly cheerful'. Their main complaint was the transport problem. Two tunnels across the river were outofactionandno ferry service had been organised. Other reports here cover, for instance, a visit to Paddington Rest Centre after a raid and local versions of a bomb incident in Putney Bridge Road, including rumours circulating about the number of dead. M-O questionnaires, known as directives, can also be useful. In September 1940 the regular respondents were asked what effect the air raids had had upon them. One Londoner replied 'I don't think my mental attitude is affected, except perhaps in my attitude to radio. As a general rule I hate the wireless...', but he quite liked to have it on in air raids.

Mass-Observation diaries, sent in monthly, give insights into morale as, of course do those diaries kept elsewhere. Fluctuations of mood about the war and its dangers could be recorded in private from day to day without bringing accusations of defeatism or of undue optimism from those around. Understandably, it was not the military and political news of the war that usually had the greatest impact, but incidents affecting the diarist personally. Mrs M. Cossins worked at the British Museum in 1944. Her diary, in IWM Department of Documents 92/25/1, records a walk round the Inns of Court on 3 June 1944, seeing the results of recent raids. 'First I viewed the ruins of the church, etc. very very dreadful... How many people were killed I wonder. Buried under heaps of rubbish. I think that at first I could not have borne to see it, but one gets hardened to chaos'.

# BUSINESS AS USUAL: THE WORLD OF WORK

London was as central to Britain's business life in the late 1930s as it was to the nation's system of government. Hundreds of banking, insurance, shipping, wholesale and retailing firms were based in the City or the West End, and many industrial firms had London head offices even if their factories were elsewhere. The diversity of manufacture was very wide, and accounted for much of the city's prosperity. Old-established industrial premises were still to be found in central London, like Berger Paints in Homerton and the furniture and clothing workshops in Shoreditch. Out in the suburbs the growth of light industry between the wars had lined main roads with modern factories such as those of the Hoover and Firestone companies beside the A4. The war brought great changes to all these firms. Many lost key staff to the call-up. Some evacuated their work to the provinces, at least for a time. And industrial premises producing non-essential items were liable to be diverted to war production of munitions or other vital war requirements. Fords, for example, manufactured army trucks instead of private and commercial vehicles; Bryant and May made detonators instead of matches. Volumes in the *History of the Second World War UK Civil Series* including those on the *War Economy, British War Production, Works and Buildings, Contracts and Finance, Factories and Plant, Manpower,* and *Labour in the Munitions Industries* cover the economic problems in great detail, many with specific references to London. The volume *Civil Industry and Trade* is excellent on commercial policy in general, including price control, import and export controls, the retail trade and the textile industries in wartime.

## *National records*

Government involvement with every aspect of economic life at this period is reflected in records at the PRO, many of which are of particular London relevance. John Cantwell's book *The Second World War: A Guide to Documents in the PRO* is again valuable here. Material on London topics occurs in many Board of Trade records, for instance in the papers of the Bankruptcy and Companies departments, BT 37 and BT 58, and of the Industrial Supplies Department, BT 96. Perhaps unexpectedly, the London fashion industry was encouraged to continue manufacturing and exporting *haute couture* through the Cotton Board and Textile Council. It encouraged sales drives in South America and the United States, commissioning famous artists, including the cartoonist Fougasse, to produce fabric prints. *Vogue*'s June issue in 1941 illustrated many of these designs. The Cotton Board's papers are in BT 175. Adverse economic effects of the war can be traced in BT 226, bankruptcy applications put to the High Court by the Official Receiver, with some public examinations of individuals. Unfortunately only representative samples of cases after 1931 have been preserved, but some of them relate to London firms.

Ministry of Labour records such as BK 29, BK 35, on the London Docks Labour Board and LAB 100, the Port of London Registration Committee, and Ministry of Supply records including SUPP 4, contracts, also yield information about London business and industry. The London Regional Group's records on control and rationing are among those preserved in the files of the Ministry of Fuel and Power in POWE 3. Many London firms sustained bomb damage and it is sometimes possible to find detailed reports including plans and photographs in HO 192, the Ministry of Home Security Research and Experiments Department's registered papers. For example, HO 192/632 covers bomb damage to the heater and cooker manufacturers Falk Stadelmann & Co Ltd, of Onslow Street EC1, in

August/September 1944, with 35 accompanying photographs. IR 36 and IR 37, the papers of the War Damage Commission, may also be useful in this context. Even the Ministry of Agriculture records reflect economic activity in the London region. The National Farm Survey, MAF 32, covers farms in the Greater London area; indeed it allocated a file to the City, though it contains no documents. MAF 32/844/402, for example, deals with Hornchurch, Essex, now part of the borough of Havering, with detailed coverage of land allocation, labour, livestock, and a Ministry assessment of the farm's condition and efficiency, including 'personal failings' of the farmer, if relevant. Also vital for the full picture of London's wartime supply are the Port of London Authority's archives in the Museum in Docklands.

## Commercial records

Some firms, such as major banks and insurance companies, retain their own records, others have been deposited in local record offices and libraries. For many department store records, including Selfridges, Fortnum & Mason and Bourne & Hollingsworth, as well as those of other firms, a search of the National Register of Archives' catalogues leads the enquirer to the Business Archives Council for advice on access. The records of Heal & Son are in the Victoria and Albert Museum's Archive of Art and Design; the Army & Navy Stores records and those of Dickins & Jones are on deposit in the Business Record Centre in Glasgow University. Others are in local authority collections. Those for Berger Paints, for instance, are with Hackney Archives; J. Lyons & Co are in the custody of London Metropolitan Archives, with many other commercial archives. Westminster Archives have Gillows, the furnishing company's archives, and those of the clothing firm, Jaeger.

A good set of records can shed light on the wartime difficulties of operating the particular business, perhaps concerning change of use of machinery, shortage of equipment or raw materials, transport and distribution problems, staffing difficulties and war damage to the premises. Many firms increased their use of female labour considerably to replace the male staff who were called up. Information about wage-rates and labour troubles may also emerge. The records frequently include details of ARP provision for staff and visitors, with plans of air raid shelters and photographs of staff in gas masks, firewatching, or taking shelter. Large institutions were very conscious of the risk to their record-keeping from bomb damage and made careful arrangements to duplicate data elsewhere. Each branch of the National Provincial Bank, for example, prepared duplicate records for storage at some other, distant, branch. 'The maintenance, for over four and a half years, of these duplicate records added considerably to the work of our depleted staff, but their value was proved on many occasions', wrote the Bank's Inspection Department after the war (National Westminster Bank Archives NPB 3878, 26 November 1945). Smaller organisations did not necessarily anticipate the problem. The Cooks' Company, one of the ancient City livery companies, suffered badly in the great fire raid of late 1940. The Company minutes for 1941, in Guildhall MS 3111A/1 pp. 1–2, give details: 'The Clerk reported that his offices at 34 and 36 Gresham Street were totally destroyed by fire on December 29th in the enemy raid on the City and that all his papers, books and documents (including many original documents) also the Poor Box and its contents Ballot Box Beadle's Staff and Staff Head and Master's Ivory mallet were consumed in the flames...' The loss of so many records caused various complications for the Company, including losing track of those entitled to pensions — 'The Clerk reported that owing to the destruction of all his papers and books he was not in a position to communicate with the Pensioners, but that he thought it probable

# WESTMINSTER BANK LIMITED

## BLOOMSBURY BRANCH

Telegrams : Alabamian Westcent London
Telephone : Holborn 7254/5/6
Please address reply to
THE MANAGER
quoting full postal address

214 High Holborn
London, W.C.1

29th March, 1938.

J. Greenhill, Esq.,
    Joint General Manager,
      41, LOTHBURY, E.O.

Dear Sir,

        With reference to the subject matter discussed at the Managers' Conference held on Thursday afternoon last, I beg to submit the following suggestions for your consideration:-

*No* Protective Measures at Branch.

*as a principle.—No*

        It appears necessary that any arrangements made for protection will have to include the Staffs employed in the Offices above the Bank, in view of the fact that the Holborn Council's arrangements stress the necessity for people in one building making communal arrangements. It is calculated therefore that it may be necessary to provide protection for, say, 80-90 people, made up as follows:-

| | | |
|---|---|---|
| Staff and messengers | | 40 |
| Messenger's family living in flat above offices | | 3 |
| Number of persons in offices above Bank | Say ... | 30 |
| Customers in Bank at time of raid | Say ... | 12 |
| | | 85 |

        It would appear that the most suitable part of the

-1-

A Westminster Bank manager rejects the idea of admitting non-staff to his bank vault shelter
*(NatWest Group Archives D6854)*

that he should hear from them' (p. 5). They were also unable at first to locate the position of a past Master's grave in Highgate Cemetery when the time for the current Master's annual visit and inspection of it was due.

The London Chamber of Commerce was actively concerned with wartime arrangements for business, issuing monthly war circulars in its *Journal* from the outbreak of hostilities. These noted and explained restrictions on trade, new government orders and reports, covering their effect on imports, exports, finance, rationing, postal arrangements, censorship, travel restrictions, replacement of called-up staff and mutual assistance between firms in case of bomb damage. They are very detailed and informative, and can be found in Guildhall Library MS 16,487/1.

Many large firms, like other institutions, were proud of their performance during difficult times and commemorated it after the war in published accounts of how they had coped. Examples of these are listed in the bibliography; John Wadsworth's informative and very readable *Counter Defensive* (1946) is a good example. Subtitled 'the story of a bank in battle' it is dedicated to his colleagues at the Chancery Lane branch of the Midland Bank 'with whom the author shared the exhilarating days and nights of air-raids, flying bombs and rockets'. Like many of these published wartime histories it was intended for limited circulation, mainly within the firm concerned. Indeed, Wadsworth's book assumes throughout that readers will know that the bank in question is the Midland without naming it, though its identity becomes apparent through photographs of war-damaged branches. Some wartime retrospectives, though prepared with publication in mind, never in fact appeared in print. Where these drafts survive among the firm's archive they provide a useful key to the subject. Staff magazines often carried this sort of material in a series of articles just after the war, and they are worth checking.

## Trade Union records

Trade union activity continued throughout the war, though emergency conditions and regulations necessarily restricted its scope, and affected unions in a variety of ways. The National Union of Seamen, for example, had to relinquish its new headquarters building in Clapham for civil service use for the duration. Other unions with London bases — like the Amalgamated Engineering Union, in Peckham — also evacuated to the country to carry on their work. Theirs, and the national records of many other trade unions, are held at the Modern Records Centre at the University of Warwick. These records frequently contain material of London interest either because the union had London office premises, or was active in metropolitan industries, or both. Local branch and district records are more usually deposited in local record offices, thus the MRC has the national records of the National Union of Teachers, but LMA has the records of its London and Middlesex Associations, in LMA ACC 2902.

A particularly productive source at the MRC is the records of the Trades Union Council, MSS. 292, containing files on an extensive range of topics, like rationing — they were concerned about a shortage of alarm clocks for shift workers — canteens, travel difficulties, the need to relax trade practices, labour supply, and post-war reconstruction. Records of the British Employers' Confederation, also at MRC, provide a contrasting range of concerns.

## Mass-Observation

Mass-Observation was interested in the economic effects of the war and, as so frequently, did some of its research in London. M-O file 267 contains a report on the subject by Charles

Madge, undertaken in July 1940. The areas surveyed were Islington and Coventry. He found that in Islington the great majority of working class families were now forced below their peacetime standard of living, whereas in Coventry nearly half had increased their income. 'Islington had, pre-war, its considerable quota of satisfied C class workers. It is these people who are now pinched and in varying degrees unhappy. The extent of their deprivation is probably greater than most people in official circles realise'. Among other subjects, the report found that eighty per cent of the Islington inhabitants and eighty-five per cent in Coventry had insurance policies — a figure unaffected by the war.

The same M-O file also includes a typewritten account of 'The City, Feb. 3 1941' by YL, surveying public utilities, catering, trade and general business, and concluding 'The general atmosphere was one of complete normality and preoccupation with everyday affairs'. Mass-Observation diarists frequently recorded their impressions of economic life as it affected them. R.J. Nichols, a park keeper, noted in September 1939, N5163, that 'Many shopkeepers are up to their old game of making hay while the sun shines. In a chemist's shop at Woolwich I saw gas mask waterproof covers marked 1/6d each, identical and obviously made by the same firm as those being sold by Woolworths at 6d'.

## Personal experience

Memoirs, diaries and oral history collections may also have useful material on working and trading in London during the war. The IWM Department of Documents has a copy of C. Gaylor's memories of life at Frederick Sage & Co Ltd, normally a shopfitters' firm, but turned over to building aircraft components for the war. He describes the practical and technical difficulties of getting parts in wartime London, and how they were overcome. Mrs R.E. Uttin worked in an aircraft components factory in Wembley, as directed labour, in 1942–3. Her diary, in 88/50/1, records the experience. The IWM also holds, for instance, an unpublished history of Tough Bros Ltd, small boat builders of Teddington, covering the effects of the war and the requisitioning of small Thames vessels for the Dunkirk evacuation, in Misc 1047. And interwoven with the Home Guard reminiscences of G.D. Simons is an account of how the air raids affected his working life as a senior employee of the Royal Arsenal Co-operative Dairy in Mitcham, in 94/2/1. The diary of Miss F.M. Speed, 86/45/1, covers the destruction of her family's clothing business in the City, and other varied topics. The 'City Lives' series of recordings at the National Sound Archive contains recollections of working life, such as John Oliver, on C409/016 C1, talking about difficult times at Lloyds of London during the Blitz, and the evacuation of his office to Beaconsfield, and Hilton Clarke, on NSA C409/011 C1, a dealer at the Bank of England in the Foreign Exchange section, who explains how the legendary vaults were converted into dormitories with showers and lavatories for the staff who worked ten days on and three days off duty.

Most employers made efforts to stay in touch with their workers who were away in the Forces. A deposit in the IWM from A.C. Walker includes circular letters from his firm Barry & Staines Linoleum Ltd about the effect of war on business with news of other employees. Among the J. Lyons archive in LMA ACC 3527/289 are copies of their staff magazine *Lyons Mail* which carried regular messages from called-up staff, like the chocolate factory worker who wrote 'Remember me to all in the Moulding Department'. Similarly, the London Passenger Transport Board's staff magazine *Pennyfare* featured articles on the exploits of its staff away at war. Evacuated staff, too, felt the need to maintain contact with their dispersed colleagues. The Westminster Bank's Clearing Department, evacuated to Trentham, in Staffordshire, chronicled its activities in a journal ironically named *The Outcast*.

## Transport

A properly functioning transport system was vital to the London economy and the government made strenuous efforts to ensure that it did not collapse through bomb damage or other strains. The papers of the Ministry of Transport, later War Transport, contain considerable material of London relevance, particularly in the papers of the Railway Executive Committee in PRO AN 2, AN 3, RAIL 1080, RAIL 1135 and RAIL 1172. The use of the underground railways as deep shelters, discussed in the section on Civil Defence, resulted in additional documentation among the papers of the Ministry of Home Security (HO), and the Ministry of Health (MH).

The London Passenger Transport Board played a crucial role. Its records for the wartime period are divided among the PRO, LMA and the London Transport Group Archive. In addition, the London Transport Museum and its Photograph Library have important holdings illustrating all aspects of the Board's wartime work including the extensive use of its premises for munitions work and aircraft production by the London Aircraft Production Group, a combination of the LPTB and a number of London motor firms, as well as for public shelters. There is much, too, on the increased employment of women, for the Board realised very early on that this would be essential as the men went into the Forces. The Board had pioneered this in the First World War, and found once again that it could also make useful publicity for their activities. LT file S94144, 'The women', for example, contains facts, figures, draft articles, press releases and cuttings generated by the Public Relations department about female employment within the LPTB. Among the human interest stories are accounts of husband and wife teams operating buses, an Icelandic conductress at work, and articles about older women, who had worked in public transport during the First World War, returning to do the same again in the Second.

London was the terminus of all the major railway companies. Their services enmeshed with those of the LPTB, and their records, now in the PRO, contain London material. Further information on the London area occurs among the National Railway Museum's collections in York. Wartime film shot by many of the railway companies to record services and bomb damage is held by the Imperial War Museum's Film and Video Archive. Trade union records, such as those of the National Union of Railwaymen, at the Modern Records Centre of the University of Warwick, MSS.127, are another useful source.

Transport disruption bulked large in the daily experience of Londoners during the war and is often mentioned in diaries and letters. It was an annoyance for commuters, while for business travellers it could make work almost impossible. W.W. Churchill was a salesman for Whiffen & Son Ltd, manufacturing chemists of Fulham. Based in Chorlton-cum-Hardy, he needed to travel all over the country. His letters to Fulham in the autumn and winter of 1940–41 record a continuing experience of missed connections, late starts, slow journeys and lack of information: '...the general opinion of travellers is that the Rly companies are taking the fullest advantage of the situation... One man told me that it took him 19 and a half hours one day last week to get from Newcastle to London in an express' (LMA B/WHF/29. 18.1.41). But many were grateful that services continued at all. Emerging from her overnight shift at the Central Telegraph Office on 10 May 1941, Miss N.V. Carver saw the results of a terrible raid on the City. She walked with difficulty across Blackfriars Bridge towards Waterloo station, but it was closed. She could not get to the Elephant and

Castle for the fires along Waterloo Road. 'When we arrived at Lambeth Baths...I was thrilled to see a number 3 coming along so I jumped on, and was I thankful to get out of that ghastly mess!' (IWM Dept. of Documents, 90/16/1).

## The postal system

Business and public administration depended heavily on a reliable postal service. Travel delays and bomb damage could affect this seriously, but the Post Office had made detailed contingency plans in advance, and coped well in wartime. The Post Office Archives include the London postal region war diary, 1939–45, (56/152 PSD/HMB), which begins with a useful survey of the main problems faced. These included a serious loss of trained manpower necessitating a cut in postal deliveries in London to three a day, working difficulties resulting from the blackout, confusion arising from redirection of mail to evacuees, and air raid interruptions. During one very bad raid twenty-three London Post Offices were hit, but they were opened again, or an alternative provided, within twenty-four hours. Throughout the war, postal delays seldom exceeded forty-eight hours, a matter for some envy today. The war diary is in typescript and contains an account of the City fire raid of 29 December 1940 and the damage done to the Central Telegraph Office where Miss Carver, mentioned above, worked. The Post Office realised the value of good public relations, and the collection contains photographs and publicity material about its services, showing, for instance, a mobile Post Office operating in a bombed-out district, and postmen sorting sacks at Euston station in the blackout (56/14).

## Work discipline

In spite of official worries about general morale, absenteeism and sick leave did not emerge as a serious problem for London employers even during the Blitz and the flying bombs. Many Londoners seem to have drawn strength from the pursuit of normal routines in stressful times and it became a matter of pride that service to the public should resume as rapidly as possible after air raid damage to premises. Plate glass was in short supply, so damaged shops had to replace their big display windows with smaller versions, decorating the surrounding hoardings with murals, cartoons and slogans like 'Smaller windows...yes, but there are big values inside!', or 'Business as usual, Mr Hitler'. Business and institutional records can yield insights into the realities of 'carrying on as normal'. Bishopsgate Institute's librarian reported to his committee in October 1940 that: 'Two members of staff — Miss Reid and Miss Daniels — have had to evacuate their homes in Stepney owing to the serious damage caused by bombs; but I am happy to state that beyond shock they are well and have loyally attended to their duties here'. Muriel Quinn, sub-librarian at the University of London library, kept a work diary chronicling the difficulties of working properly in wartime conditions: 'The staff has been short owing to illness recently and as the glass lost from the windows has never been replaced since the air raids the Library Rooms are too draughty and cold' (UL 3/3 5 February 1943). Cold or not, staff were expected to put up with the situation. The Ministry of Labour could prosecute slackers in essential occupations; Petty Sessions registers regularly record fines for those who were persistently late for or absent from work without reasonable excuse.

Background information about the workplace sometimes occurs in unexpected sources. The Public Morality Council became concerned in 1943 that '...young girls some of them just leaving school, aged 14–15, were being enticed into the blind alley occupation of the manufacture, testing and packing of contraceptives, by large wages offered'. They were earning £2.5.0. a week, very good pay for their age at a time when adult female munitions

Staff attitudes to attendance at work vary

*(Bishopsgate Institute. From the Bishopsgate Foundation Librarian's report for 2 October 1940*

workers got £2.16.0. The PMC tried to get a minimum age limit set on this work but the government refused, pointing out that the girls took up the work of their own accord, often because an older relative in the same firm had got them the job (LMA A/PMC/10. 16.9.43). The flourishing state of this firm, presumably supplying the commercial market, would have annoyed the formidable birth control reformer, Marie Stopes, as she tried to run her free contraception clinics. Her papers, in the Wellcome Institute Contemporary Medical Archives Centre, document her ceaseless skirmishes with the 'enraging' Rubber Control at the Ministry of Supply which was unwilling to divert supplies for her clinics. She wrote to the London Rubber Co in December 1944, '...the position I maintain is that the commercial trade, touting in garages and barbers shops, should have no supplies at all while we are short' (PP/MCS/B.29).

## Munitions work

Munitions of all kinds were manufactured throughout the London area in a variety of premises, such as converted factories, underground railway shelters and private basements. The *History of the Second World UK Civil Series* volumes on *Labour in the Munitions Industries, Factories and Plant* and *British War Production* all contain some material on London factories, especially the Royal Ordnance factories at Enfield, Woolwich and Waltham. One of the more unusual examples was the Palace of Westminster's Munitions Factory, documented in files MF/1–6 in the House of Lords Records Office. Volunteers, including members of the Houses of Commons and Lords as well as staff, were invited to sign up for a regular shift assembling instruments. Initially this was done at the Westminster Technical Institute, but when the accommodation there was needed for full-time workers, attempts were made to find space within the Palace itself, causing great alarm to the Lord Great Chamberlain who supposed that explosives would be involved and ruled that 'under no circumstances will he, as being responsible for the safety and well-being of the Palace, allow this scheme to be carried out' (MF/2 15 December 1942). Only the personal intervention of the Minister of Production changed his mind. The scheme became successful, with more than a hundred part-time workers by 1944. All were paid, unless they were civil servants of the higher grades. Some produced torque amplifiers for anti-aircraft guns, some assembled detonator holders and fuses, and others inspected shell fuse parts. The House of Lords Record Office has interesting photographs of this work in progress.

## FAIR SHARES: RATIONING AND SHORTAGES

Diverting the country's manpower and production into the war effort meant that consumer goods of all kinds became scarce and shortages were inevitable. To ensure an equitable distribution of basic essentials, rationing was imposed through a 'points' system and prices were controlled. Ration books and clothing coupons were issued to all, with adjustments to meet special needs, like pregnant women, young children and vegetarians. By and large the public supported rationing as ensuring fair shares for all, and though a black market developed it never seriously threatened the system. It is generally accepted that food rationing improved the nation's health through the imposition of a balanced diet with essential vitamins. The *UK Civil Series* volumes on *Food* and on *Civil Industry and Trade* have detailed information about the policy behind rationing and its implementation. Meat, butter and sugar were rationed from early 1940, other foodstuffs, including tea, were added later, and entitlement varied at different times during the war. Bread, potatoes, coffee, vegetables, fruit and fish were never rationed, though choice and availability of the last three were often limited. 'The main grouse of people at the moment is that they are not able to buy all they want at the shops, especially in the food line. It isn't the rationing they complain of, but their inability to buy unrationed goods', wrote a Harrow cinema manager to the Ministry of Information in March 1941 (IWM Department of Documents, SMB collection box 5). Clothing was rationed from 1941, and fuel was subject to restrictions from early in the war.

Cabinet-level policy decisions on rationing are documented in PRO CAB 75, in BT 64, Board of Trade Industries and Manufacturers Department papers, and in POWE 3, Solid Fuel and Rationing where the representation papers have information on clothing and fuel rationing. Some matters of wartime diet and nutrition are covered in MH 56, Foods.

The Ministry of Food had begun as a department of the Board of Trade just before the war, and was later absorbed into the Ministry of Agriculture. Its records therefore have the prefix MAF. They reveal the great spread of its responsibilities, working through Food Control Committees for local authority areas. The Supply Departments, covered generally in MAF 67, were subdivided by type, the Cereals Group in MAF 84, the Dairy Produce and Fats Group in MAF 85, the Meat and Livestock Group in MAF 88, and others. MAF 99, the records of the Distribution Group, concern emergency services, rationing and communal feeding arrangements. The Food Standards Group, in MAF 101, was concerned with standards and labelling and the distribution of welfare foods such as cod liver oil and orange juice. The Wartime Meals Division encouraged the setting up of industrial canteens, and lent local authorities money to start British Restaurants for the public. But the wartime Londoner's main contact with the Ministry would have been through the Local Food Offices, documented in MAF 100, which issued and replaced ration books.The IWM has an interesting painting by Grace Golden, 'The Emergency Food Office', showing a patient queue waiting for new ration books in the incongruously stately surroundings of St Pancras Town Hall. Their Department of Documents has some official correspondence and papers of F.A. Bates, Area Bread Officer for the metropolitan area, in 94/24/1, and the diary of Miss J.M. Oakman, in 91/20/1, describes working in the Chelsea Food Office in the war. Fred Barnes was a Food Officer, enforcing rationing regulations and investigating the black market under cover in Whitechapel, his recorded memories are in the IWM Sound Archive, on tape 11852/2.

Food rationing loomed large in most Londoners' lives and receives frequent attention in letters and diaries. Ration books effectively tied people to one butcher and one grocer, with whom it paid to stay on good terms. Queues were inevitable, imposing an extra time-burden, particularly on working women with household responsibilities. 'Home to lunch at 1.15. Stewed rabbit — and lucky to get that by all accounts', wrote Anthony Heap, whose long-suffering mother had probably queued half the morning at the butchers (LMA ACC 2243/15/1, 5 January 1941). The demoralisation resulting from queues and shortages of food was recognised by the editor of the *Times*, R.M. Barrington-Ward, in a letter to the Minister of Information at the height of the flying bomb attacks on 27 June 1944 (HO 262/15 HI 1033/1, Morale of civilian population at home). He pleaded for greater public acknowledgement of Londoners' sufferings. Could more food be diverted to South London, he asked: 'I am told that the food queues, especially it seems, for fish and vegetables, are adding a great strain to the life of women in these vulnerable places, and they have already stood a great deal'.

The system permitted a little extra for special family celebrations where possible: 'With Ma to Food Centre to get extra for our Golden Wedding. Ma left her book behind so I went for it whilst she went to Meads. Jumbo [the dog] and I went to meet her...', wrote Byron Penn, of Hendon, in his diary for 27 March 1945 (Barnet Archives MS 6111/1–12). Although everyone had enough to eat, the lack of variety became boring. Any novelty, such as fruit sent from friends in the country, was especially welcome — Mrs Macmullan's letters, in Kensington Local Studies Library MSS 36148–247, contain annual references to gifts of plums sent by her family in Cambridge.

The Ministry of Agriculture's 'Dig for Victory' slogan encouraged people to grow fruit and vegetables on any available land — gardens, parks, allotments. Records of local allotment associations survive in some local collections; Kensington, for example, has correspondence concerning the use of two tennis clubs as allotments in the war, in 940.5317 AR/A, and Guildhall Library has material from the Metropolitan Public Gardens' Association's wartime allotments scheme in MS 22,293. The London Passenger Transport Board supplied its staff canteens with vegetables grown alongside railway tracks. Some people kept pigs, rabbits and chickens in suburban gardens to supplement their diet, feeding them on household scraps.

Maximum Price Orders and Current Price Orders, imposed by the Ministry of Food, proved a very successful method of price control. Human nature inevitably led some people to make illicit attempts to get round the rationing and price restrictions, and examples are common in the court records. The Marlborough Street Petty Sessions register, for instance, records frequent cases of 'unlawfully acquiring rationed goods', or of overpricing. John Gilbert 'did expose for sale strawberries at 10/- and 15/- per 2 lb basket which exceeded the maximum price' and was fined £2, with fourteen days to pay, on 10 July 1944, documented in PS/MS/A2/113. The fine cannot have made a serious dent in his profits.

## *Eating out*

Meals eaten away from home, whether in expensive West End restaurants or industrial canteens, were 'off ration' and a popular alternative with Londoners who could afford them. The conspicuous ability of the rich to enjoy almost pre-war levels of gastronomy at top hotels led to such resentment from Londoners at large that the government prevented restaurants charging more than 5/- a meal from 1942. This curbed the most ostentatious examples, though it did not completely solve the problem. Other restaurants fell more within the average Londoner's experience, especially the country-wide chain of Lyons' tea shops and Corner Houses. Reliable and reasonably priced, they provided a respectable meeting place for all and were popular right across the social spectrum.

Among the records of J. Lyons & Co in LMA is a detailed account book of meals served daily at the Oxford Street Corner House from 1928–52, ACC 3527/58, just one of many branches in Greater London. It remained open throughout the Blitz except for three days in September 1940 when they had no water supply, but even then the 'Front Shop' managed to continue trading. Examples of the meals on offer can be found in the folder 'Wartime menus', ACC 3527/371. A table d'hôte menu from 1941–2 lists a choice of two starters, seven main courses and four puddings and a small coffee, all for 1/6d. A tea shop menu lists tea at 3d per cup or 4d per pot (per person) with scones at a penny halfpenny and Bath buns at twopence halfpenny. 'FOOD is a munition of War Don't waste it' warn all the menus sternly. In the early 1990s the firm appealed for ex-'Nippies', as Lyons waitresses were called, to write in with their memories; a file of correspondence is in ACC 3527/235. Mrs Edith Walsh, from Streatham, remembered the importance attached to staying open however difficult the conditions. She worked in the largest of the Brixton teashops in 1941, arriving one post-raid morning, after a bad journey, to find that the nearby railway bridge had been hit. They opened up the shop: 'Word soon got round that Lyons were open and serving food and drink (we had our own generators). It seemed that the world and his wife came into our shop that day. Mrs Hedley (our

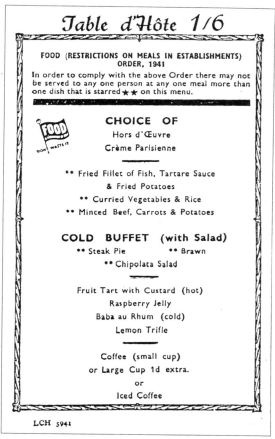

Rationing affects choice when eating out: Lyons menu
*(LMA ACC 3527/371)*

manageress) told us not to try to keep to our own "stations" just give the people the drinks and food as the counterhands placed it out for us. The teashop was so crowded we couldn't recognise who we'd "put what down for" so we just gave a bill for what we thought was OK. That night we couldn't believe how many bill books we'd used and how much adding up we had to do from the slips at the top. As you can imagine our commission was the best we ever had'.

British Restaurants supplied another almost universal experience of eating away from home. Here a three course meal cost only 9d. Standards varied, but the best were greatly appreciated and had a large regular clientele. British Restaurants were run by local authorities, who set them up in a variety of different premises such as schools and church halls. They evolved from the LCC's Londoners' Meals Service which originated in September 1940 as a temporary, emergency system for feeding those who had been bombed out. By mid-1941 the LCC was operating two hundred of these restaurants. Records of this service are in the LMA, among those of the Restaurant and Catering Department in LCC/RC/GEN. LCC/RC/GEN/2/1, for example, relates to negotiations to take over the Bun House Restaurant, 111 High Holborn WC1 — 'practically facing Holborn Tube Station' — from March 1943. The LCC already ran a British Restaurant in Princeton Street nearby and required different premises. They rejected Slaters at 55–6 High Holborn as too badly damaged and the Express Dairy, 294 Holborn, as too small. Records for British Restaurants beyond the LCC area are scarce. Hertfordshire RO has some menu books for the restaurant in Rickmansworth — strictly speaking outside the Greater London borders, but only just — in ACC 2908.

British Restaurants were open to all, but mainly served office and industrial workers. The one in Standard Road, Acton, catered for nearby factories without their own canteens. In January 1943 the *Acton Gazette* reported that the local Food Executive Officer had criticised it as inadequate — 'Workpeople do not like the place', they wrote, there had been 'quite a number of complaints'. Taking up the cudgels on behalf of his borough's catering sub-committee, the Town Clerk wrote to the Food Executive Officer to protest that eight hundred people regularly patronised the Restaurant quite contentedly. The FEO denied any slur on the borough's arrangements, saying he had been misreported. The Acton Borough Minutes, November 1942–3, contain further details.

Londoners proved fonder of British Restaurants and their equivalents than did inhabitants of the rest of the country. The Wartime Social Survey monitored public attitudes to food and rationing in some depth between February 1942 and October 1943, presenting the results in the report 'Food during the war' by Gertrude Wagner (PRO RG 23/9a) quoted earlier in the section on morale. They found that in the main people had accepted rationing, would not object if it continued after the war, and welcomed price control in this context.

The food trade made special arrangements for wartime, and the records of some trade associations may prove useful as most were based in London. For instance, the Soft Drinks Industry (War Time) Association's records are in the Bodleian Library MSS Eng Misc b 389–92, c 819–40, d 1237, and Guildhall Library MS 19,816 has the minute book of the London Wholesale Fish Trade Ltd, set up to deal with arrangements for fish distribution if Billingsgate market were badly damaged or destroyed. Fortunately it was never needed and the organisation was wound up in 1945, but the records contain information about the wartime fish trade. The Modern Records Centre at the University of Warwick has records of several other food-trade associations, including the British Dextrine Manufacturers' Association, MSS. 200, and the Edible Nuts in Shell Association, MSS.313. The experience of an individual potato merchant, including his acrimonious relations with the Ministry of Food, is covered by E.F. Franklin's diary in IWM 91/5/1.

## Clothing

Clothes were not rationed during the early part of the war, but by the start of 1941 it was clear that shortages would soon be felt if some restrictions were not imposed, so the Board of Trade brought in a system of coupon allocation for the civilian population. 'Quite a shock for us all this morning. We are to have clothes rationing now! Very clever of the Government to announce this over the Weekend!', wrote Miss Carver in her diary on 2

June (IWM 90/16/1). Clothes rationing was not popular, but it ensured fair shares of essential items. The Board of Trade exerted close control over the textile and footwear industries which produced 'Utility' goods, cheap but durable versions using a minimum amount of materials, from August 1941. Correspondence and papers of the Industries and Manufacturers' Department are in PRO BT 64. Many of the clothes for women were created by members of the Incorporated Society of London Fashion Designers, and represented very good value for money. Trade association records can provide extra information about clothing manufacture and its problems at this period. The University of

Clothes manufacturers make a virtue of necessity
*(Daily Telegraph, 27 March 1944)*

Warwick's Modern Records Centre has the archives of the London and District Wholesale Clothing Manufacturers' Association, the Women's Fashion Export Group, the Wholesale Fashion Trades Association, Clothing Manufacturers' Federation of Great Britain, the Tie Manufacturers' Association, and others, all at MSS. 222.

Londoners, like everyone else, were urged to be frugal and to make clothes last as long as possible, unravelling and reusing the wool from old jumpers, cutting down adult clothing for children's use, and retrimming ageing dresses with scraps of contrasting fabric. In normal circumstances people managed quite well, but they could encounter problems if they needed to replace an entire wardrobe after bomb damage. Salvage sales, with bargains from damaged premises, were popular. Voluntary bodies collected unwanted clothing at home and distributed gifts from overseas through outlets such as the WVS clothing depots and Salvation Army clothes shops.

Other shortages, for example of household utensils or toilet goods, caused great irritation. Anthony Heap recorded shortages of shaving soap, toothpaste and especially of razor blades in January 1941. 'The chemist told me his supply is limited to 14/6 worth for three months — the quantity he normally sells in two days. A preposterous position' (LMA ACC 2243/15/1). 'It is getting very hard to obtain matches', wrote Charles Ritchie in his diary *The Siren Years* during February 1941, '...at the Indian restaurant they give you curry without onions that tastes like hot mud. There is a shortage of French novels and French wines, of glass for spectacles, of rouge. I do not speak of necessities like butter and eggs'. Shortages were not confined only to such everyday needs. In November 1941 the Bishops' War Committee was worrying about the supply of wine for Holy Communion. They approached the Ministry of Food for clarification. If supplies were short, could the churches have priority? Lord Woolton reassured them that no problem was anticipated (Lambeth Palace MS 2448, Minutes of the BWC). Grand Lodge had to relax dress requirements for Freemasons' Lodge meetings according to Keith Flynn's *Freemasonry at War*: 'Gloves too were dispensed with as they quickly became unobtainable', and 'Regalia quickly came into very short supply and an enthusiastic second-hand market quickly established itself'.

## CAPITAL OF CRIME: MAINTAINING LAW AND ORDER

The rosy retrospective view of London as relatively crime-free during the war has long been demolished, notably by Edward Smithies in *Crime in Wartime* (1982), and it is now recognised that many criminals continued their normal careers, seizing the fresh opportunities presented by emergency conditions. The blackout, in particular, provided good cover for criminal activities of many kinds, usually less alarming than the serial killings by Frederick Cummins in February 1942 that spread panic for a time. Theft and prostitution rackets flourished. Confidence tricksters found a new crop of victims among the many servicemen and other visitors passing briefly through London. Rationing 'fiddles' and pilfering offered easy profits, and most Londoners took advantage of the black market in scarce goods at some point, however minimally. Police and the courts were busy throughout the war and their records reflect the continuing problem, though it never became a serious crime wave. Newspapers, both national and local, are an invaluable source for this topic as for so many others.

Looting from bombed buildings was quite common; premises with particularly valuable contents were guarded as soon as possible after the raid, often by Home Guards. Newspapers carried frequent accounts of looters' court appearances. On 8 November 1943 the *Yorkshire Post* reported a destructive raid on Putney High Street, though it was not named in the article. The bombs had hit a dance hall, with considerable loss of life, but local opportunist thieves had got busy in nearby premises: 'LOOTING CHARGES — Youth accused of rifling milk bar till'. Roy F.D. Ford (17) was charged with stealing £1 cash, a half-pound of tea and 520 cigarettes from a bomb-damaged milk bar. He had been spotted by a police constable sent to collect the till money for safe keeping. In a separate case arising from the same raid, a Canadian Army corporal was remanded in custody for stealing a coat from a shop in the High Street. Some thieves did not scruple to rob the dead and the injured. As Mrs Blair-Hickman lay injured in the rubble of the Café de Paris a man came past and — as she thought — felt her pulse. He was stealing a ring from her finger. Her taped memories of the incident are in the IWM Sound Archive, on 2302.

### The records

The records of law and order in the wartime capital are spread among a variety of repositories. Those relating to London are divided between the PRO, LMA, the county and borough record offices and some specialist collections. They fall within three main groupings — records of policing, of the courts, and of prisons. For all three groups as represented at the PRO Michelle Cale's *Law and Society: An Introduction to Sources for Criminal and Legal History Since 1800* (1996) is very helpful.

### Policing London

Most of the Greater London area falls within the Metropolitan Police district, the chief exception being the City, which has its own police force. Both forces have museums, open by appointment only, the Metropolitan at New Scotland Yard and at Wapping, the City at Wood Street. The records of the Surrey and Essex forces, relevant for some outer London areas at this period, are with their respective County Record Offices. Specialist forces policed the docks, canals, railways and underground network. Later absorbed into the modern British Transport Police, their records are stored with that force's archives. Overseas troops had their own military police, the American 'Snowdrops' in their white helmets were a familiar sight near the U.S. Forces' clubs around Piccadilly.

REPORT OF PATROL WORK........NOV 1941.

NIGHT CLUBS........Reported  2I,
                    Previously reported, now Convicted, 7,

HARBOURING PROSTITUTES....Reported,I,
                    Previously reported, now convicted, 2,

SOUTENEURS, ........Previously reported,Now convicted, I,

DISORDERLY HOUSES,...Reported, 8,
                    Previously reported, now convicted, 2,

NOTES. The NIGHT CLUBS reported are all situated in the
central area, the offences being, gaming, illicit
drinking or harbouring prostitutes, or similar
charges.
Of the present convictions, ALL were fined, the total
being £450,-4 were struck off the Register & premises
disqualified,(Gaming took place at 3).-I Club was
closed under the Emergency Powers Act, for 2 years
the premises not to be used for any form of amusement,
2 others have been closed for I2 months.
One of the convictions reported last month was then
fined £373 for Gaming. He is now sent to prison for
4 months . He is said to have inserted lead in the cogs
of a fruit machine so as to make it impossible for a
winning combination to take the jackpot or pool.
(The man is called Maurice Conley- he was born Cohen).
The Souteneur was sentenced to prison for 4 months.
The Disorderly Houses now reported are being used,
one in particular by Canadian Soldiers, & Norwegian
Seamen. The 2 houses convicted were fined £47-I0-0,

It is interesting to note that the Police are now
taking a new kind of action against Night Clubs in
certain bad cases, by closing them under the E.P.A.,
from 2 p.m., till 6 a.m., which effectively prevents
any abuse. Such a case on the present list is the
PARADISE, Regent St, and LA CONGA, Denman St.

The CAFE now closed,(SAM'S, Rupert St) from 6 p.m. to
6 a.m., was the resort of criminals, male & female
prostitutes & was often the scene of drunkenness &
disorderly conduct.

SHEPHERD MARKET. This is a complaint by Lt Col Hill,
late of the Scots Guards who states that the neighbourhood is over-run by both English & Foreign prostitutes,
who are established in nearly all the flats of the
district. A leakage of military information, he suggests
occurs when Naval, Army & Air Force Officers go to
these places under the influence of drink.
A preliminary survey shows that there is substance in
this complaint.Legal action can only be taken when the
flat is used by more than one woman.The Police can
challenge these women to produce their identification
cards, but not to give proof of having registered for
National Service & many of them are apparently flouting
the law in this respect. One of the Clubs complained of
was registered by a man who had been convicted 3 times
previously- now he opens a club & sells drink without
needing a licence. It would seem worth while to explore
the possibility of influencing Parliament to pass a
Bill enacting that "No NEW club shall be opened without
the approval of the Police

The Public Morality Council polices loose behaviour
*(LMA A/PMC/10)*

*The Metropolitan Police*

Unlike police forces elsewhere in the country, the Metropolitan Police is directly responsible to the Home Office. As a result, its administrative records are public records, preserved at the PRO under the class reference MEPO. HO classes often contain relevant material also. However, some records for the war period are still closed under the seventy-five year rule. For operating purposes the Metropolitan Police area is sub-divided into twenty-one divisions, each known by a letter of the alphabet. A is Westminster, for example, G is King's Cross, W is Clapham. Incomplete records for some of these divisions are held by the Metropolitan Police Museum at New Scotland Yard.

The Annual Reports of the Commissioner of Police of the Metropolis, published as *Parliamentary Papers*, give a good overview of police work in London in wartime, including the impact of the many extra duties resulting from Civil Defence and other emergency work. H.M. Howgrave-Graham's short history *The Metropolitan Police at War* (1947) outlines the problems. MEPO 2–4 contain correspondence and papers from the Commissioner's office on varied aspects of policing including personnel, pay and conditions. War measures are dealt with in some detail in MEPO 2/3386–3729. Many of the files draw attention to the additional tasks mentioned above — MEPO 2/3386 relates to Civil Service billeting, for instance, MEPO 2/3391 to police at tube and rail stations, MEPO 2/3395 to early ARP arrangements with the London CD Region, MEPO 2/3411 to the London area Home Defence scheme, MEPO 2/3424 to court procedures under war conditions, and MEPO 2/3676 to anti-sabotage patrols at Avon Wharf, Bow.

MEPO 3, Special series files, is a varied class including not only instructions for action in the event of an invasion, but folders relating to individual police investigations. Some of them illustrate the way in which wartime conditions influenced crime. MEPO 3/2234, for example, concerns a murder case in 1942 resulting from an ill-fated wartime love-affair. A Polish lieutenant had shot his mistress and then himself in a suicide pact in Hyde Park. The folder contains a report to the Detective Inspector of 'A' division describing the arrival of two constables at the scene and the subsequent findings of the Westminster coroner's inquest, which was murder, and suicide while of unsound mind. Both victims had left diaries which helped the enquiry. The lieutenant's read 'To make things easier I inform you that we both spent 10 days Colosseum Terrace 13. We are absolutely 2 broken people. We are finish with money to stay in hotel thats that. She give up always everything for me also her life'. His mistress wrote a message for her mother: 'Dear, Just in case anything happens to me today — Ronie is still here. He should have returned yesterday but says he cannot live without me in the awful place where his Regiment is. He threatens all the time to kill himself and me. I love him — but don't want to die...' A *News of the World* cutting relating to the tragedy is enclosed headed 'Death Threat Story in Park Drama'.

MEPO 4, Miscellaneous books and papers, has war diaries, casualty lists compiled by the Central Casualty Bureau at Scotland Yard, a set of the Commissioner's *Annual Reports*, and attestation ledgers with the signatures of recruits and their witnesses. MEPO 6 is a register of habitual criminals known to the police, but many pieces are closed for seventy-five years.

MEPO 20, a register of deaths by violence in the metropolitan area, including deaths as a result of abortions, contains some wartime cases in MEPO 20/3. Case J30 relates the grisly story of a Hackney housewife suffering from depression because of the air raids, who on 1 October 1940 murdered her elderly husband with a chopper and severed his head. The case came to trial in November, the woman was found guilty but insane, and sentenced to be detained at His Majesty's pleasure. Curiously this case is mentioned by the anonymous writer of a Kensington diary (Kensington Local Studies Library 940.548 EVE AR/RS), who recorded on 24 October: 'Madeleine Shearing who knits with much skill leant against her basement mantelpiece telling me of her friends, one has been a hard working wife and made things, her home was bombed, she had a knife sharpened and nearly severed her old husband's head from his body as he lay on the bed, covering him up with a cushion she sat for an hour with him... now she is sent for trial and the funeral is over, she is most worried as to whether they will get the insurance money, she is mad, as mad as the world is at present'.

Most of the cases in MEPO 20 make no specific reference to war conditions, though its stresses may have occasioned some of the suicide pacts, often by gas poisoning, and the septic abortions listed there. These cases can frequently be tied in with the records of the Central Criminal Court, the Hackney example above, for instance, is also found in PRO CRIM 1/1239.

Like other police forces, the Metropolitan Police needed extra manpower in wartime. MEPO 7, on personnel matters, contains material on special constables, reserves and auxiliaries. MEPO 8 includes the *Official Handbook for the War Reserve* and other instructional leaflets. The very wide-ranging class HO 45, Home Office registered papers, has material on the police, such as HO 45/11830 and /19068 concerning the Police War Reserve, and /20601, about auxiliaries' strength, allowances and sick pay. HO 45/20651–4 concerns the release of policemen for service in the armed forces and the RAF police. Other HO papers can shed light on police matters, HO 341, for example, relating to communications procedures for the police and CD services. Representative records from various police units, in MEPO 11, are potentially useful but most of the class is closed for seventy-five years. Many of the papers in it came from West End Central police station. Photographs, drawings and plans of police stations are to be found in MEPO 9, 13 and 14, but plans of stations still in use are not available for current security reasons.

The Metropolitan Police retain many records at New Scotland Yard. These are outlined in Bridgeman and Emsley's *Guide to the Archives of the Police Forces of England and Wales* (1989). Preservation of police archives has been patchy, but records of London relevance survive from the war years, including some charge books and charges, 'refused charge' books, complaints registers, occurrence books, warrant registers, CID memos, and air raid casualty lists for various Divisions. There are also some Special Constabulary occurrence registers, for instance, from Kensington sub-division, civilian personnel records, including women clerks, 1915–64, and recreational records, like the Brixton Police Concert Party records, 1943–50. The occasional notoriety surfaces among hundreds of exemplary employees — Christie, the mass murderer, was a Police Reservist with 'X' Division at Harrow Road Police Station for part of the war. The Metropolitan Police's Thames Division, the river police, faced particular wartime difficulties. The docks were a target for criminals as well as the Luftwaffe. The division's surviving ledgers are at Wapping Police Station Museum. Police pensions records for the wartime period are held by the Metropolitan Police Office.

### The City Police

The City Police retain their own records, which are listed briefly in Bridgeman and Emsley's *Guide*. The wartime holdings include, for example, registers of prisoners, police orders, emergency instructions including an 'invasion book', a Special Constables' order book, and a set of the famous Cross and Tibbs war damage photographs already mentioned. There are also excellent personnel records. Some police air raid reports, mainly from the Snow Hill station, survive in the CLRO in Police Papers Box 2.8. These printed forms are filled in in typescript, giving the name and number of the officer making the report, the time and date of the occurrence, the position, number of casualties, services in attendance or *en route*, whether there was a fire, and the names of any roads blocked. Thus on 11 September 1940 Sub-Inspector 8 'A' Charles Crutchet reported an incident: 'An enemy high explosive bomb dropped penetrating roof of Central Telegraph Office St Martin-le-Grand, causing slight damage and fire. The fire was extinguished at 20.50 hours by fire fighting squad on the premises before the arrival of the Fire Brigade. Angel St and St Martin-le-Grand closed to traffic owing to broken glass'.

Railway police were employed by the different companies, the PRO's useful *Source Sheet 13* provides an introduction. British Transport Police archive, for instance, has a railway police minute book covering 1942–7.

### Personal memories

Written or recorded memories of wartime policing in London exist in several collections. The City and Metropolitan Police archives, predictably, have some. The Police History Society is engaged upon an oral history programme which includes the war years, the tapes are in the National Sound Archive. Police material sometimes occurs elsewhere. The IWM Sound Archive, for example, has a tape of an East End policeman, Geoffrey Taylor, recalling his duties during the evacuation scheme, on IWM 5221/2.

## The Courts

Court proceedings often contain useful material for the social historian as well as for the student of legal history. Much information about London in wartime emerges from this source, at all levels from serious criminal cases to minor infringements of the blackout regulations. Although the records of most courts are in fact public records, the more local ones are customarily held by county or borough record offices for ease of access.

### The Central Criminal Court

The chief criminal court for London and the Home Counties is the Central Criminal Court, commonly referred to as the Old Bailey. In many respects it fulfilled the function that Assize courts had for the rest of the country. Records of trials for murder, sedition, treason, riot, conspiracy and 'other matters of historic interest' are preserved in the Public Record Office in the series CRIM. The records include depositions and indictments and their calendars in CRIM 1–4, court books in CRIM 6, and details of convicted persons in CRIM 9. Some classes have been weeded so that only a representative selection of cases remain, and some records for the war years are closed for seventy-five years because they contain personal information about people who may still be alive.

All these classes can provide a quarry of London material of all kinds, though the findings are unpredictable because of the sampling mentioned above. CRIM 1/1351, *Rex* v. *Andrews*, is a murder case, resulting from a brawl in the street in Kensington in October 1941. Apart from Andrews' deposition, the file contains photographs of the crime scene, handwritten notes from the jury foreman to the judge — 'My Lord, is it possible for the Jury to see a photograph of the deceased's face and head taken after death?' — evidence from eye witnesses, and from the distinguished pathologist, Sir Bernard Spilsbury, who performed the post mortem, and a report on the accused from the Medical Officer at Brixton Prison. Not all the cases in CRIM/1 are so serious. Lesser charges also made their appearance at the Old Bailey in wartime. CRIM 1/1465, for instance, relates to the case of *Rex v. Mariani*. Bonaventure Guglielmo Cipriano Mariani ran a café at 5 Pilgrim Street, EC, and was being tried on two counts under the Rationing (General Provisions) Order of 1942. He had failed to keep an accurate record of meals and drinks sold, lied about it to the Food Officer, and had used a false name to sign official forms. Asked to estimate his weekly takings, he said £50, but it turned out to be nearer £200. His defence was an implausible one of mere carelessness. The case had been sent on from the Mansion House Justices and the file contains the handwritten Mansion House depositions. CRIM 2 contains useful calendars indexing cases sent to the Old Bailey from coroners' and magistrates' courts.

### Quarter Sessions records

The Quarter Sessions with London jurisdiction until 1971 were London, Middlesex, Essex, Hertfordshire, Kent, Surrey, the South East London Sessions at Croydon, and West Ham. County of London and Middlesex Sessions records are deposited in LMA, the City in CLRO. The other counties are with their respective county offices, the Croydon records being with Surrey RO. West Ham Quarter Sessions rolls for this period are in Newham Local Studies Library. The records list the cases that came before the court and the judgment reached. Some series have calendars of indictments and of prisoners.

### Civil law

Useful material on Civil Law cases relating to London may be found in the published Law Reports. Some classes in the PRO can also yield London information, especially those concerning bankruptcy such as LCO 28, Registers of county court judgments; BT 39, Registers of deeds of arrangement, and BT 226, High court papers. Practical emergency arrangements concerning the Royal Courts of Justice in the war years are described in WORK 28/22–46.

### Local courts: Petty Sessions

Even more informative, for many historians of London, are the proceedings of local courts in wartime. Only a small minority of Londoners charged with a criminal offence ended up at the Central Criminal Court. Their first appearance would be at Petty Sessions, sometimes known as police or magistrates' courts, before either the City or the Metropolitan justices or, if on the suburban fringes, before the local bench. Only more serious but non-capital cases would normally be sent on to Quarter Sessions, capital cases went to the Old Bailey.

Typical magistrates' court holdings are court registers, giving the name of the accused and brief details of the offence and action taken, letter books and minute books. Sometimes the separate records of the associated juvenile court are kept with them. These were also empowered to deal with children who had not actually committed an offence, but were thought to be keeping dangerous company. Magistrates' courts dealt with a wide variety

Mr. Hawke prosecutes

CENTRAL CRIMINAL COURT.

THE KING -v- BONAVENTURE GUGLIELMO CIPRIANO MARIANI.

BONAVENTURE GUGLIELMO CIPRIANO MARIANI is charged with the following offences:-

Count 1.          STATEMENT OF OFFENCE.

MAKING FALSE STATEMENT contrary to section 30(1)(a) of the Rationing (General Provisions) Order 1942.

PARTICULARS OF OFFENCE.

BONAVENTURE GUGLIELMO CIPRIANO MARIANI on the 29th day of July 1942 in the City of London for the purpose of obtaining rationed food recklessly made a statement which was false in a material particular to wit in the return of hot beverages and meals served at the M.C.Restaurant 5 Pilgrim Street E.C. from the 29th day of June to the 26th day of July 1942.

Count 2.          STATEMENT OF OFFENCE.

FAILING TO KEEP REDORD contrary to section 13(b)(1) of the Rationing Order (General Provisions) Order 1942.

PARTICULARS OF OFFENCE.

BONAVENTURE GUGLIELMO CIPRIANO MARIANI on the 22nd day of August 1942 in the City of London being a person having control of a watering establishment at 5 Pilgrim Street E.C. failed to keep on the premises an accurate record showing the meals and hot beverages served in the establishment.

ROLAND JOHN MORGAN
GEORGE KEEN PITHERS

The bureaucracy attached to rationing offers ample scope for fraud
*(PRO CRIM 1/1456)*

of offences, such as licensing matters, infringement of blackout and motoring regulations, black market sales, theft, illicit betting, loss of identity cards, drunkenness and soliciting and as well as more serious crimes like assault and child neglect.

At this Petty Sessional level, LMA holds most of the records of the magistrates' courts and former police courts, including the juvenile courts, for London and Middlesex, except for the City and Mansion House Justice Rooms' records which are in CLRO, and some Westminster records, for example Paddington Petty Sessions, which are in Westminster Archives. Occasionally the records have been retained by the borough — Southwark Local Studies Library has the wartime registers of Newington Petty Sessions. Some outer London boroughs formerly in counties other than Middlesex hold local sessions records too. Bromley has those for Bromley and some for Penge (ref. 788), comparable Kingston-upon-Thames records are at Kingston Heritage Centre. But some have gone to the relevant County Record Office — Romford magistrates' court records, for instance, are in Essex RO, in P/RO.

LMA's wartime holdings are extensive, including Bow, Brentford, Clerkenwell, Feltham, Greenwich, Hendon, Highgate, Holborn, Marylebone, Thames, Tower Bridge, Wandsworth, and Woolwich, among others. The reference is PS/, normally followed by the first three letters of the place name, as in PS/BOW. An inspection of the registers for Marlborough Street Magistrates' Court from July 1943 to July 1944 (PS/WES) provides a flavour of their content. They give a case number, the name of the complainant, the name of the defendant with age if known, the nature and date of the offence, a minute of the adjudication and the time allowed to pay. So the London Passenger Transport Board accused William Hobson of 'travelling on the railway without having previously paid your fare and with intent to avoid payment' on 24 May 1943, and he was fined 5/-. The Ministry of Labour complained about Sidney Walker being 'without reasonable excuse, persistently late for [essential] work' in the spring of 1943; he was fined £10, with 2 guineas costs and seven days to pay. The Fire Officer for Westminster brought a case against Dillon Damen, for failing to turn up for fireguard duties on numerous occasions. His case was eventually dismissed but he had to pay three guineas costs.

Police courts dealt swiftly with minor offences such as being drunk and disorderly, vagrancy, soliciting and begging. Marlborough Street Police Court register for May–October 1943, (PS/MA/A1/188), reveals a good cross-section of such cases. Similar to the Sessions register described above in appearance, it additionally gives the time charged and the time bailed, the doctor's fee if applicable, and the defendant's occupation. On 23 October 1943 the court dealt with Stellios Yiannis, a cook accused of keeping a brothel at 1 St Anne's Court, W1. He was fined £50 with 30 guineas costs and given three months to pay. Henry Phillips, street trader, was gaoled for a day for begging, Edward Byrne, labourer, was gaoled for fourteen days for assaulting a police constable and damaging his overcoat, and Frank Tweedie, motor driver, was fined £10 for stealing eight ingots of electrical bronze valued at £6.10.0. Shoplifting, gaming, living on the earnings of prostitution were other typical charges. Deserters from the Forces appeared before this court, as did aliens absent from their residence overnight, and people who used false names, or who had failed to report the loss of identity cards.

*Coroners' courts*

Coroners' courts investigate sudden or suspicious deaths, and a seventy-five year closure rule applies to their records. LMA has the records of the coroners' courts for the counties of London and Middlesex over the war period; the CLRO has those for the City, including fire inquests, 1940–7. Coroners' records for parts of outer London later absorbed into Greater London are with their former county record office, Surrey, Essex, Kent or Hertfordshire.

Coroners' record books give a date and case number, the name, age and sex of the deceased, the coroner's findings, whether a post mortem was held, the fee due and the name of the authority responsible for payment. The record book for London's Southern Division 1937–54, (COR/A/27), gives entries such as: 'September 12 1941. Ward, Joseph. 73. M. Accidental asphyxia — foreign body — plumstone. Tooting Bec. p.m.£4.4.0', and 'July 16 1942. Unknown child. Newborn. F. Want of attention at birth. p.m. £4.4.0. Wandsworth'. Characteristically, for wartime London, this register records many traffic accidents and suicides, some judicial hangings — Wandsworth Prison was within the court's jurisdiction — but comparatively few deaths due to enemy action, such as: 'November 5 1940. Riches, Kate. 64. F. War operations. £2.2.0. Southwark'.

### Civil courts

County Courts dealt with civil litigation and their records have been transferred from the PRO to local record offices. Those for the London area — Bow, Edmonton, Lambeth, Southwark, Wandsworth, West London and Woolwich — are in LMA. Records for the Mayor's and City of London Court are in CLRO. Surrey RO has the records for Kingston-on-Thames County Court including the war years.

## Prisons

The London prisons, like those all over the country, were the responsibility of the Prison Commissioners, working closely with the Home Office's Criminal Department. Surviving papers are in the PRO in the PCOM classes — PCOM 2 covers prison records to 1951, PCOM 8 and 9 are registered papers on a variety of criminal matters including staffing. PCOM 13 has Treasury authorities for expenditure on prisons. However, many of these records are closed for seventy-five or a hundred years.

The Commissioners' *Annual Reports*, published as *Parliamentary Papers*, provide a valuable source for prisons in wartime. That for 1939–41, for example, Cmd 6820, describes the early discharge of prisoners with under three months still to serve, and the evacuation of prisoners from the large London gaols to provincial ones, sometimes with unfortunate effects: 'The "London recidivist" is a special type, and the influx of parties of these difficult men, resentful of removal from London and the consequent loss of visits... had a very disturbing effect on the discipline of some provincial prisons'. The London gaols soon filled up again as life proceeded almost normally during the phoney war. In the summer of 1940 the influx of aliens under internment orders, and security detainees under Regulation 18B presented difficulties, for they had to be segregated from ordinary prisoners, with laxer rules, and there were also language problems. In London the main burden fell on Brixton, Pentonville and Holloway. At Holloway 'both detainees and internees were not clean in their habits and it was hard at times to resist the temptation to send a cleaning party of convicted prisoners among them to clean and show an example...'. German women detainees were said to be particularly unpleasant to the prison staff.

The published reports also detail air raid damage to London prisons throughout the war. Seventeen people died at Pentonville on the night of 10–11 May 1941, for instance. The report for 1942–4, Cmd 7010, covers V1 damage which particularly affected Brixton. The report notes that the wartime labour shortage meant that prisoners could easily find employment when their sentences were over: 'The war years have provided golden opportunities for cases such as ours who have to bridge a gap of a minimum of two years in their employment record'. The last of the reports to deal with the war years, 1945, Cmd 7146, noted a V2 hit at Wandsworth, and observed that the increase of the female prison population had greatly exceeded the male. Four main offences had swollen it: shoplifting — a reflection of clothes rationing —, neglect of children — 'the broken home'—, brothel-keeping — the 'armed camp atmosphere' —, and industrial absenteeism.

Wartime records for most of the London prisons are still in the care of their respective Governors, though the Home Office is actively encouraging their deposit in local record offices. Direct approaches can be made to the prison authorities, but access is at the discretion of the Governor. In the case of Wandsworth Prison the records can be consulted at LMA, in ACC 3444. They include committee minutes, letter books, reports, correspondence and prisoner and staff records.

Additional sources can add to the picture of prison life at this period. M-O file 2198, Holloway prison, by a prison officer, is a lengthy report written in January 1945. The author was a temporary officer who served there for four months. She had had no previous experience of the prison service. There is considerable and varied detail on conditions and pay, the formalities of joining and the uniform, day-to-day routines, bribery and tobacco-smuggling. 'Staff conditions generally are slack. The majority of the regular officers are extremely dull, mentally and physically.' She clearly found the experience unpleasant, complaining of unhappy, bitchy staff and dirty, smelly prisoners. The worst duty, she said, was on the VD wing. 'The women inside for neglecting their children are the most despised, and next to them the petty pilferers. The drug addict is considered to be of a higher rank than the majority, but the most respected are the abortionists and the grand-scale shoplifters (hoisters is the expression used).' Evidence from the prisoner's side, at an earlier stage in the war, comes from some oral history recordings in the IWM Sound Archive, where Nora Page on 4659/7, and Stella St John on IWM 4997/3, both absolutist religious pacifist internees in Holloway in 1943, recall their memories of prison life. The Sound Archive at the IWM has nearly four hundred recordings relating to wartime imprisonment of all types.

Frank Norman, another religious pacificist, was sent to Wormwood Scrubs in 1942. His recorded memories are on IWM tape 4652/4. Interned for quite a different reason was Douglas Peroni, on IWM 3866/7, a porter in a block of flats who had joined the BUF in 1936 and become branch treasurer. He explains what attracted him to the BUF at first: '...they looked clean, they looked orderly, they looked a very patriotic group... And they were heckled and shouted at by people who basically looked to me quite the opposite. They looked ugly. They looked over-emotional...'. He and his wife were surprised to find themselves interned. 'We regarded ourselves as very small fry. The thought that we would be Churchill's prisoner never entered our head.' Far more famous detainees, of course, were the Mosleys, detained in Holloway under Regulation 18B. Home Office papers contain information on their detention, PRO *Source Sheet 26* provides a useful introduction.

## TEACHING FOR TOMORROW: EDUCATION

### *The University of London, colleges and public schools*

The government's advance planning had assumed that little educational activity would take place in London once war had broken out. State schools were to be evacuated. Colleges of all kinds, including those of the University of London, public and private schools had all made arrangements to continue their work out of the danger-area, taking over premises in the country or sharing accommodation with similar institutions. Many remained in the provinces throughout the war. St Paul's choir school moved to Truro, Dulwich College to Tonbridge, the Mercers' School to Horsham. Records of the colleges and public schools mostly remain with their parent body or its successor, though leasing and property arrangements, and any resultant problems, are often documented in the records of the host institution. Records of denominational schools and colleges, if not still with the originators, are sometimes among collections relating to the religious group concerned. The Hartley Library at the University of Southampton, for example, has records of Bayswater Jewish School, in MS 211, as well as material from the Jewish Religious Education Board, MS 157, and the Education Aid Society, MS 135. The Church of England Records Centre has the records of Anglican schools in the dioceses of London and Southwark.

Parts of the University of London were relocated far afield. Bedford College and the London School of Economics went to Cambridge, Westfield College to Oxford. Their London premises were taken over for official purposes of various kinds. Bedford College's Regent's Park buildings were used at different points by the BBC, and by the Netherlands government in exile. Published histories, available for most of the colleges, give the details and their published annual reports are also informative. A spate of college amalgamations since the war has resulted, for instance, in Bedford College's records now joining Royal Holloway College's archive and Westfield's going to Queen Mary College. Typical holdings are minute books of the governing body and of academic committees, student and staff records, prospectuses, calendars, college magazines, often full of wartime detail, and photographic collections. Staff memoirs sometimes cover the war years. The memories of a London School of Economics student, Renate Simpson, evacuated to Cambridge to do her degree, are recorded on an IWM Sound Archive tape IWM 11886/5; Eileen Round, on NSA tape C 642/07/01–01 C1, had a similar experience. Alfred York, recorded on NSA C642/72/1–2 C1, gained a place at London University early in the war but had to take it up at his college's temporary home in Wales, which seemed a foreign country to him. Pauline Harris, another London University undergraduate, on NSA tape 642/87 C1, ended up reading for her London degree in Bristol.

The staff of the central University, displaced from Senate House by the Ministry of Information, worked at Royal Holloway College at Egham where many of them 'lived in', sharing the building also with an Officer Training Unit of the ATS. The records of the central university are held by the University of London Library. They cover student sporting and cultural activities as well as academic and administrative committee papers. Birkbeck College, where students in full-time work could study in the evenings for an internal degree, could not be evacuated to the country because its students were unable to follow it. After initial fears that the college would have to close for the duration, arrangements were made to do most of the teaching at the weekend, by daylight, and its work continued in spite of the inevitable difficulties. There is useful material on the

---

**13.—Refund of Late-Entry Fees at Higher and General School Examinations, Midsummer 1943.**

REPORTED:—(1) That the last date for the receipt of entries for the above examinations is 726 21 April, but entries may be received up to 1 May with an additional fee of 10s. for each candidate entered. If all the entries of a school are late a maximum fee of £10 shall be payable.

(2) That in the case of two schools, St. Helen's School, Northwood, and South Hampstead High School, the entries were late and the maximum late-entry fee of £10 has been paid.

(3) That the Head Mistress of St. Helen's School, Northwood (evacuated to Three Cocks, Brecon), wrote (20 April) as follows:—

I much regret that I am sending the enclosed forms a day late, but the only available taxi was engaged all day. My own car is in the repair shop and I could not manage the eight-mile walk to the Post Office in Hay to get this registered.

Trusting that I shall not have inconvenienced you by this unavoidable delay.—

and again (12 May) as follows:—

I wish to explain why I was two days late in sending in the School Examination forms.

I was ill at the end of term and when my Secretary read me the various dates for important meetings and correspondence I evidently confused two dates and noted that I was to send in our forms before April 24th. It was therefore a shock to me when I was getting ready the forms on Tuesday, April 20th, to find that was the last day for entry.

Tuesday is early closing day in our neighbourhood—even in the Post Office till 6 p.m. All maids leave by 4.30 p.m., and I could not leave Tregoyd empty to go to Three Cocks and register the form envelope at 6 p.m. Tuesday is market day in Hay 4 miles away and no taxi will come out that day. As I was still suffering from rheumatism I did not feel I could manage an 8 miles walk.

It was stupid of me to fail to ring up the University and explain and I regret that I did not do so.

M.&S.E.C.;    (4) The Head Mistress of South Hampstead High School (evacuated to Berkhamsted) wrote
C.R.F.C.    (30 April) as follows:—

I was unspeakably shocked to receive your letter this morning and to realise that our entries for the Higher and General School Examinations had not reached you. I left them with my Secretary, all ready to be posted, on April 7th, and I am quite certain that she posted them within the next few days. Unfortunately she is travelling south from Yorkshire to-day so that I cannot get into touch with her before the evening.

The University was subsequently informed that the Secretary forgot to post the envelope containing the entries before the school broke up for the Easter vacation.

The University of London hears about evacuated schools' difficulties
*(University of London Library, Minutes of Senate 1943–4)*

wartime organisation of universities in the PRO in UGC 5, University Grants Committee Miscellanea. War damage claims for educational premises of all kinds occur in IR 37. IR 37/15, for example, contains damage claims on behalf of the University of London in 1941–2.

## State schools

The government evacuation scheme provided for the removal of staff and pupils of state schools to safer areas where they would share teaching premises with the local schools and be billeted nearby. London school buildings were frequently assigned for other wartime purposes, for use as information or food offices, stores depots, or rest centres. The rapid drift of evacuee families back to London in the autumn of the phoney war forced the authorities to rethink their plans, for it was essential to provide the children with an education.

The fluidity of the situation was a problem throughout the war as children moved to and fro to avoid bouts of enemy raiding. Schools opened and closed in response to the changing circumstances, teachers collected groups of children and taught them wherever accommodation could be found. By the end of the war numerous children had suffered from a greatly disrupted schooling. The history of wartime education is inextricably bound up with that of the evacuation scheme, discussed earlier. Files of the *Times Education Supplement*, which continued to publish through the war, contain many references to London educational matters.

National records relating to wartime education in London are mainly to be found in the PRO among the papers of the Board, later the Ministry, of Education. An official history of the department's wartime work was planned, to be published in the authoritative *UK Civil Series*, but unluckily progress was slow and the death of the editor, Dr Sophia Weitzman, after twenty years resulted in the abandonment of the project. Drafts of the work are in CAB 102, CAB 238–9 and also in ED 138. ED 138/32 relates to evacuation and education in London, taken from LCC notes and Ministry files.

Among the most useful ED classes are ED 10, General files, which has a 'WAR' section with material on the release of teachers for National Service, ARP, the organisation of evacuation, the requisition of premises for use as ARP posts, gunsites, hospital or first aid posts or rest centres. ED 10/309, for instance, deals with varied wartime problems such as the use of schools as feeding stations, rodent infestation, the financial position regarding education affected by evacuation and similar complications. ED 11, Elementary education general files and ED 12, Secondary education general files, do not relate specifically to London but contain matters of general relevance. ED 16, Elementary education local education authority supply files, are very significant for London, with borough files such as ED 16/665 for Ilford BC, /666 for Leyton BC, /699 for the LCC, /700–9 for Middlesex, 732 for Richmond, and so on. ED 18, Elementary education local education authority attendance files, relating to the enforcement of attendance, are subdivided in a similar way, ED 18/479 covering Barking BC, 1943, /552 the LCC, 1939–44, and /553–64 Middlesex. The School Health Service and its wartime problems is documented in ED 50, for example ED 50/211 reports on investigations into the height and weight of evacuated schoolchildren. The main series of LEA files on secondary education is in ED 53. Borough material is easy to find in ED 134, Miscellaneous wartime general local education authority files: ED 134/71–97 covers London, /98–104 Middlesex and /154 on Croydon, for instance.

*Local records*

The London County Council was the chief education authority for much of the London area, running elementary, secondary and technical schools, as well as adult education classes. The LCC was responsible for the teachers who accompanied the evacuated schoolchildren, though the reception area authority was then in charge of their education. The Middlesex County Council was responsible for secondary and technical education throughout its area, but for elementary education only in its rural parts. Its involvement in the evacuation scheme was therefore minimal compared with that of the LCC. Middlesex County Council Education Committee minutes LMA MCC/MIN/13, and 54 have useful material on Middlesex schools. Departmental papers, MCC/EO/WAR, relate to wartime measures, with evacuation returns, files on reopening schools, on blackout arrangements and school milk provision.

A Chief Inspector's report to the LCC Evacuation Committee in December 1939, LMA LCC/MIN 4984, is enthusiastic about the positive results of a move for some London schoolchildren. 'The improvement in the general poise, bearing and intelligence of the children is in some cases startling. Frankham Street [Deptford], for instance, billeted in small villa residences in St Leonards, is a most striking example of what "early to bed" methods, regular food and a quiet life can do for children. They are rosy, full of life, their eyes sparkle and they are eating up their school work. If ever a justification were needed for a forcible improvement of environment and general living standards, this school offers it abundantly' (p. 8). An appendix contains reports from many teachers and inspectors about their evacuation experiences, good and bad.

The main source for LCC educational material, held in LMA, is the Education Officer's Department, LCC EO. EO/WAR/1 is a collection concerning emergency wartime measures, including evacuation. EO/WAR/2 deals with special categories of evacuee and their educational needs, as in EO/WAR/2/46 on Jewish school children, and /50 on bombed-out TB contacts. EO/WAR/3 relates to schools remaining in London. EO/WAR/3/2 is a census of children in London in November 1939, /18 contains reports by inspectors on school conditions during flying bomb attacks in the summer of 1944, /79–91 is about the use of school premises for CD and other purposes. EO/WAR/4 is a collection of photographs and press cuttings, EO/WAR/5 comprises a useful miscellaneous group containing school magazines and evacuation diaries. EO/WAR/5/1, for instance, is the school diary of Harbinger Infants' School, Milwall, during its evacuation to Abingdon from 1939–44. EO/WAR/5/2 has Putney County High School's magazine for October 1940, while billeted in Woking. The logbooks of Silwood Street School, Rotherhithe, which was in Worthing from the outbreak of war until June 1940, are in EO/WAR/5/14, and /22 are those of Anerley Residential Deaf School which moved between Uckfield, Exeter, Banstead and Rotherham during the war. Other log books kept by evacuated school staff are among miscellaneous deposits, like the log for Shillington Street School, Clapham Junction, in ACC 3531/1. Austin Brewer, the Headmaster, kept it in a Surrey Education Committee exercise book, from September 1939 to August 1943 when he retired. The school was sent to Cranleigh, in Surrey. Mr Brewer describes the early days — 'Billeting, re-billeting, outdoor lessons and nature walks occupied the first three weeks during which excellent weather was a great saving factor' — and the amalgamation with two other evacuated London schools from May 1940. He notes staff names and the dates when they returned to London. There are accounts of the pupils' local activities, like winning allotment prizes, and giving a 'Thank you, Cranleigh' concert and so on. Comparable items occur in other collections, too, such as C.H. Lee's evacuation diary of Wimbledon Central Schools to the Chichester area in 1939–40, in the IWM Department of Documents. Material on evacuated schools may sometimes be found in the record office for the reception area, as with the Huntingdonshire examples mentioned in the evacuation section, and in local newspapers there. Sometimes the log books of non-evacuated schools, like Biggin Hill, kept in Bromley Archives, can be very revealing about the difficulties and exhausting work of the staff who stayed behind. The school was not evacuated until 1944.

The LCC had been proud of the wide range of evening classes it provided in the 1930s. Wartime circumstances meant that Evening Institutes ceased to operate, their premises being needed for other purposes. The classes found a new public in the air raid shelters, where they provided a worth-while diversion. Draft 'Notes on LCC Evening Institute Classes held in Air Raid Shelters', in ILEA/PS/CE/44/1, give several examples of the success of this enterprise. Evening Institute principals organised classes on current events, travel talks, first aid, needlework, knitting and singing. By February 1941, 464 classes were running on this basis. Plays were even produced in these unpromising circumstances. Miss Peter, from Daniel Street Women's Institute in Bethnal Green, put on a performance of *Pygmalion* in the Bethnal Green tunnel shelter, having held rehearsals in the crypt under Shoreditch church (ILEA/PS/CE/44/1).

## *Personal memories*

The numerous diaries, memoirs and oral history recordings by evacuees who were children at the time often stress the billeting arrangements that seemed so strange, and sometimes alarming, to them rather than their continuing schooling. Those by teachers are usually more informative about the educational side. Some examples have been given in the evacuation section. The Hartley Library at the University of Southampton has the diaries of the headmaster of the Jews Free School, Mr S.M. Rich, in MS 168. Also relevant are accounts by Miss J. Male of her experiences as a pupil at an evacuee school in Cornwall in IWM Department of Documents 90/10/1, and tapes by Nellie Bray-Jones, a teacher in Acton and Ealing throughout the war, who was briefly evacuated to Teignmouth, on IWM Sound Archive tape 5386/4. From a different viewpoint, Monica Pittman, on IWM tape 5397/4, describes her wartime administrative work with the LCC Education Department.

## FIGHTING FIT: HEALTH CARE

A healthy population was vital to the war effort, so the government needed to ensure sensible public health measures and a good diet as well as providing care for the sick and injured. The pessimistic pre-war estimates of likely bomb and gas injuries have already been mentioned in the section on Civil Defence. Fortunately they proved exaggerated, though the toll of death and injury was bad enough, with 30,000 dead and 50,000 seriously injured in London during the war.

As war approached, plans were made to evacuate existing hospital patients of all kinds to institutions outside London, freeing their beds for the expected rush of casualties, including psychiatric cases that were expected to outnumber the rest by three to one. This evacuation was carried out through the Ministry of Health's Emergency Medical Service and is described in detail in Richard Titmuss' *Problems of Social Policy* in the *History of the Second World War UK Civil Series* which also deals with other aspects of the Ministry's wartime role, such as evacuation of and provision for the homeless. Ferguson and Fitzgerald's *Studies in the Social Services,* in the same series, has considerable coverage of maternity provision and the nursing services. Both contain information on the London situation. Drafts and papers used in preparing the published histories are in PRO CAB 102. For medical detail on disease and injuries, the separate *Medical History of the War* series should be consulted.

### *The Emergency Hospitals Service*

Hospitals, whatever their administrative status, pooled their facilities for the duration of the war on a regional basis. In the London area they came under the direct control of the Ministry of Health, which financed the building of bomb-proof operating theatres and shelters, and put existing staff under direct contract. Its records in PRO MH are therefore essential sources for the subject. As a result of postwar reorganisation of departmental responsibilities some of the records of its special wartime services were allocated to the new Ministry of Housing and Local Government, and so carry the prefix HLG.

Some of the most useful records for London purposes are in HLG 7, Special wartime functions, which has a 'London Region general file' series containing items such as HLG 7/545, proposed medical rest centres for Jews in Middlesex, and HLG 7/612–808, covering Emergency Hospital schemes. HLG 7/763, for example, relates to civilian wards in the metropolitan boroughs, /767 to those in Middlesex. HLG 68, the '100,000 series' of formerly confidential files, contains a wide variety of topics including health matters. Another important group is MH 76, Emergency Medical Services. In this group MH 76/409–86 comprises a series of files for the London CD region, 'Region 5', but material on London also occurs elsewhere in the series. MH 76/99 covers negotiations with London Voluntary Hospitals just before the war, MH 76/252 relates to moving the civilian sick out of London in 1940, MH 76/185 to the evacuation and return of London hospital patients in 1944, and MH 76/182 to setting up a Yugoslav hospital in London. MH 76/351–6 are Port of London Authority papers, covering first aid posts and ambulance services there. MH 79 is a class relating to wartime medical services. MH 79/507, for instance, concerns a recurrent fear that too much detail entered on hospital admission sheets might possibly provide spies with information about troop movements, or munition factory activities. 'It is not suggested that the Hospitals of this country are honeycombed with medical fifth columnists and spies!', wrote the security officer, drawing it to the Ministry's attention nevertheless. MH 79/565 discusses medical arrangements for war refugees including their reception in London.

## *Hospital records*

Both the LCC and the MCC maintained hospital services at the outbreak of war, surviving records are mostly in LMA. LCC/PH/HOSP/3 deals with individual LCC hospitals and other medical establishments. The LCC was responsible for dozens of hospitals of all kinds, the MCC maintained five large general hospitals and two sanatoria at the start of the war, as well as dispensaries and convalescent homes. Both authorities also had mental hospitals situated beyond their boundaries.

In addition, London had many voluntary hospitals including the great teaching hospitals like St Mary's and University College Hospital, and many non-teaching general hospitals, as well as mental and maternity hospitals and specialist establishments. Some still retain their own archives, like Great Ormond Street Children's Hospital, the Royal London, and St Bartholomew's, others have deposited them with LMA, such as Guy's, St Thomas's and the Westminster and others. The Hospital Records Register compiled by the Wellcome Institute and the PRO, available at the latter, lists all the known surviving hospital records in public repositories, and their locations.

When London hospitals cleared their wards at the outbreak of war to await the expected rush of air raid casualties, some patients were discharged early. Long-term patients, including children and mental cases, were moved to hospitals on the outskirts of the city or beyond. The London Passenger Transport Board was heavily involved in this evacuation, and the LT Museum's photograph library has shots of patients being loaded onto converted buses for journeys to the country. Later in the war the LPTB's Greenline buses were used to take the survivors from Dunkirk to hospitals all over the South East.

Shortage of medical staff for civilian patients, coupled with the unavailability of hospital beds in the central area meant that Londoners were poorly served with health care during the phoney war. The voluntary hospitals, effectively paid by the Ministry to keep their wards empty in case of a crisis, came in for particular criticism. When the air raids failed to come, the situation was gradually rectified, and when the Blitz arrived it caused fewer casualties than planners had envisaged.

Most London hospitals sustained some degree of air raid damage, sometimes of great severity. The direct hit on St Thomas's on the night of 8–9 September 1940 was very destructive of lives and of buildings. King Edward's Hospital Fund for London, a medical charity which raised money for the voluntary hospitals, enlisted the poet John Masefield to write an account of their experiences during the Blitz. The book was apparently never published, but the records in LMA are interesting. The Fund had asked hospitals to submit accounts of their Blitz experiences for Masefield to work from. A/KE/244 is a collection of letters from hospitals designated 'less badly affected' for purposes of the book. The Matron of Albany Deptford Babies' Hospital related that only a week after they had moved out at the insistence of their medical superintendent, their building suffered a direct hit crushing their 'safest' basement shelters where the babies might have been. Charing Cross Hospital's letter remembered 8 March 1941: 'This was the night when the Café de Paris was bombed. Good work was done by one of the hospital sisters in relieving the immediate agony of patients on the spot. 53 very seriously injured cases were admitted into the hospital and 38 major operations, apart from minor casualties,

# Young Nurses Braved Bombs to Save Patients

### By Daily Mail Reporter

**T**HERE were 300 heroines of the Outer London hospital which was three-quarters destroyed by bomb blast and fire in the air raid early yesterday.

They were the nurses and probationers, some of them only 16 and 18 years old, who, like seasoned troops, sprang calmly and courageously to their stations when the first bomb fell.

Seven patients out of 1,128 and five members of the staff were killed and a small number injured. But for the precision and discipline with which the nurses and medical staff rescued patients from blazing and shattered wings these numbers would have been considerably increased.

Half the nursing staff was sleeping in the Nurses' Home outside which the first bomb fell, killing a fireguard and a fireman.

Stumbling over wrecked doors, broken glass, and through clouds of dust and smoke, the nurses and probationers hurried out of their home just as another bomb fell, blasting and setting on fire an adjoining wing containing many men patients.

Sister Agnes Kavanagh, of County Monaghan, received a special word of praise from the matron, who was herself described to me as "magnificently cool in directing rescue work."

### Escape by Crater

Sister Kavanagh told me that when a bomb fell close to the children's ward she was with her patients, aged from 20 months to seven years.

RELATIVES of patients in the hospital in the London area which was bombed early yesterday crowd round the entrance for news. Some turned away to mourn. Top picture shows nurses retrieving stores. Story in BACK Page.

*The* Daily Mail *reports another London hospital bombing, 20 April 1944*

were treated here'. St Mary's wrote that '...it was not until the night of 13–14 October [1940] that really heavy demands were made on the casualty service. During that night a bomb fell across the road onto the open air platform of the Metropolitan Railway. A Sunday night, the station was crowded; there were men of the Forces returning to their units after leave, parents who had been to see their evacuated children... Ten minutes after the shattering thud of the heavy bomb, the first of the ambulances arrived and a long line of 30 to 40 stretchers was admitted... Part of the nightmare was the blackened skins of the victims, covered with soot and dirt from the blast and with only the whites of their eyes and terrible injuries standing out like some dreadful mark.' The King's Fund records contain other material of relevance to the position in London, like the papers of the British Hospitals War Emergency Committee in A/KE/70/1–3, reports on the shortage of maternity accommodation in A/KE/350 and maps of the location and availability of London hospitals at various periods. Annual reports of the voluntary hospitals provide valuable information on their wartime work, the King's Fund records contain a good set. Published histories of the hospitals invariably cover the war years, usually with illustrations, as in L.A. Amidon's *Illustrated History of the Royal Free Hospital* (1997).

Records for the LCC and MCC hospitals vary considerably in their coverage. Some, like those for St Mary Abbot's Hospital in Kensington are quite full, with inventories, patients' registers, accounts, minutes, nursing and staff records in H17/SMA, for others there are only the minutes. Photographs of staff and patients in wartime are frequently preserved among hospital records. St Bartholomew's Hospital and the Royal London Hospital archives, for example, both have extensive collections of contemporary photographs showing bomb damage, air raid precautions, medical staff and patients on the wards and similar subjects. The IWM has several paintings of hospital scenes and medical staff, including Kathleen Guthrie's 'Bombed hospital ward' and an interesting view by Evelyn Dunbar of nurses and doctors on a train, knitting and reading while they wait in a siding to be moved into a bombed area after a raid.

## *Shelter health*

Hygiene in the air raid shelters concerned the Ministry of Health greatly. Large numbers of people cramped in hot, airless, insanitary conditions for hours at a time provided ideal conditions for the spread of infections, and, sometimes, of infestation. In the early days of the Blitz this hazard was demonstrated very clearly, and the problem is documented in a number of files in MH 76. In September 1940 the Ministry circulated all the boroughs, urging careful attention to sanitation in public shelters of all kinds. Kensington's Medical Officer of Health replied promptly: '26 September 1940. You may rest assured that we are doing everything we can to meet your wishes that air raid shelters should be clean, healthy and comfortable', adding a list of measures already in place (MH 76/586). Other boroughs were less virtuous, the 'laissez faire attitude of one or two of the Medical Officers of Health' was criticised by the Ministry in an internal memo. Medical considerations relevant to the new tube shelters planned after the Blitz are covered in MH 76/539.

Respiratory diseases spread rapidly in shelter conditions; attempts to deal with the problem have already been mentioned in the section on public shelters in 'Civil Defence'. MH 76/547 concerns attempts to encourage the general use of germ-masks in shelters generally. Individual borough shelter inspection reports in MH 76 contain comments on the progress of this policy, MH 76/590, on Poplar MBC in April 1944, for example, comments that 'Face masks have been kept in store and never issued'.

Pests of various kinds were another problem. The boroughs were responsible for maintaining hygiene by regular cleansing of the shelters, but bed bugs were common, brought in on dirty bedding. Distasteful, but not dangerous in themselves, it was their association with other forms of vermin like lice and fleas that made them a hazard. MH 76/538 is a file of detailed reports on vermin at tube station shelters, in one of which a London Region CD doctor outlines the risks: '... the possibility of a great increase in lousiness during the coming winter with its attendant danger of an outbreak of typhus, and a serious outbreak of this disease would probably result in an immense crippling of our war effort. Further, in one large shelter, Bethnal Green tunnel, fleas have been reported in large numbers and also black rats. As this tunnel is situated in the East End of London and not very far from the docks, I do not think the risk of plague can altogether be ignored' (2 September 1941). The Ministry took the problem very seriously, for instance complaining to the Medical Office of Health for Merton and Morden on 31 December 1943 that 'It has been reported to me that a bug has been found on bunk no. 42, southbound platform [of South Wimbledon station]'. The MOH reported 'Bunk inspected 1.1.44. No evidence of vermin. Bunk occupied by Mrs Spring, 8 Nelson Grove Road'. More material on this problem, including insecticide trials and their results, is in HO 207/359.

Mosquito infestation made conditions very unpleasant at some stations, and raised fears of malaria. Liverpool Street, Bond Street and Charing Cross were the worst affected when the problem was first noted in 1940, but other stations suffered too and 'mosquito gangs' worked throughout the war trying to kill the larvae which also affected Liverpool Street underground station, and a malaria expert was called in to advise (MH 76/546).

First aid posts were provided in most underground air raid shelters to deal with minor injuries, often caused by shattered glass, and routine health problems. Their provision, staffing problems and work are documented in HO 207/411, /445; inspections of the posts are covered in MH 76/537.

## Voluntary bodies

Voluntary bodies assisted with paramedical work in several ways, including helping at first aid posts, ambulance driving and stretcher-bearing. The Friends' Ambulance Unit was active in this work, its records are at Friends' House. The Joint War Organisation of the British Red Cross Society and the Order of St John of Jerusalem were also extensively involved. Among the Red Cross archives relating to London in wartime are the Society's County of London branch minutes, annual reports and bulletins, in ACC 750; City of London branch minutes, and detachment registers, ACC 920; Richmond Centre detachment records ACC 1254; Greater London Blood Transfusion service circulars and reports and Voluntary Blood Donors' Association minutes, ACC 345 and 562.

The Red Cross collection also contains unpublished reminiscences by wartime personnel, such as Joyce Dowse's 'Recollections of my days working for the BRCS at St James's Palace' 1943–5, where she was a secretary, T.M. Bullock's personal account of service at the BRCS First Aid post at Dulwich College Cricket Pavilion, and 'Sheltering the homeless', Eileen Barralet's memories of work at the Red Cross first aid post at Knightsbridge underground station. Three VADs who served in Hammersmith recorded their reminiscences for the Red Cross's collection, on tape ACC 759. Examples of first aid class notes and certificates awarded by the Red Cross or St John's survive quite widely, as in the ephemera collection in the Museum of London, boxes A3, A5, and Kensington Local Studies Library, in 940.5475 WW.

## Personal memories

Memoirs and recordings of medical work in London are also represented in other collections, notably those of the Wellcome Institute and the IWM. The Wellcome has reminiscences of life as a wartime probationer at St George's Hospital, Hyde Park, by Mrs P.M. Clewett, in CMAC GC/41. The IWM Department of Documents has nursing memoirs by probationers at the Royal Free, in Misc. 168, 2581, and the diary of Miss G. Thomas, a nursing sister at Highgate Hospital between August 1939 and January 1943, and later at Lewisham Hospital, in 90/30/1. P. Lambah, a medical student, composed a verse account of his experiences as a medical student in the Blitz, in 88/49/1 and Miss M.I. Wilson wrote letters home to Northern Ireland while nursing at Bart's in 1939–41, in 89/11/3. Memories from the patient's viewpoint are less common, but C. Jory, sub-editor of the *News Chronicle* kept a diary, now in the IWM Department of Documents, which describes a V1 hitting the roof of his block of flats while he slept, and his subsequent medical treatment.

The IWM Sound Archive has over six hundred recordings of nurses, doctors and other medical staff. Peter Horsey, on tape 13925/2 recalls his time as a medical student at St Thomas's Hospital during the flying bomb attacks, and an anonymous Jamaican nurse, recorded during the war, on tape 2292/G/A, describes working at night on a busy ward through the Blitz. She said it was less terrifying than people supposed, because of the need to be so busy. Even four year olds now knew the difference between bombs and gunfire — 'ducking when bombs fall' became automatic. Dr A.S. Till, on National Sound Archive tape C410/06 C1, talks about treating German pilots for burns at Woolwich, and about coping with lung blast, crush syndrome and gas gangrene injuries.

# FAITH IN ADVERSITY: RELIGION

*'But gracious Lord whate'er shall be*
*Don't let anyone bomb me...'* (John Betjeman, 'In Westminster Abbey')

The bulk of the surviving records relating to religious affairs in London during the war refer to practical matters of administration, to claims and repairs for damaged buildings, and to welfare work undertaken among evacuees, the bombed-out, refugees and the air raid shelterers. National records in the PRO reflect this to some degree, but do not provide the deep vein of information about religious matters that they do for so many other topics. The more spiritual side is much harder to document, though personal papers, letters, diaries and occasional reports can yield insights into this aspect. Denominational newspapers and magazines, like the *Church Times*, the *Catholic Herald, Methodist Recorder, Baptist Times, The War Cry, The Friend, Jewish Chronicle* and others, are invaluable sources for their activities and views at this time, frequently covering London topics. In an impressive outbreak of ecumenism the *Catholic Herald, Church of England Guardian, Jewish Chronicle* and a Christadelphian publication all shared editorial premises in High Wycombe from the outbreak of war.

The main link between the government and religious bodies during the war was provided by the Ministry of Information's Religions Division. It arranged tours for clergy, distributed publicity and news items for the press, and produced weekly religious news sheets. Surviving records are in INF 1 and INF 2. Occasional information about church activities in London emerges incidentally from such PRO records as the air raid shelter inspections in MH 76, such as MH 76/590, concerning the notorious shelter at Christ Church, Cubitt Town quoted in the section on Civil Defence, and HO 207, as in HO 207/422 on church crypts as shelters. The high level of bomb damage to churches, chapels, synagogues and other ecclestastical buildings is reflected in the records of the War Damage Commission. IR 37 contains many examples. IR 37/47 refers to damage claims on behalf of the Convent of the Holy Child Jesus in Cavendish Square, a convent and training college with a chapel, school and infirmary. It suffered superficial damage from a high explosive bomb in 1940, and fire damage in 1941. The claims were all handled by an architect on behalf of the convent, and the folders contain detailed plans of the building. IR 37/94 deals with the Dutch Church, Austin Friars, and IR 37/86 with damage at Westminster Abbey. This last file is closed till 1999 because claims went on being made until 1969; a reminder that archival closure periods run from the date of the most recent document added, even when the bulk of the contents dates from an earlier period.

At the outbreak of war, religious observance levels in London were not dissimilar to those of the rest of the country, and scarcely justifying the Public Morality Council's view of the capital as the 'modern Babylon'. During the war, Mass-Observation conducted several surveys around London to investigate the role of religion in daily life. An early one, in 1939, looked at the churches and evacuation, especially their activities in the reception areas. In 1940 they conducted interviews, mostly by telephone, with London clergy of all denominations, to find out what effect the war was having on church activities. Almost all respondents mentioned the problems that evacuation had brought in terms of loss of congregation and choir members, and the practical difficulties caused by the blackout regulations. As the war went on, Mass-Observation's reporters attended a cross-section of church services around London and commented on what they found. All give the numbers attending, some also describe the congregation and give a résumé of the sermon. The churches are named (M-O Religion Box 1 Folder F). Then, towards the end of the war, respondents were asked whether their views of religion had changed as a result of it — this drew a predictably mixed response. Mass-Observation concluded that those who already had a fairly deep faith found that it was strengthened in wartime, those with little found it weakened still further. The M-O book *Puzzled People* (1947), is based on a survey on atttitudes to religion done in 1944, almost certainly in Fulham.

Congregations looked to their clergyman, whatever his denomination, for an example in very difficult times, and they were not usually disappointed. Clergymen were designated as being in a reserved occupation, but many, especially the younger ones, volunteered for Forces service as chaplains. Those who stayed behind mostly threw themselves wholeheartedly into the care of their congregation both materially and spiritually. In many cases their behaviour was not only dedicated but heroic during air raid rescue operations. Some were killed or injured, many lost their own homes in the bombing. The damage toll to religious buildings was enormous. Relevant records are available in a range of repositories.

Like all other organisations, religious bodies and their local 'branches' set up some sort of emergency committee to deal with the problems brought by wartime circumstances, and to settle matters of general policy. Churches, chapels and synagogues had to contend with air raid precautions, the blackout regulations, staffing difficulties due to the call-up, bomb damage to their buildings, firewatching rotas and shortages of essential supplies, as well as trying to carry out their normal religious activities.

## *The Anglican church*

The records of the dioceses of London and Southwark are, of course, of most direct relevance to the history of the capital, but there is useful material, too, among the archbishops' papers at Lambeth Palace Library. The Bishops' War Committee minutes reveal concern about a variety of wartime problems such as training chaplains for the Forces, moral issues, like 'unmarried wives' of servicemen and their financial support, VD, and contraceptives, and also financial ones, such as how to adjust the stipends of clergy who were chaplains but still had benefices. In November 1939 the bishops worried about burials after air raids. Local authorities had power to use any cemetery if necessary, but the committee hoped that common sense would prevail if it became necessary to bury German dead in large quantities. They hoped that the authorities would not antagonise local communities by insisting on filling up small parish burial grounds for this purpose, displacing the parishioners. By July 1940 they were considering what to do if services were interrupted by air raids. They decided that the service should continue till guns or bombs were heard. And in November 1940 blackout restrictions were discussed. It was impracticable to black out huge church windows, so services must be held in the early morning, using the minimum light necessary to read (MS 2448).

Lambeth Palace itself was badly damaged by an air raid in 1940. The Lang Papers, in Notebook transcripts 223 f. 265, record Archbishop Lang's own experience: 'The night bombing of London reached its highest intensity on the nights of September 7–11. No one who has not gone through it can realise the almost intolerable strain. All night long, from about 9.30 to 5.30 a.m. usually, a continual droning of German aeroplanes and crashing of bombs — sometimes it was hard to believe the house itself was not hit'. On 20 September it was, but the Archbishop had moved out three days earlier. His successor, Archbishop Temple, was determined to move back in, and his wife has left a graphic description of the palace's bomb-damaged state and the extensive work it took to make it habitable again, in Fisher 5 ff. 250–74.

The Archbishop's correspondence and official papers, in Lang 88, reveal a flurry of public concern about evacuation and its effect on churchgoing in 1939. Members of the public wrote to stress the need for evacuated children to attend church and Sunday School. The Bishop of Salisbury reported complaints about over-zealous Catholic priests and teachers accompanying children evacuated from the diocese of Southwark, but Lang replied in December 1939 that he could not 'but admire the zeal with which these Roman Catholics try and minister to the spiritual needs of their scattered flock.'

The Fulham Papers, from the diocese of London, are also held by Lambeth Palace. Churches in the City of London suffered badly from air raid damage. The bishop, Geoffrey Fisher, set up a small committee to consider their problems; later it became the Bishop's Commission on City Churches, chaired by Lord Merriman, which planned the fate of the damaged buildings after the war. The Committee papers reflect concern about the safety of the structures, their contents and fittings, and relations with the City Engineer's Department over clearing debris. The file contains reports on individual churches, listing the incumbent, maintenance and fabric grants, current arrangements for services, payments being made to cleaners, caretakers and organists, and any drop in collection money compared with pre-war. A memorandum dated 26 June 1941, for instance, noted that the Rector of St Bartholomew the Great, Smithfield, was charging 6d entry fee and that 'The church is in a most deplorable and filthy state and I hope that no one will be permitted to go in unless it is cleaned. The dust and dirt everywhere is pathetic. Dead flowers in dirty vases are an eyesore'. Detailed lists of plate, registers, fixtures and fittings follow, with a note of where they are stored for safe keeping. Finding firewatchers for City churches, a legal requirement from early 1941, was difficult because so few parishioners lived locally. The Bishop wrote to the Lord Mayor to ask for help in July 1941 (Fisher 8).

Apart from the Fulham Papers the bulk of the diocesan records for London are kept in the Guildhall Library Manuscripts Department. There are samples of the Diocesan Registrar's correspondence about wartime cases, such as the use of church land for Civil Defence purposes, which include an agreement between the vicar of St John the Evangelist, Kingston-upon-Thames, and the National Fire Service for the erection of a static water tank in the churchyard; the disposal of rusting tomb railings for scrap at Stoke Newington, Chiswick and Enfield, and the emergency storage of valuables from All Saints, Fulham (MS 24,778). The records of the diocese of Southwark are at LMA.

Guildhall Library and LMA have the records of many Anglican parishes, including wartime material where it survives. Some local record offices have diocesan deanery minutes. Hackney Archives has those for Hackney and Stoke Newington Rural Deaconal Chapter, for example, and for Shoreditch Rural Deanery. A feeling for life at parish level in wartime can be gleaned from parish magazines, of which LMA has a good collection. The magazines for St Barnabas, Dulwich, in 1940 (P73 BAN 489), report that ENSA entertained servicemen in the parish hall in February, that ladies replaced evacuated schoolboys in the choir from April, that English classes and social events for refugees were held in September and that shorter, earlier services to beat the blackout were scheduled from October.

Guildhall Library has many of the records of St Paul's cathedral, but among those still retained by the cathedral library are some of wartime interest. They include firewatchers' logbooks and expenses and attendance registers, with a collection of photographs of the firewatchers at work, taken for use in a recruitment drive. When not patrolling, the firewatchers performed other useful tasks, gardening in Amen Court — there is a photograph of Canon Mozley admiring a crop of beans — or oiling the lift in the choir school. A.S.G. Butler's letters to his mother describing firewatching in the distinguished company of other architects, sculptors and artists have already been mentioned in the section on Civil Defence; they are also valuable for his comments on London more generally, as is his published memoir *Recording Ruin.* Patrolling the complex building was confusing for newcomers. Butler wrote a short guide for new watch members, 'Learning St Paul's', in which he suggested thinking of the great building in terms of the different decks of a ship. St Paul's library also has the manuscript of W.R. Matthews' *St Paul's in Wartime* (1946), with related correspondence.

Westminster Abbey's muniments contain correspondence files relating to ARP precautions at the abbey (61250–79), including official dealings with London Region CD headquarters as well as 'in house' handbills and posters explaining what to do if a service was interrupted by an air raid. The choir had special ARP duties, while the congregation headed for the shelters under the Methodist Central Hall. If the interrupted service was a VIP funeral, such as Lord Willingdon's in 1941, special instructions applied. Royal representatives and the Cabinet went to the crypt, the diplomatic corps to the Pyx chapel, members of the family and members of Parliament to the Norman undercroft and 'other members of the congregation would be accommodated in the Dark Cloister, as far as space allows...' (61250). Correspondence concerning war damage claims (61587–61605) covers rebuilding plans after air raid damage. Canon Don, the Dean, suggested to the Planning Committee that future housing arrangements should be practical and should not assume that new canons would have private means to support elaborate establishments (61594). Not

---

**NOT TO BE TAKEN AWAY**

### Westminster Abbey

#### AIR RAID WARNINGS

In future, and until further notice, the following procedure will be adopted when an Air Raid warning is given:—

1. ON WEEKDAYS the Services will proceed as usual irrespective of the siren, since the Abbey can offer adequate protection for the small numbers concerned.

2. ON SUNDAYS (except at the 8 a.m. Service) services will be suspended on the sounding of a siren, and no Service will be commenced until a quarter of an hour after the "all clear" has been given.

This precaution is necessary in view of the fact that no adequate shelter is available for the larger numbers attending the Sunday services, nor is it desirable to dismiss the congregation into the streets after the "alarm of imminent danger" when shrapnel may be falling.

When a Service is thus suspended the congregation are urged to disperse at once, but the Clergy and Vergers on duty will remain in the Abbey until the Congregation have had an opportunity to leave.

N.B.—The Public are advised that the Abbey is not a safe place during an Air Raid—and are strongly advised to take shelter as recommended above.

PAUL DE LABILLIERE,
*Dean.*

*October,* 1940

Church services might be interrupted by air raids
*(Westminster Abbey Muniments 61250b)*

---

all his colleagues were convinced. 'Canon Donaldson put in a caveat about the suggestion that houses should be modest in size. He thought that on an optimistic view large families might occur [this replaces "be usual" on the document] and domestic service be available' (61595). There are also records of the abbey firewatchers in 61462–90. Schedules of war removals (63099 A–B), relate to the abbey's treasures, stored in various country houses and parts of the underground for safety. There is a collection of wartime service sheets and other ephemera including lecture programmes for the abbey's contribution to the 'holidays at home' campaign, and photographs of activities continuing amid war damage. Canon Don's diaries, with a good account of the severe air raid of 10–11 May 1941 and others, are in Lambeth Palace Library MS 2861–71.

Books and articles on the church's wartime work were published at the time, such as the Bishop of Stepney, R.H. Moberley's 'East London in wartime — what is the church doing?' in the *East & West Review* (April 1941). Several London clergy wrote accounts of their parishes' sufferings during the Blitz, for example H.A. Wilson's *Death over Haggerston*. R.C. Taylor, vicar of St Bartholomew, Shepperton Road, Islington, kept a diary of his life in the parish during 1941, illustrating typical problems of a difficult year: 'We had nice services in the Tube only on one platform and one stair II K.VII. Prayer in Canonbury Sq. shelter' (23 February 1941, LMA, in P83/BAT/015). Unpublished memoirs and tape recordings can be found in some collections. The rector of St Peter Walworth, J.G. Markham, wrote a memoir called 'The church under fire' which is now in the IWM Department of Documents in 91/5/1. He was an Air Raid Warden, serving later as a District Warden and a Bomb Reconnaissance officer. Miss M.S. Smylie's poem 'London church, October 1 1944' (IWM Misc.161 2479), describes a service in the ruins of St Silas, Nunhead, after heavy V1 damage. She also drew a picture of the scene.

Photographs showing clergy taking services in air raid shelters are quite common. Ministry of Information shots in the Museum of London's collection include, for instance, the Revd. Mackay holding a service in a shelter 'under a religious institution' in North London (8851), and another shelter service in progress (8872).

An interesting angle on religious observance during the war comes from the papers of the Church of England Advisory Board on Spiritual Ministration, set up by the LCC in 1932 to oversee 'matters of spiritual ministration to patients and inmates of the Anglican Faith in the Council's hospitals and institutions'. These were categorised under the headings Hospitals; Social Welfare establishments, such as homes for the aged; Mental Hospitals, and Educational Establishments, like children's homes. Surviving records include agenda papers, LMA LCC/MIN/12,606, though February 1940–November 1944 are missing; minutes, LCC/MIN/12,608; general papers, CL/SPC/4/1 and presented papers, LCC/MIN/12,612–16. The last class is the most informative, with correspondence about appointments and salaries, annual reports from each chaplain with information about his work, and inspection reports from members of the Board who visited a selection of institutions each year to gauge the effectiveness of the ministry there. The Church of England Records Centre has the records of the Church Commissioners, including material on Church House, as well as collections relating to Anglican voluntary societies and schools active in London.

## *The Roman Catholic church*

The Catholic diocese of Westminster covers Greater London north of the Thames. Its archive holdings cover the administrative records of the diocese, parochial records are mainly still in the care of individual parishes. South of the river Catholic parishes belong to the archdiocese of Southwark. Among archdiocesan archives are papers on its work with refugees and evacuees, its chaplaincies, bomb damage and compensation claims for churches, and the removal of their iron railings for the scrap metal campaign. The records of religious orders are usually retained by the order, either centrally or at the convent concerned. The *Directory of Catholic Archives* (Catholic Archives Society, 1984) provides further guidance.

Barnet Archives holds a copy of an air raid diary kept by nuns at the Convent of the Good Shepherd, Finchley in MS 16526, entitled 'Summary of air raids in Finchley starting from August 1940'. As a teaching order they had the safety of their pupils to worry about as well as that of the sisters. Although the primary purpose of the diary was to record air raids as they affected the convent, the two auxiliary nuns who made the entries sometimes added comments on the political news they had heard on the radio, and on their daily lives more generally. The first entry is for the feast of the Assumption, 15 August 1940, when an air raid warning sent the Children of Mary rushing to the convent's shelter. On 30 August there were three raids. During the third 'After one particularly large explosion Mother Superior brought Father Ryder round and he gave us a General Absolution. We really thought we were going to die and made preparations for Death'. Catholic as well as Anglican clergy acted as shelter wardens, the Museum of London's collection contains several photographs of the basement gymnasium of a North London college in use as an air raid shelter in the care of a priest, such as 8847.

## Nonconformists

Nonconformist records for London are found in a variety of record offices and libraries. Some are in specialist repositories, others have been deposited in local authority collections for the appropriate area.

### Baptists

Baptist Union records for this period, kept at Regent's Park College in Oxford, are full of references to the war, its War Damage Committee papers deal with damage to London churches. Private papers of Baptist ministers, such as Dr James Rushbrooke, of Highgate and Hampstead Garden Suburb, are also potential sources of London information. Church minutes and deacons' minutes for several London churches are kept in this collection, including Bermondsey, Hanwell, Chelsea and Holborn Kingsgate. Records of some other Baptist congregations have been deposited in local record offices. Southwark, for example, has Sunday School teachers' minutes for Walworth Road Baptist Chapel in 7023, LMA has records for Upper Holloway Baptist Church in ACC 2541, and for Ferme Park Baptist Church, Hornsey, in ACC 2732, 1412, 1466 and 1361.

### Congregationalists

The records are either still held by the churches concerned or have been deposited at LMA or other local record offices. LMA has the records of the London Congregational Union, in N/LCU, and of a range of London churches including, for example, Lavender Hill Congregational Church in ACC 2998, Isleworth Congregational Chapel in N/C/10 and Park Chapel, Hornsey in ACC 1413. Typical records are minutes, registers, correspondence, accounts and photographs. Hackney, Southwark and Camden, among other borough collections, have also taken in local examples.

### Methodists

The Methodist Archives and Research Centre at the John Rylands Library, University of Manchester, holds many of the Methodist archives, including those of its War Damage Commission, which predictably has considerable London material. Other potentially useful sources are the records of its Division for Social Responsiblity and Divison of Education, as well as individual ministers' diaries. Lord Soper was very active in London during the war, his papers are now in the Methodist Archives and Research Centre at the John Rylands Library. Records for metropolitan Methodist churches and circuits have been deposited in London repositories. Southwark has an extensive collection including the records of the South London Mission, while Hackney, for instance, has some for Dalston Methodist Church, D/E 234 A6, and for Packington Street Methodist Church in Islington, D/E 234 PAC; LMA has circuit and church records for many more. They include registers, minutes, accounts, magazines and photographs. The *Catalog of Methodist Archival and Manuscript*

*Collections* Pt. 6: *Great Britain and Ireland* (World Methodist Historical Society, 1985) provides further information.

## *Quakers — the Religious Society of Friends*

Quaker records, at Friends' House, have some important sources for wartime London, including documentation on the work of the Friends' Relief Service, previously called the Friends' War Victims Relief Service, or the Friends' War Relief Service, especially active in evacuation and hostel work for Londoners. Friends' House has a run of the Service's annual reports, photographs, publicity material and the archives of its central office. Another important facet of Friends' war work was the Friends' Ambulance Unit; again Friends' House has its archives as well as annual reports and publicity material. Published histories of both these services are included in the bibliography. During the war many non-absolutist pacifists chose to do their war service with the Ambulance Unit, the IWM Sound Archive has a tape of Alan T. Taylor remembering the experience, on tape 13649/2. The collection has over a hundred other recordings of conscientious objectors of all kinds in London.

Records of London Quaker meetings may be useful. The regional organisation was based on the London and Middlesex Quarterly Meeting. The area was subdivided for Monthly Meetings like the Westminster and Longford MM, for instance, or the Kingston and Wandsworth MM. Within each Monthly Meeting area there were local Preparative Meetings, the equivalent of local congregations. Friends' House has the archives of the Quarterly Meeting and its constituent subordinate meetings.

## *The Salvation Army*

Salvation Army citadels usually keep their own records, but the SA Heritage Centre has some material on the Army's wartime activities. In keeping with its emphasis on practical Christianity the Army worked hard for Forces welfare, providing 'Red Shield' clubs abroad as well as all over the UK. In London it ran a hotel for Canadian servicemen in Southampton Row, and station canteens to feed troops and other travellers. For the civilian population more generally, the Salvation Army staffed mobile canteens taken to air raid shelters and to bombed areas to feed survivors and the rescue services. Where they had halls close to underground stations, as in Hampstead and Marylebone, they opened them for light refreshment provision. Like other denominations, the SA suffered serious bomb damage to their premises, the Centre has a looseleaf binder detailing 'Properties damaged by flying bombs, 'Battle of Southern England', 1944 in the box marked Red Shield/Wartime giving the address, date of damage and whether the freeholder had been notified. The box also contains two copies of an account of 'East London Division in the Battle of Britain', covering August 1940–October 1942, written at the request of the Salvation Army authorities with a view to publication, but never issued. Pasted into one copy is the editorial department's conclusion, dated April 1943, that it was now too late: 'The events recorded lie so far back... there are hardly any real "stories" and the whole would compare rather unfavourably with quite a few little books that have been published by vicars and ministers in East London...' The text has sections on East End work in general, and borough by borough activity: 'Dagenham and Becontree: many bombs have fallen, causing great suffering. Adjutant Mabel Gainey and Adjutant Tompkins have done Mortuary Duty (not a particularly pleasant task) which has put them in peculiar and effective touch with the people'. The collection also has useful runs of the *War Cry* and

*Red Shield Bulletin*, in addition to many Red Shield information booklets and photographs of officers at work.

## Jewish communities

Jewish religious observance was affected by wartime conditions in similar ways to that of other denominations. Synagogues, like churches, were awkward to adapt to ARP regulations, and services were often held in halls instead. Efforts were made to retime services so that they could be held by daylight. On important Holy Days larger synagogues found it necessary to hold extra services to fit in all the people who wished to come, because gatherings of over 250 were prohibited for safety reasons. Synagogues evolved new welfare activities. West London Synagogue, for example, opened a club for Jewish Forces personnel, with a canteen, reading room, refreshments and entertainments. When local schools closed for evacuation, some East End settlements organised daytime activities for children who would otherwise have nothing to do. The Jewish authorities worried about the special needs of evacuated children, especially the provision of kosher food for them, and their religious education and observance. Ministers held services in air raid shelters, and helped with welfare work for the bombed-out and the bereaved. On 2 January 1941 the *Jewish Chronicle* reported that Chanukah services had been held in several shelters, including the one at Dickins & Jones. The festival coincided with Christmas, and non-Jews had joined in too, ending with a mutual exchange of good wishes.

Many synagogues look after their own records, which commonly include minutes, annual reports, committee papers, financial and membership records, newsletters and correspondence. The National Register of Archives lists many examples, with synagogue addresses. Others have deposited them in the Jewish Museum, at LMA, or the Hartley Library at the University of Southampton. LMA has records from the New Road Synagogue, ACC 2943, and the United Synagogue, ACC 2712, as well as those of other Jewish organisations, including the Chief Rabbi's office, ACC 2981 2805, Federation of Synagogues, ACC 2893 and other Jewish organisations such as charities, such as Food for the Jewish Poor, ACC 2842, the Jewish Bread, Meat and Coal Society, ACC 2944, and clubs like the Victoria Boys & Girls Club, ACC 2996. Permission is needed from the depositors before these records can be consulted. The Hartley Library has some other synagogue records, including deposits from the West London Synagogue, MS 140, the United Synagogue, MS 145, and Machzike Hadath Synagogue, MS 151; youth club records: Notting Hill, and Stepney Jewish Lads' Clubs, MS 116/82 and MS 172; institutional papers: Jewish Friendly Societies, MS 214, Jewish Care, MS 173, and educational holdings. Still more records are deposited locally. Tower Hamlets Local History Library has records from Princelet Street Synagogue, Spitalfields, in TH/8262, for instance.

Reminiscences, diaries and memoirs in the Hartley Library are also useful for London, such as the papers concerning Diana Silberstin, a refugee in London, MS 93, and Edith Ramsey's memories of life in Stepney, MS 116/82. Additional material is available in the Jewish Museum, including a good collection of photographs showing damage to synagogues, and welfare activities at East End settlements. The museum has a collection of oral history tapes, some of which relate to London in the war. The IWM Sound Archive has hundreds of recordings of British and refugee Jews in its collection. The Jewish Studies Library at University College, London is a valuable source of secondary literature, some of which covers London Jewry in the war, like the published synagogue histories. It also has an easily accessible run of the *Jewish Chronicle.*

## OUT ON THE TOWN: LEISURE AND THE ARTS

### *Literature and the arts*

In spite of manifold practical difficulties literature and the arts flourished in Britain during the war. Any imaginative escape from grim reality was welcome, but there was also a conscious feeling that cultural matters must not be overwhelmed by the sheer struggle to survive, and reading, listening to music, art appreciation, theatre and concert-going probably had a wider audience than in peacetime. Books, poetry and music of lasting importance were written and paintings made, as well as an impressive quantity of less enduring work that was nevertheless enjoyed at the time, and now provides a flavour of the period. A great deal of this activity took place in London. Robert Hewison's *Under Siege: Literary Life in London, 1939–45* (1977) is an invaluable guide.

Many writers and artists served in the Forces, or were employed in some capacity by government departments, like the Ministry of Information, during the war and information about them can sometimes lie among departmental records in the PRO. The government's main effort in cultural matters, however, was channelled through the Council for the Encouragement of Music and the Arts (CEMA), which was to evolve later into the Arts Council. The Pilgrim Trust provided its initial funding, with a matching grant from the Board of Education which provided a chairman, Lord MacMillan, officers and staff. Its papers in the PRO are in classes EL 1–3. It organised cultural events and concerts of all kinds, including entertainment for factory workers. The War Artists' Advisory Committee, set up by the Ministry of Information and documented in PRO WORK 54, also played an important role in cultural affairs by commissioning artists to record Britain at war.

### *Reading*

Reading assumed greater importance to many people in wartime circumstances. Hours of sheltering during air raids, ARP and firewatching duties, slow and delayed journeys by public transport could all be enlivened by an interesting book or magazine. 'Blacked-out evenings — take home some books', urged posters on railway bookstalls. Paper rationing restricted the size and quality of book production, but the advent of the cheap paperback, pioneered by Penguin Books in the thirties, opened up an enormous range of choice covering everything from favourite classics, crime fiction, new poetry and novels to non-fiction 'specials' on current events, history or politics. Other publishers maintained a steady output. The public libraries, and subscription libraries like Boots, supplied some of it. Voluntary societies organised book collections, particularly for the troops, and friends lent each other favourites from their own collections. There was a marked revival of interest in classics by Jane Austen, Charles Dickens and Anthony Trollope through which people could lose themselves in the safer and more reassuring world of the past, though some preferred stronger meat. George Orwell pointed out the enormous popularity of James Hadley Chase's brutal thriller *No Orchids for Miss Blandish* during the Battle of Britain and the Blitz. 'It was, in fact, one of the things that helped to console people for the boredom of being bombed', he wrote in his 1944 essay 'Raffles and Miss Blandish'.

Magazines like *Picture Post, Illustrated, Horizon, Lilliput, Punch, Women's Weekly, Times Literary Supplement, The Listener, Contemporary Review, Fortnightly Review* and many more, were comparatively cheap, catering for all tastes with a mixture of war-related articles and others to take the reader's mind off the subject. They provide a useful guide to current preoccupations from month to month. Newspapers of all kinds were widely read, too.

Novels, short stories and poetry written during the war can provide background information about attitudes, expectations and social conventions of the period, frequently conveying a sense of atmosphere lacking in more factual material. Leisure reading inevitably had some influence on public opinion, making imaginative as well as factual literature worth considering as an additional historical source.

It is, of course an enormous field. The bibliographical section of this guide includes some titles about wartime fiction, notably Mary Cadogan's *Women and Children First,* which deals with both World Wars, and Alan Munton's *English Fiction in the Second World War.* Neither sets out to concentrate on London in particular, though plenty of London examples are included. The bibliography in Philip Ziegler's *London at War* also lists some relevant novels. Many writers lived in London anyway, many more worked there in wartime and drew on the experience for fictional purposes. The pivotal importance of the capital in the experience of war, and especially the effects of the Blitz, made the subject matter compelling. The examples that follow provide a small sample from the vast range available.

Established novelists were quick to turn their wartime lives into potential copy. E.M. Delafield, already popular for her *Provincial Lady* books, based the *Provincial Lady in Wartime* (Macmillan, 1940) on her experiences as a volunteer ARP canteen helper at the Adelphi station, deep under the Savoy Hotel, in the autumn of 1939. The passages describing this establishment, with its motley staff and customers, during the phoney war, with food still plentiful and no urgent incidents to deal with, carry the ring of authenticity: 'Trousered women are standing and walking about in every direction, and a great number of men with armlets... Rather disquieting notice written in red chalk on matchboard partitions, indicates directions to be taken by decontaminated Women, Walking Cases, Stretcher-bearers and others... Canteen is a large room, insufficiently lit, with several long tables, a counter with urns and plates, kitchen behind, and at least one hundred and fifty people standing and sitting about... Atmosphere thick with cigarette smoke and no apparent ventilation anywhere...'. Later passages relate the Provincial Lady's attempts to persuade the Ministry of Information to give her a job — a popular ambition of many writers at the time — where an official says 'that what those whom he designates as "All You People" have got to realise is that we must all go on exactly *as usual*. If we are novelists, we must go on writing novels; if poets, write poetry just as before... But keep away from war topics. Not a word about war.'

Elizabeth Bowen's great novel *The Heat of the Day* (Cape, 1949) came later, but is generally agreed to give a vivid picture of London life in the war. Here Stella, the central character, reflects on life in the autumn of 1942: 'And it was now, when you no longer saw, heard, smelled war, that a deadening acclimatisation to it began to set in. The first generation of ruins, cleaned up, shored up, began to weather — in daylight they took their places as a norm of the scene; the dangerless nights of September two years later blotted them out... This was the lightless middle of the tunnel'.

Marghanita Laski's cheerful satire *Love on the Supertax* (Cresset, 1944) is 'a story of the spring of 1944' and follows the adventures of Clarissa, daughter of a duke, and her infatuation with Sid Barker, a Communist activist. The plot is slight, but there are some intriguing sidelights on social life. Clarissa visits Lyons Corner House for the first time and finds the queuing arrangements an improvement on those at expensive restaurants: 'At last they arrived at the door. There had been none of the pushing and shoving Clarissa was accustomed to, no specially favoured patrons wheedling their way in out of turn. Instead they were taken in charge by a courteous Viennese refugee who led them to an admirable little table just sufficiently far from the music'. She found the food an improvement, too: 'Every dish on the menu looked as if it might represent real, solid food, and none of them was crossed off'. 'Clarissa, while she ate, had no words. She had completely forgotten what it was like to feel completely satisfied...'

Graham Greene's *Ministry of Fear* (Heinemann, 1943) and George Orwell's *1984* (Secker, 1949) are both said to owe something to their authors' employment in the Ministry of Information at Senate House. Greene's *The End of the Affair* (Heinemann, 1951) contains a vivid description of an air raid and its aftermath. Evelyn Waugh's *Put Out More Flags* (Chapman Hall, 1942) carries the atmosphere of the phoney war, with a billeting officer taking bribes from householders wanting to avoid awful child evacuees. Scores of other titles also convey some flavour of life in London at this time. Some written long afterwards, like Muriel Spark's *Girls of Slender Means* (Macmillan, 1963) are nevertheless useful for this purpose.

## *Poetry*

Wartime London life also provided inspiration for poetry, yielding both individual poems, such as Desmond Hawkins' 'Night Raid' and volumes focused on London, like W.C. Reedy's *London Garland* (Fortune, 1942), Olga Katzin's *London Watches* (Cape, 1941) and Stowers Johnson's *London Saga* (Fortune, 1946). C.W. Reilly's *English Poetry of the Second World War: A Biobibliography* (Mansell, 1986) gives a useful list.

Diarists sometimes mention their wartime reading among other leisure activities. Miss D.L. Uttin of Wembley, a clerical assistant, writes mostly about her free time, in IWM 88/50/1. Henry St John, whose diary is in Ealing Local History Library, in 68/21, lists books he has read, adding critical comments — he thought Cronin's *The Stars Look Down* 'sordid'. Anthony Heap, whose diary, in LMA ACC 2243, has been quoted earlier, was a regular user of Boots library. Librarians' reports illuminate the problems of the time, some eagerly seizing the chance for a clearout in aid of the waste paper drive. In July 1940 the librarian of the Bishopsgate Institute wrote: '...in response to the call for waste paper I would further recommend that I be instructed to dispose of all old magazines, periodicals and journals purchased prior to the opening of the Institute in 1894, together with out of date, worn out and little used books...'

Mass-Observation carried out an investigation of wartime reading in March 1940, the results are in M-O file 47 Wartime reading. The study was conducted in London, using facts and opinions from libraries, publishers, book and magazine sellers. Everyone remarked on a drop in reading in first week of war. Suburban libraries only issued fifty-six per cent of normal loans. Then it picked up again. London librarians remarked an increased demand for books about international politics and current events. Books about modern Germany were particularly popular, but so was country life and travel in England, as Wandsworth Library reported to M-O. Battersea Library had found that indoor hobbies were more popular. The Psychic Book Club noted no increase in interest since outbreak of war. Booksellers reported that sales had dropped. Later in the war the position changed considerably. Later M-O surveys on 'Books and the Public' revealed that reading was widespread as was a taste for escapist fiction. But some claimed not to read at all: 'I never read — I've far too much to do, what with factory work, shopping and managing the flat', stated a twenty-five year old woman in 1942, in M-O file report 1332.

## Art

The earlier section on evacuation drew attention to the way in which all the major galleries and museums made arrangements for their greatest treasures to be stored safely in the country, away from possible air raid damage. PRO EB, the papers of the Museums and Galleries Standing Commission, contain information about the evacuation and the reopening of galleries in 1940. Ironically, the circumstances which enforced the removal of the most important works of art and museum exhibits sizeably increased the potential audience for them in London. Shift workers, office staff in their lunch breaks and troops on leave were glad of free access to museums and galleries where they could meet friends and pass some leisure time in congenial surroundings, without expense. Most of the institutions managed to stage temporary exhibitions, either on their own or with the help of CEMA, and would bring one or two treasures out of store for short periods. The National Gallery's 'Painting of the Month' was a famous and very popular example of this system. Exhibitions of new work, such as paintings by members of the Fire Brigade or the Forces, were set up in the ample available space at the National Gallery and others.

Early in the war the Ministry of Information set up the War Artists' Advisory Committee (WAAC) to commission artists to draw or paint aspects of the war effort. The Committee suggested subjects. Many were related to Forces' operations and training, but there was also a policy of reflecting civilian life and the home front. Prominent artists recorded scenes of various kinds. Among those depicting London from different aspects were Graham Sutherland, Henry Call, and Ruskin Spear who all painted scenes of bomb damage, Edward Ardizzone's paintings of Home Guard manoeuvres, and Meredith Frampton's and Eric Ravilious' depictions of behind-the-scenes work in CD Control Rooms have already been mentioned. Henry Moore's well known shelter drawings convey a powerful sense of the claustrophic tunnels where people were trying to sleep; Feliks Topolski also drew the hunched shapes of tube shelterers. Muirhead Bone painted the *Graf Spee* victory celebration in Horse Guards' Parade. Other painters show evacuees, wartime traffic on the Thames, bombed hospital wards, and food queues. The National Gallery made exhibition space available to show these new WAAC works throughout the war. Afterwards some went to the Tate Gallery, but most paintings joined the Imperial War Museum's collections where they can still be seen. Another project to record Britain in wartime was organised by the Pilgrim Trust, which encourage artists to contribute to its 'Recording Britain' scheme. The results were exhibited at the National Gallery in a series of shows. Wartime paintings can also be found elsewhere, such as H.S. Merritt's view of the Bank bomb crater, in the Gresham Royal Exchange collection or the London Transport Museum's paintings by the bus driver, Henry Stockley. William Roberts' *The Demolition Squad*, showing soldiers clearing a City church, is currently on display in Guildhall Library. The Museum of London's collection also contains many wartime scenes.

Diarists sometimes comment on gallery visits and other cultural events. Mrs M. Cossins worked at the British Museum and was interested in art exhibitions and concerts, which she describes in her diaries, in IWM 92/25/1. Robert Ramsay, whose diary is in LMA F/RMY/37, also had wide cultural interests, including the theatre, and music, as will be seen below.

## Music

For many Londoners and visitors to London, the chance to listen to classical music was a welcome distraction from the problems of war. Orchestras, like theatrical companies, suffered from the loss of front and back stage staff to the call-up. Financial aid from CEMA helped them to continue, using mainly older players, and sharing scarce soloists with other ensembles. The famous Queen's Hall, home of the pre-war Proms, was destroyed in a raid in 1941 only hours after a London Philharmonic concert; the orchestra lost all its instruments as a result. Concerts continued at the Coliseum instead, and in the summer the Proms found a new home at the Albert Hall, attracting large audiences. Lunchtime concerts were popular. Lasting just over an hour they attracted a wide public who came to hear top soloists like Dame Myra Hess and Isobel Baillie, with the Boyd Neel Orchestra and others, at the National Gallery or the Royal Exchange. Robert Ramsay, (LMA F/RMY/37), enjoyed attending the National Gallery events, saving the programmes among his papers. On 26 June 1941 he described the

> **NATIONAL GALLERY CONCERTS**
>
> *Brahms Programme*
>
> MYRA HESS (*Pianoforte*)
> THE GRILLER STRING QUARTET
> SIDNEY GRILLER (*Violin*)        PHILIP BURTON (*Viola*)
> JACK O'BRIEN (*Violin*)        COLIN HAMPTON (*Violoncello*)
> DENNIS BRAIN (*Horn*)
>
> I
>
> QUINTET FOR PIANOFORTE AND STRINGS IN F MINOR, OP. 34
> Allegro non troppo
> Andante, un poco adagio
> SCHERZO : Allegro
> FINALE : Poco sostenuto—Allegro non troppo
> MYRA HESS and THE GRILLER STRING QUARTET
>
> II
>
> TRIO FOR PIANOFORTE, VIOLIN AND HORN IN E FLAT MAJOR, OP. 40
> Andante
> SCHERZO : Allegro
> Adagio mesto
> FINALE : Allegro con brio
> MYRA HESS, SIDNEY GRILLER and DENNIS BRAIN
>
> Fifteenth and last of a Series of Brahms Programmes
> which has included all the Chamber Works
>
> STEINWAY PIANOFORTE
>
> TUESDAY, AUGUST 25TH, 1942        PRICE ONE PENNY

Lunchtime concerts were popular
*(LMA F/RMY/37)*

procedure: '...you buy your shilling ticket, deposit your hat on a chair and go downstairs to the buffet where you can have your choice of sandwiches and sweets and a cup of coffee. With these you return upstairs, however you may take your eatables into the gallery, you must consume your coffee outside... There was a delicious programme of Mozart arias, duets and terzetti. The concert lasted from 1 o'clock until 2.10'. Joyce Grenfell regularly worked at the National Gallery canteen in 1939–40 and reported to her mother on the huge quantities of sandwiches consumed —'We had 1,280 people and they ate 1,500 sandwiches...' (*Darling Ma*. Hodder 1988) — as well as on the music. Biographies and memoirs of prominent musicians, such as Sir Henry Wood, Sir Malcolm Sargent and Sir Thomas Beecham are useful for background on this period.

Three ballet companies managed to keep performing in London throughout the war in spite of production and staffing difficulties, and ballet became very popular. Sadlers Wells Ballet, whose records are in Finsbury in the Islington Local History Collection, and the archives of the Ballet Rambert contain wartime material. Opera was less well represented, probably because of the greater expense and elaboration of its staging, though the Carl Rosa company performed for several wartime seasons.

Music societies of various kinds continued to operate at this period. LMA has the records of the Royal Choral Society, ACC 2370; Greenwich Libraries have the minutes and accounts of the Blackheath Music Society, in Strong room 1, G/13, and a scrapbook of material about the Erith Municipal Music Society's wartime activities is in Bexley Libraries, CS/EMM.

## Dancing

Dancing was a passion that crossed class barriers. Whether at dinner dances in West End nightclubs or at public dance halls such as the converted Royal Opera House, where onlookers sat in the boxes, or the Hammersmith Palais and others all over the city, enthusiastic crowds danced to live bands night after night, undeterred by occasional disasters like the destruction of the Putney dance hall and the Café de Paris bomb when most of the musicians, as well as many patrons, were killed. Survivors of that terrible incident always remembered that 'Snake-Hips' Johnson and his band had been playing the song 'Oh Johnny' when the bomb fell. The favourite tunes of the day are widely available on recent compilation tapes, and the National Sound Archive has a full range of contemporary recordings and relevant oral history interviews. Mass-Observation's topic collection 'Music and Dancing' contains detailed reports on dance halls, their appearance, social ambience, and the behaviour and clothing of the patrons. The collection also contains interviews with people in the music business and some contemporary sheet music.

## Theatre

The fear of immediate air attack led the government to close places of public entertainment as soon as war broke out, to avoid putting large numbers of people at risk. The entertainment world had known this would happen, '...so that the grave dislocation of the theatre industry throughout the country, with its attendant distress and unemployment, was not unforeseen', wrote the editor of *Theatre World* in October 1939, noting that most suburban and provincial houses had now reopened as the government gradually relaxed the rules when no enemy action materialised. Only a handful of West End theatres had, as yet, risked it. It rapidly became clear that the continuation of normal leisure facilities would be essential to maintain general morale and some sense of normality. Londoners and visitors alike needed some distraction from long working hours, CD commitments, travel problems and air raids, and theatre-going was a popular pastime.

The West End theatres faced grave operating difficulties, not least because so many of their staff — actors, stagehands and box office workers — were eventually called up for war work. Stage costumes and makeup were rationed, late afternoon or early evening performances became common because the blackout deterred suburbanites from travelling in. Air raids disrupted performances. These problems were ventilated regularly and fully in trade journals like *Theatre World* which lamented in October 1940 that due to the Blitz 'The choice of the Londoner is now restricted to the delights of the Revudeville at the Windmill and the lunch-time ballet hour at the Arts Theatre Club, to which must be added the brave venture of Shakespeare at the Vaudeville, matinées only'. Things got easier once the Blitz was over, but the flying bombs of 1944 brought another crisis, closing many shows although *Theatre World*'s editor noted in August that 'the remaining plays have certainly shown increased takings as Londoners accustom themselves to the new form of aerial attack and begin to put on a bolder front'. Troops were an important component of the West End audience. When Army leave in London was banned in the early summer of 1941 their absence was keenly felt by the box offices. The Theatre Museum has runs of *Theatre World* and other theatrical journals and files on many West End theatres with wartime programmes, reviews, newspaper cuttings and publicity material. The programmes always include instructions on what to do in the case of an air raid. Audiences were warned that an air raid was in progress through illuminated signs, and were free to leave for a shelter if they wished: 'All we ask is that — if you feel you must go — you will depart quietly and without excitement', as the programme for Olivier's *Richard III* at the New Theatre put it in September 1944. Many theatregoers preferred to stay put and enjoy the play.

Some entertainment choices in late 1943
*(Sunday Times, 28 November 1943)*

Records for several theatres at this period survive in the Theatre Museum's collections, the Ambassadors, St James's, the Unity, the Windmill, Wyndham's and the Tennant Theatre Company among them, while Bristol University's Theatre Collection has others, including Her Majesty's. Biographies and autobiographies of leading actors and impresarios of the period often contain useful background on London theatrical life. Tapes of several actors in the IWM Sound Archive mention their professional work in the war as well as their other activities, such as Ballard Berkeley on 5340/2; Maurice Denham on 11811/1 and John Houghton on 11346/2. London productions through the war years are meticulously recorded in J.P. Wearing's *London Stage, 1940–49*. Theatre premises, like others used for public entertainment, were subject to LCC safety regulations, which required detailed plans to be submitted for inspection. The LCC's Safety Committee papers, LCC/PC/ENT, described below in the cinema section, can prove useful for specific buildings.

## ENSA

The theatrical profession banded together to entertain serving troops through the Entertainments National Services Association, affectionately known to the Forces as 'Every Night Something Awful'. ENSA was based at the Theatre Royal, Drury Lane, where the stalls bar was also used as a studio for broadcasts of 'London Carries On'. ENSA's Controller was Sir Seymour Hicks, and the impresario Basil Dean was its Director. His papers are in the University of Manchester's John Rylands Library. Walter Legge was director of music, and Geraldo, the bandleader, managed ENSA broadcasting. Hundreds of artists auditioned at the Theatre Royal before joining concert parties, plays and musical entertainments to travel all over the country and overseas. Some travelled as solo entertainers, especially to small anti-aircraft and searchlight batteries, 'to keep up the sing-song spirit'. ENSA was a division of the NAAFI (Navy, Army and Air Force Institutions), and came within the remit of the Ministry of Labour and National Service. It even had its own uniform. By August 1940 the Ministry of Labour, responsible for the welfare and productivity of vast numbers of factory workers, many billeted away from home, saw that ENSA could perform a similar task for them. ENSA therefore arranged munitions concerts in factories, and also some shelter concerts in London during the Blitz. For the most part, however, ENSA concentrated on troop entertainment, and CEMA, set up later in 1940, made comparable provision for civilians. ENSA records are in the PRO, in classes WO 32 and WO 163. The Imperial War Museum Department of Documents has the private papers of several of those closely involved, notably Mrs Vernon, ENSA's Chief Welfare Officer. Theatrical memoirs of artists who served with ENSA usually describe their experiences. Joyce Grenfell denounced the organisation in a letter to her mother as 'third rate, inaccurate and in a mess. We all hate it...' (*Darling Ma*. Hodder, 1988), a view widely shared by other performers.

Amateur acting remained popular. Local operatic and dramatic societies managed to keep going in spite of the obvious complications of wartime conditions. Big employers, like the London Passenger Transport Board and J. Lyons, had a large pool of potential amateur talent to draw on. Lyons' Club's revue section produced the *Lyons Troop Show* and offered it to ENSA, proudly claiming that 12,000 members of the Forces had seen it by June 1941. The July issue of the staff magazine, *Lyons Mail*, in LMA ACC 3527/289, urged employees to sign up for free tap dance classes with Buddy Bradley, who had taught such famous names as Jack Buchanan, Jessie Matthews and Jack Hulbert. 'We want to train more girls to dance for inclusion in the chorus! Don't say "You didn't know".'

## Cinema

Perhaps the most universal leisure activity was cinema-going. West End and suburban cinemas flourished throughout the war, once they were allowed to reopen after the initial scare. Cinemas were cheap, comfortable and available to all. The traditional pattern of newsreel and information shorts, 'B' feature and 'big' picture, ensured that the picturegoer absorbed some government messages as well as enjoying escapism. Many people went at least twice a week to 'the pictures'. Guy Morgan's *Red Roses every Night* (1948) describes the life of a London cinema manager at this period. Individual cinemas' programmes can be checked in the local press; *Film Weekly* and *Picturegoer* give an idea of the films' contemporary critical reception. Hollywood films were particularly popular because they provided such a glamorous contrast to most viewers' daily lives. Many of the feature films Londoners watched during the war are still shown occasionally on British television: *Gone with the Wind, Casablanca, Dangerous Moonlight, Let George Do It, In Which We Serve, The Maltese Falcon,* and *Millions Like Us* to name but a few; documentary films from the Crown Film Unit and others are listed in *British Official Films in the Second World War* by Frances Thorpe and Nicholas Pronay. The IWM Film and Video Archive has an extensive collection of these. The BFI, which also has prints of the British feature films and the papers of prominent filmmakers like Sydney and Muriel Box, has an extensive library of books about films and the cinema. Halliwell's *Film Guide* gives a short résumé of the plots, though it is not comprehensive.

Diarists were often enthusiastic film-goers. Anthony Heap, in LMA ACC 2243/15/1, saw *Lucky Partners* at the Kings Cross cinema on 4 January 1941 and effused to his diary: 'I like Ronald Colman. I like his well-bred poise, his polished finesse, his twinkling eyes...' Violet Tyler, an office worker from Lewisham, was another diarist with a keen interest in filmgoing, her papers are in Lewisham Local Studies Centre, in A/98/9. Mass-Observation dutifully investigated films and the effect they had on the public. Many Londoners reported on their film-going habits and opinions for M-O, some are included in *Mass-Observation at the Movies*, edited by Jeffrey Richards and Dorothy Sheridan. Ministry of Information files in the PRO cover the control of film making and the commissioning of official films. The Wartime Social Survey undertook an investigation of 'The Cinema Audience' in June–July 1943 (RG 23).

Cinema premises, like theatres, dance halls and night clubs, had to be approved by the LCC's Public Control Department from the safety point of view. Plans and diagrams often survive, for example in LCC/PC/ENT/1–2. This department's committee papers contain applications for licences to show films — the Institut Français acquired one for a single showing on August 25 1943 —, for permission to instal a café, as at The Odeon, Edgware Road in June 1943, or to store more film than was normally permitted, as at the Brixton Pavilion in August 1943. All these cases are taken from LCC/MIN/9884. The same file contains several letters asking special permission to take wheelchairs into cinemas. Mrs E. Dorling, of Brockley, complained that when she took her son, who had had both legs amputated on active service to a local cinema: 'I was turned out of the Ritz after paying for admittance and told a bath chair was not allowed... I hope they will not treat all our boys that way when they come home wounded'. Letters from the Ritz and from another Brockley cinema, the Rivoli, explained that they would like to admit Mr Dorling, but it would contravene safety regulations — would the LCC waive them in this case? The committee gave permission for him to attend matinées only, sitting always in a specified place, and with an able-bodied adult in attendance. Records of individual cinemas have not survived well, though examples are sometimes found in local history collections. Islington Libraries, for example, have correspondence files for the Blue Hall Cinema, Islington, in wartime.

## Broadcasting

Listening to the wireless to catch up with the day's news, and for entertainment, was as important to Londoners as it was to their compatriots in the rest of the country during the war. The BBC's landmark headquarters, Broadcasting House in Langham Place, remained open throughout the war, suffering damage in several air raids. Live broadcasts, with background noises of anti-aircraft fire, were made from the roof of Broadcasting House during the Blitz, and are available in the IWM Sound Archive collections at 15365/C/C, 2277/E/B, 2278/E/C and 17699/W/J. Reporters like Raymond Glendenning interviewed shelterers and ARP personnel for *London Calling* and other topical programmes. The Sound Archive has nearly five thousand other BBC broadcasts, mostly news and commentary, but also some entertainment material as well as interviews with wartime reporters and correspondents. The National Sound Archive also has copies of many BBC recordings, including Robin Duff's 'A typical London air raid', from 1940, Ed Murrow's 'The blitz in London' recorded live in Trafalgar Square in 1940, and Audrey Russell's 'Surviving an air raid', from 1944. Most BBC departments had been evacuated for safety at the outbreak of war with Variety travelling to Bristol and later to Bangor, Schools to Wood Norton, and Religion to Bedford. Written records are in the BBC Written Archives Centre at Caversham. These include files about contributors, policy matters, programmes of all kinds, scripts, news bulletins and daily logs of output, as well as a full register of bomb damage to Broadcasting House and its effect on programming. The Listener Research Department of the BBC monitored audience reaction to programmes of all kind and its records provide further evidence of public morale throughout the period. Volume 3 of Asa Briggs' authoritative *History of Broadcasting in the UK* (1970) gives more detail about this material, and the bibliography section of this guide lists some publications by and about leading broadcasters of the time. Leslie Mitchell, the well-known broadcaster who enrolled in the Home Guard, talks about his experiences on IWM Sound Archive tape 5364/1. The *Radio Times* was published through the war giving details of BBC output week by week, and the BBC Written Archives have programme indexes.

Until February 1940 the BBC operated the Home Service only, mainly broadcasting talks, plays and serious music. Then the Forces Programme was inaugurated, providing an alternative diet of records, live dance band music and variety shows. Regular broadcasts by the 'Radio Doctor' were popular, as were comedy programmes like *Band Waggon* and *ITMA*. Their catch phrases and jokes studded their listeners' daily conversations. *Music While You Work*, *Works Wonders*, and *Workers' Playtime* brought cheerful light music programmes to factory workers, helping to maintain morale and productivity. Many popular songs made no direct reference to the war or its problems, but a few, usually comic, did. George Formby's 'I did what I could with my gas mask' is an example. Some mentioned London in particular, like Caroll Gibbons' 'I'm going to get lit up when the lights go on in London' (1943), Suzette Tarri's 'London will rise again' (1942) and Ronald Frankau's appeal to the parents of evacuees 'Don't bring the children back to London...let them stay where birds are birds and raspberries are fruit' (1940). Florence Desmond's 'I've got the deepest shelter in town' has already been mentioned, and Noel Coward's 'London Pride' is still familiar.

## Pubs

Public houses continued to provide an important leisure facility for Londoners, as for the rest of the country. Beer and tobacco were never rationed, though supply difficulties sometimes led to shortages. Ever alert to social changes, Mass-Observation monitored the opinions of pub-goers at various stages in the war. In 1943 they published *The Pub and the People*, and particularly investigated attitudes to women in pubs, quoted earlier in the section on Allied troops. Interviews on this topic were written up for the *Mass-Observation Bulletin* in February and in file report 1611. In June they narrowed their focus area with a report on the 'Behaviour of women in public houses in certain London areas', M-O File Report 1835. This looked at the way young women behaved in public houses in some areas and specifically aimed to investigate allegations that young women were being plied with strong drink, especially by Allied troops with dishonourable intentions. The areas studied were around Victoria Station and Covent Garden, with a small control study around Paddington, which had not been the subject of similar rumours. Colourful detail emerges from this report, which found that both target areas witnessed a good deal of drinking among very young women and had 'a free and easy atmosphere in which it was very easy and usual to pick up with a member of the opposite sex'. M-O concluded that the men were not taking girls to these pubs to get them drunk, but they were meeting women who had gone there in the hope of an exciting evening out at American or Canadian soldiers' expense, whatever might happen later. And the pubs' immoral reputations were usually worse than the reality.

Novels can convey something of the atmosphere of wartime pubs. Elizabeth Ferrars' detective story *Murder among Friends* (Collins, 1946) has her characters on a pub-crawl in the area of the Strand and Covent Garden: 'They went in, walking into darkness and swaying shrouds of blackout curtain that smelt of dust and old clothes and alcohol. Managing to find the opening they walked through it into warmth and light'. 'The second pub was very much fuller and slightly more colourful than the first. Besides the usual mixture of nondescript civilians and soldiers of a dozen nations with their pick-ups, there was a group of gentle-faced young men in very pretty clothes who were earnestly interested in one another, and some girls in slacks and bright blouses with rather unkempt hair.' Julian Maclaren-Ross's encyclopaedic knowledge of London pubs emerges in his *Memoirs of the Forties* (Cardinal, 1991). From the Museum Tavern to the Highlander in Dean Street, a favourite with the documentary film-makers from the Ministry of Information, Maclaren-Ross knew them all and devotes a special section — 'Fitzrovian Nights' — to Rathbone Place, off Oxford Street, which had at least five pubs of varying character and reputation.

## Clubs

Records of clubs of all kinds, from grand West End establishments such as Brooks's, in LMA ACC 2371, 2796, to wartime groups like the Kingston Women War Workers' Club, Kingston Heritage Centre KT 2/25, survive in London collections. Youth clubs were considered particularly important in wartime, to counteract the disruptive effects of evacuation and bombing on young people. National concern is documented in PRO ED 124, General files on youth welfare. Records of varied youth groups are available, for example University College Manuscripts Department has some papers of the St Christopher Working Boys' Club, in Fitzroy Square; Tower Hamlets Libraries have records of the Cambridge and Bethnal Green Boys' Club, in TH/8458; Barnet Libraries have Friern Barnet Boys' Club, MS 19199, and Newham Local Studies Library some registers of the local Kensington Youth Club.

The Boys' Brigade, Girls' Friendly Society and some similar organisations preserve local groups' archives at their headquarters, others, like the Scouts, have little of local relevance centrally, though records can sometimes be found in other libraries and repositories. Hammersmith and Fulham Archives, for instance, have the records of two Fulham scout companies, in DD/575 and DD/786, Hackney Archives and Greenwich Local History Library each have comparable deposits for their areas. Among the entries for a competition associated with the *Making of Modern London* television programme is a short tape about scouting in wartime, now in the collection of the Museum of London. Religious denominations often ran their own youth groups, the records of which can sometimes be found in the appropriate specialist repository. The Hartley Library at Southampton University, for example, has records for various London Jewish clubs, including Stepney Jewish Lads' Club, MS 172 and West Central Jewish Working Lads' Club, MS 152.

Diaries sometimes add information on this subject. F.B. Breakspear was a conscientious objector released on appeal to do full-time social work. He ran a boys' club and became an organised games leader at LCC Play Centres, his diary is in IWM 87/63/1. Mrs C. Eustace, another IWM diarist, was Assistant District Commissioner for the Scout Movement in Chiswick. She describes the effects of the Blitz and the war on scouting in general and her Cubs in particular.

## *Holidays*

Non-essential travel was discouraged during the war in order to conserve fuel supplies and ensure that train accommodation was available for troop transport and other official purposes. Private cars were mostly 'laid up' for the duration because of petrol rationing. 'Is Your Journey Really Necessary?' asked the posters, not always effectively. 'I wish more people would heed the official notice...', wrote Joyce Grenfell during a theatrical tour in August 1943, 'Mine is, but theirs, at the moment, isn't. It's the holiday season and crowds pour all over the country and are a hell of a nuisance to people who must travel' (*Darling Ma.* Hodder, 1988). Londoners could not resist the temptation to get away for a break. The seaside resorts of the South and East coast were ruled out, their beaches being barricaded with barbed wire and their hotel accommodation mostly requisitioned for military use. But there were parts of the country which, by London standards, seemed almost untouched by the war. Peace, relaxation and fresh local food sent visitors back to face London life in a better state of health.

Mass-Observation investigated holiday behaviour, as it did so many other aspects of life. Its boxes covering 'Holidays 1937–51' contain material of all kinds including cuttings and questionnaires relating to how people spent August Bank Holiday in 1941, in File C, and travel out of London for Easter 1942, in File F, for which observers counted the number of people queuing with luggage for tickets at Euston, Charing Cross, Waterloo and other mainline stations, and noted their comments and conversations.

Official attempts to dissuade people from making such trips led to the campaign for 'Holidays at Home' in 1942 and 1943. The scheme encouraged local authorities to draw up a programme of events and amusements for the summer months, using local parks and sports facilities. M-O's Holidays 1937–51, in File E, deals with the 'Holidays at Home' campaign for 1942, and contains programmes, newspaper cuttings and reports on events in various London areas, including Beckenham, Willesden and Paddington. Open air concerts, dances, children's games, swimming galas and other sports competitions were typical 'Holiday at Home' events. Other institutions added their own contribution, like Westminster Abbey's historical lectures. There was a special cricket match at Lords over

**13.** **Report of the Special "Holidays at Home" Committee.**

20th August, 1943.

*Old English Fair.*

1.—As the Council are aware an Old English Fair was staged on the bombed site in Camden High Street, adjoining the Bedford Theatre, from the 27th August to the 18th September.

An estimate in the sum of £100 was received from the Borough Engineer and Surveyor for levelling the site, and Mr. Harry Gray, who is responsible for providing the fair side of the show, has forwarded to the Borough Treasurer a cheque for this amount, so that no cost will be incurred by the Council. In addition to this payment he agreed to instal electric lighting and provide a microphone in the Council's exhibition marquee, and so enable the Committee to stage their own exhibitions and shows.

*Dog show.*

2.—In connection with the above we arranged an Everyman's Dog Show on Saturday, 28th August. The show was of a purely informal character, and Mr. Gordon Knight, M.R.C.V.S., of the Royal Veterinary College kindly consented to act as judge. The Mayoress presented prizes to the value of £4 18s.

We recommend—

**That** the action taken be approved. **[Approved.**

Local authorities operate 'Holidays at Home' programmes
*(Camden Local Studies and Archives Centre, St Pancras Borough Council Minutes)*

August Bank Holiday weekend in 1942, Middlesex and Essex played Kent and Surrey, attracting a crowd of 22,000. Local collections often contain programmes and publicity material about the arrangements, usually preserved with the Parks Department records. Among the records of the LCC Parks Department is correspondence about outdoor summer entertainments such as Sadlers Wells' ballet season in Victoria Park in July 1942, LCC/MIN 9014. Council Minutes may refer to the appointment of temporary organisers for such schemes. East Ham, for example, advertised for one in *Theatre World* in 1943, offering £6 a week from April 12 to August 31.

Interesting background on the organisation of a large-scale wartime outdoor event at local level is provided by Hendon Ministry of Information Local Committee's material on the 'Rout the Rumour Rally' held in Hendon Park on Sunday, 21 July 1940. A bound volume contains cuttings, photographs, posters, correspondence, stewards' instructions, song sheets, draft and finalised programmes and other ephemera, in Barnet Archives L940.66. Designed as a morale-building event, the programme presented an afternoon of sketches, songs and music intended to reinforce the message that gossip and rumour prejudiced the national war effort. An official speaker from the Ministry of Information was to come — the organisers hoped for Duff Cooper, but got Harold Nicolson — and an impressive array of stars. Renée Houston, Will Fyffe, Flotsam and Jetsam, Jack Hawkins, Jack Warner, Lucan and McShane and others gave their services free. Among the correspondence are letters of complaint from local clergy about the rally profaning the Sabbath with 'entertainment', an accusation vigorously refuted by the Committee Chairman in letters to the local press: 'Yes, we are going to have flags and marching and stirring music by the Band of the Grenadier Guards, and why not?... No better day is available for the vast number of the general public who will attend. The Artistes, too, could not have come on a weekday'. Other protestors objected to local authorities about Sunday activities on occasion. In August 1942, for instance, the Lord's Day Observance Society tried but failed to overturn the LCC Parks' Department's proposal to open children's gymnasia and playgrounds on Sundays, in LCC MIN 9014.

Some large employers sometimes offered holiday provision for their workers. Lyons' active staff club, which had extensive grounds at Sudbury, ran a 'holiday camp' there for employees and their families in the summer of 1942. It was advertised in the house journal, *Lyons Mail*, in July 1942, promising a tent with four bunks for 30/- a week, or a bunk in the communal tent for only 10/-. Three meals a day for seven days cost adults £1 and children under twelve 12/6d. There was an organised programme of entertainments every week. *Lyons Mail* is in LMA ACC 3527/289.

## *Sport*

Football, cricket, boxing, athletics, horse and greyhound racing and other organised sporting events attracted large crowds and were therefore cancelled, like other entertainments, as soon as war broke out, to prevent the risk of large-scale loss of life in air raids. They were sorely missed by the public, especially as the phoney war brought no immediate danger. Quite soon the government relented. The Home Office permitted a revised football programme as long as it did not interfere with war duties, matches were authorised by the local police, and crowd numbers were restricted. Other professional sports began to re-emerge on a similar basis. Published histories of the sports and their grounds, several of which are listed in the bibliography, give the details; the overall position is usefully set out in Tony McCarthy's *War Games*. Mass-Observation file reports and topic boxes illustrate public attitudes to sport and its continuation in wartime.

Amateur sport continued at local level, playing matches against other nearby clubs or Forces sides. The pressure to use as much land as possible for food production led to the conversion of many suburban sports grounds into allotments for the duration, but the records of a wide range of clubs can be found in local record offices as a few examples will show. Bromley Libraries have those for Bromley Lawn Tennis Club; Lewisham has those of Bellingham Bowls and Lawn Tennis Club, and West Kent Wanderers, a cricket team; Richmond has records of the Twickenham Cricket Club; Camden has minutes of the Highgate Harriers; LMA the records of the Polytechnic Harriers, Mayfield Athletic Club, Edmonton and more. The Modern Records Centre at the University of Warwick has recently acquired the archive of the London-based Cyclists' Touring Club, including its London District papers, in MSS.328.

Information about sports facilities also occurs among the papers of the LCC Parks Committee. LCC MIN 9014 notes that in May 1942 the Royal Canadian Air Force asked if they could reserve the tennis courts in Lincoln's Inn Fields for their regular use; the LCC refused because the courts were in such demand. The same minutes contain bitter complaints from the Socialist Party of Great Britain in May 1943 that they were being prevented from using their usual spot in Brockwell Park for propaganda meetings, being told it was now needed as a football pitch: '1. This ground is impossible of use as a football pitch, sloping steadily as it does in both directions. 2. This is not the football season...', they wrote. The Lyons social club had seventy acres of grounds and offered an enormous range of sporting facilities including tennis, putting, bowls, a rifle range, swimming, cricket and fencing — 'd'Artagnan had to learn!' — encouraged the *Lyons Mail* in 1941 (LMA ACC 3527/289).

# 6. Brave New World?
## Planning Ahead and Victory Celebrations

The need to look ahead to a postwar world was an official concern from an early point in the war, and a psychological necessity for the general public. There was a general feeling that things would be, indeed must be, different 'after the war' and that a population which had suffered considerable hardship for the greater good should be rewarded with a fairer world offering better housing, education, employment, health care and social equality.

In some fields, notably that of town planning, changes had been in the pipeline in prewar days. Enemy action and bomb damage cleared the way for a scale of operations the planners could scarcely have dreamt of in normal circumstances. The public was very interested and concerned about postwar developments, both architectural and social. The possibilities made a popular debating topic in air raid shelters in the Blitz.

Mass-Observation prepared several reports on attitudes to the future and its planning. In July 1943 they asked a small sample of Londoners their opinions about driving. Only thirty-two per cent of the men and seven per cent of the women had had licenses before the war. 'There will be more cars than ever, the youth of tomorrow will be car-mad', was one response, and 'I'd like to see some good road-planning', in M-O file 1869. An M-O book in 1947, *Peace and the People*, compared wartime expectations with subsequent reality. 'Should married women be able to go out to work after the war?', asked an M-O directive in early 1944, 'Married women and work', eliciting a wide range of responses from both sexes. Opinions varied, from the Wembley housewife who said 'I shall be sorry to leave my job, and the part-time hours I work could be continued *ad infinitum* as far as I am concerned', to the company secretary from Purley who was longing to stay at home and knew other war-workers who 'would be only too pleased to give up their jobs when the war is over...', providing their husbands could keep them in comfort. Further responses were reported in a *Mass-Observation Bulletin* on 'Good and Bad Omens for the Postwar World'. Three M-O topic boxes, TC 2, contain an assortment of surveys and interviews in which Londoners give their views on postwar reconstruction. Box 2/3/C, for example, contains questionnaires describing how people in 1942 imagined London would be after the war.

# I'm clocking-in -at home!

I've said good-bye to that war job, and now I'm going to enjoy the simple home life I've been so eagerly planning. Family health will be my first responsibility. I shall make sure that ' Milk of Magnesia ', which has helped to keep me free of digestive upsets in the stress and strain of war, will never be missing from the medicine cabinet.

## 'MILK OF MAGNESIA'

*'Milk of Magnesia' is the trade mark of Phillips' preparation of magnesia.*

Advertisements take up the postwar theme
*(The Observer, 19 August 1945)*

## *Planning*

The continuing growth of London between the wars had added to a general perception of the city as overcrowded and traffic-ridden. A report by the Ministry of Transport engineer Sir Charles Bressey and the architect Sir Edwin Lutyens had investigated traffic congestion in central London in 1936, mapping the bottlenecks and suggesting a network of new roads. In a GPO film unit documentary in 1939, *The City*, Sir Charles proudly shows off his series of plans in which gigantic roundabouts, viaducts and fearsome flyovers carve through the central area within the North and South circular roads, providing 'every device for facilitating movement of traffic'. The coming of war delayed the implementation of these ideas, some of which fed into later planning proposals.

The LCC and the boroughs had made a start on slum clearance programmes after the First World War, but many central areas still had large quantities of substandard housing. Evacuation of mothers and children from these areas to more comfortable homes drew public attention on both sides of the social divide to the contrast in living conditions and expectations. Very little building could be done during the war, the slums deteriorated still further, and thousands of houses were destroyed or badly damaged. The housing shortage was made even more acute by the rise in the marriage rate in wartime. Planners saw one solution in removing thousands of Londoners to new estates in the suburbs, and to new towns beyond, after the war. Social engineering on such a scale could only be achieved through national legislation.

Until the creation of the Ministry of Housing and Local Government in 1943 there had been no national planning policy. Each local authority had dealt with its own area under the general guidance of the Ministry of Health. The Ministry of Works had acquired some wartime planning functions. Recommendations of the Barlow Committee, in 1940, had urged future consistency at national level, and the need for this became increasingly apparent amid the destruction of the Blitz. Architects and planners seized the opportunity to publish ambitious designs for 'Rebuilding Britain' and the subject provoked considerable public debate. Where London was concerned, there were frequent comparisons with Wren's plans for rebuilding the city after the Great Fire of 1666. Many, like Sir Charles Bressey, felt that opportunities had then been lost: 'the forces of conservatism were too strong...', that should not be missed this time. The 'London' heading in the wartime issues of the *Subject Index to Periodicals* reveals a steady stream of articles on this theme.

Works Department papers in the PRO are informative on the background of planning and redevelopment. HLG 68/70 reviews postwar prospects for the redevelopment of bombed central areas from the papers of the Hicks Committee. HLG 71/239–262 all relate to postwar plans, London Region 1941–3 is in HLG 71/243–4. HLG 79, correspondence with local authorities, HLG 86, advisory panels and committees on reconstruction, and HLG 82, papers relating to the Nuffield College Social Reconstruction Survey, are full of London information. HLG 88 contains reports on the redevelopment of war damaged city centres, 1943–4; HLG 101, housing files, have material on the provision of postwar housing.

Many Londoners were not sorry that bomb damage would force redevelopment of what they considered squalid streets and out-of-date buildings. Much central London architecture was Victorian, a period then unfashionable and widely derided. In his 1941 book *London under Fire*, James Pope-Hennessy wrote that the bombs had hit 'mainly buildings of small aesthetic merit (and often of no historical interest)'. Ordinary Londoners tended to agree with the prevailing urge for modernisation. Anthony Heap, in LMA ACC 2243/15/1, described a walk round the City a week after the great fire raid of 29 December: '...it's been a blessing in disguise. The City so badly needed re-planning and re-building... It was a huge, intricate labyrinth of dark, narrow, twisting turnings. Its buildings were old and antiquated and in a bad state of decay. Its offices were insanitary, badly arranged and ill-ventilated. Taken all in all it was a drab, dismal, unhealthy, soul-less place to spend one's working life in. I'm glad I never did. It wasn't even picturesque. Really it was a gigantic Museum piece, a mausoleum of all that was hideous and ugly in the commercial sense during the Victorian age, when it grew up and thrived'. His view was shared by many others.

The government appointed Professor Patrick Abercrombie, an eminent town planner, to draw up plans for London. The County of London Plan, for rebuilding and redevelopment within the LCC boundaries, was published in 1943. HO 186/2552 has observations on the plan and subsequent reports on it between 1943 and 1946. Institutions and individuals studied the planning proposals for the effect they would have on their own work. The Post Office, for example, concluded that: 'The general view in this Region is that the Plan is eminently sensible and what while it will shake up the postal organisation no strong ground for adverse criticism can be found from the service point of view' (PO Archives. 56/152 P.S.D./H.M.B. London postal region war diary, 1939–45). There was a parallel plan for the County of Middlesex.

Abercrombie's Greater London Plan (1944) looked at the wider area, and provided the blueprint for the future dispersal of the London population. It advocated the decentralisation of housing and employment away from London and the suburbs to a series of new towns around the capital, to reduce crowded slum conditions. The postwar Labour government began to put this into effect from 1946, with unanticipated result, such as the spread of inner city blight, and the growth of long-distance commuting. Abercrombie's correspondence concerning the plan is in HLG 85; HLG 104 contains publicity material about it. The film *Proud City* (1945) publicised the plans, with Abercrombie himself and the LCC planners showing the look of the future. In the film *The Plan and the People* (1945) the way the plan would affect life in a local community was examined.

"*Well, anyhow, there'd be no harm in giving it a trial.*"

Fougasse's view of plans for London redevelopment
*(Punch, 11 August 1943)*

However, postwar planning covered matters beyond building and road redevelopment. All government departments were making plans for the future to some degree throughout the war, with implications for London, and most departmental files contain something on this. The Board of Education was working towards the Butler Education Act of 1944. ED 10 includes papers on postwar plans, ED 31 are Bill files, many relating to the 1943 Education Bill, ED 152 has local education authority plans for the development of primary and secondary schools under the 1944 Act. MH 77/1–4 concern early planning of the postwar health service in the London area, including preliminary survey reports on hospitals. Beveridge Committee papers relating to the planned postwar changes in social insurance can be found in ACT 1, LAB 12, PIN 4 PIN 8 and CAB 87/76–82. Every department had an eye on the future, including the Prison Commissioners, PCOM. Their published report for 1945, Cmd 7146, has an appendix of proposals for the postwar development of the prison system.

Just as the government and its departments needed to plan for the future, so local government authorities and their committees had to do the same. The LCC was heavily involved and useful material may be found in a variety of committee minutes, presented plans and departmental papers. Council minutes carry policy decisions. Committee minutes, presented papers and departmental papers relating to several departments are also worth checking, notably: Architect's, Town Planning — papers on the County of London Development Plan are in LCC/AR/TP/4 — Housing, and Education. Similar advice applies to the records of Middlesex County Council, whose early papers on the County of Middlesex Development Plan are in MCC/CL/L/PL/1, and town planning schemes are in MCC/CL/PL/07. Borough council minutes, and committee and departmental papers can also prove fruitful.

Firms and institutions also needed to plan ahead for peace, to cater for a time when trade would be less restricted, when munitions and other wartime factories would be restored to their usual purposes, and their former staff demobbed from the Forces.

The London Passenger Transport Board had its own Postwar Planning Committee; banks such as the Westminster began to consider war staffing and postwar reconstruction matters from an early stage. Institutional records of many types may contain relevant London information.

### 'Getting lit up...': Victory celebrations

The fiftieth anniversary of the end of the war in 1995 brought a flood of publications and reminiscences on radio and television about the way that victory was celebrated. The significance of the event prompted many people to commit their feelings to paper at the time, and diary entries, letters and memoirs, both published and unpublished, reflect varying experiences of the victory celebrations. Overwhelming relief was the predominant feeling.

Victory had taken a long time to arrive, and the nation was war-weary after six years of mixed hardship, boredom and danger. V1s and V2s continued to cause death and destruction in London as late as March 1945. This hazard was particularly hard to bear when everyone knew that the end of the war was so close. Hitler's suicide on 30 April convinced the public that the German surrender must come soon, in fact events dragged on until 7 May, with the public speculating as to which day would finally be designated 'V-Day'. On the evening of 7 May, they learnt that it was to be tomorrow.

The official side of the Victory celebrations is documented in HO 45/20688–90, amid the Home Office registered papers; WORK 21 also has material on the celebrations and on Remembrance Day procedures. Local collections have photographs and other memorabilia about celebrations in their area, official and unofficial, such as street parties and parades. The Mass-Observation archive's topic collection has two boxes of material on VE Day and VJ Day, TC 49, with interviews, overheard conversations, descriptions of crowd behaviour, street sellers and decorations in London.

Most people were given the day off and troops were on leave if possible. Crowds started to grow in the West End, for everyone felt drawn to celebrate in the heart of London. People travelled in from the suburbs and even further away to feel part of the great occasion. When Harold Nicolson emerged from lunch at the Beefsteak he had considerable trouble getting to the House of Commons for the afternoon sitting. He wrote to his son: 'The last few yards were very difficult, as the crowd was packed against the railings. I tore my trousers in trying to squeeze past a parked car'. After announcing the surrender of Germany, Churchill moved that the House adjourn to St Margaret's, Westminster, for a service of thanksgiving; the same procedure was followed on VJ Day, 15 August. Meanwhile the crowds continued to grow, wandering around the West End and down the Mall to Buckingham Palace to see the royal family come out on the balcony at intervals to wave. Among the many diarists to record their impressions of London that day are Miss S.M. Andrews, a teacher, in IWM Department of Documents 88/50/1, and Mrs P. Bell, in 86/46/1. Mrs Florence Palmer, from Wembley Park, in LMA ACC 3051/9, confined herself to brief notes in a pocket diary: '8 May 1945 VE Day — put out flag. Kath and I took Margaret to Mansion House, St Paul's, Fleet St and on to Trafalgar Sq. Bonfires and fireworks in West Hill. 9 May 1945 Went to Buckingham Palace. Saw royal family & also Mr Churchill — Hyde Park Corner'. The IWM Sound Archive holds many recordings relating to VE and VJ Day celebrations, as well as to wider postwar issues, and to the General Election. Interviews recorded for the LWT programme *The Making of Modern London, 1939–45* include reminiscences about VE Day festivities, in the Museum of London's oral history collection. The National Sound Archive has copies of contemporary BBC broadcasts by Howard Marshall describing the celebrating crowds outside Buckingham Palace, and Wynford Vaughan Thomas reporting from Piccadilly on VJ night, and individual reminiscences such as Maureen Steffen, on C 642/98/1–2 C1, about VE Day celebrations. Almost all observers stressed the unfamiliar and impressive effect of the floodlit public buildings, after years of blackout.

Vera Brittain, who remembered the Armistice celebrations at the end of the First World War, found the 1945 public celebrations 'so formal and "arranged"' in comparison. Her *Wartime Chronicle* (Gollancz, 1989) recorded on 8 May 1945: 'Felt disinclined to hear a "Victory" service so went to the little meeting of the London Mission at Kingsway Hall to hear Donald Soper give a really inspiring address on thanksgiving, penitence and dedication'.

Harold Nicolson finished his day rather differently. After dinner, he wrote, 'I went on to a party at Chips Channon's. Why did I go to that party? I should have been much happier seeing all the floodlighting and the crowds outside Buckingham Palace. But I went and I loathed it'. Noel Coward made sure he saw the spectacle first: 'After that I went to Chips Channon's "open house" party which wasn't up to much' (*The Noel Coward Diaries*, ed. Graham Payn and Sheridan Morley. Weidenfeld, 1982).

The IWM Film and Video Archive has some film footage of the VE Day celebrations, including the display of a captured U boat on the Thames, in COI–246–05, and colour amateur footage of the events; cinema newsreels featured the festivities extensively. Numerous press and agency photographs record the scenes. In addition, there are paintings of the occasion, such as Leila Faithful's *VE Celebration outside Buckingham Palace*' in the IWM.

On 13 May there was a special service at St Paul's Cathedral, attended by the royal family and many other distinguished guests, widely reported and pictured in the press.

On 5 July came the general election, not counted until 16 July to allow for the troops' postal votes, which changed the political pattern of the country with a landslide victory for the Labour party. One of the highest swings, by eighteen per cent, was in London, where the radical vote in the centre was huge and a Communist was elected in Mile End. Even previously safe Conservative seats were taken — Herbert Morrison was elected for Lewisham with a majority of 15,000. The optimistic public mood of expectation that good times were on the way proved short-lived because of the need for austerity in the face of financial crises brought on by the ending of the Lend-Lease agreement with the United States. The age of plenty was slow to arrive. Some felt the VE Day celebrations had been premature, with the war still going on in the Far East. When at last the Japanese surrender was officially announced, VJ Day was set for the next day, 15 August. London had already filled up while the announcement was awaited, and great crowds again gathered to stroll around the West End.

## Rolls of honour

Finally, there is the recording of civilian war dead to consider. The Imperial War Graves Commission compiled a complete, countrywide list after the war. When the list was published it was made available in borough sections, and all the London local history collections have the appropriate parts for their own areas. Some boroughs had already begun to prepare lists for their own purposes. For instance, Kensington Local History Library has a 'Register of civilian war deaths, September 7 1940 to December 13 1944', giving full names and addresses of the dead and their place of burial (940.5467/AR/A), as well as the Imperial War Graves list and a list of all war burials in Gunnersbury Cemetery from 1940–47. Other boroughs' collections should be investigated for equivalents. Civilian war dead were commemorated in a variety of ways, including firms' books of remembrance, and memorial plaques in civic or commercial buildings. The Imperial War Museum's continuing project to list war memorials in a National Inventory of War Memorials tries to identify them all. As recently as 1997 the local residents managed to prevent development on a bomb site at Heritage Wharf, Wapping, by insisting that it be turned into a memorial park for the 30,000 Londoners who died in the war.

---

Woman Police Constable Bertha Massey Gleghorn, "C" Division.

Died as a result of injuries received from a flying bomb explosion during an enemy air attack on the 19th June, 1944.

[*P.O. 20th June, 1944*]

---

An entry from the Metropolitan Police Roll of Honour 1939–45
*(Reproduced in the Newsletter of the Friends of the Metropolitan Police Museum no. 8 (1997))*

# 7. Bibliography

## CONTENTS

## INTRODUCTION TO THE BIBLIOGRAPHY

The following classified bibliography lists published works of all types relating to the history of wartime London. They have been found through the catalogues of many London libraries, especially Guildhall Library, the library at London Metropolitan Archives, the Bishopsgate Institute and the local history libraries of the London boroughs, and through footnotes and other bibliographies. The editor has tried to see them all, but a few have proved elusive, though they have not been added unless full bibliographical details could be verified. They are included in the hope that others may be more fortunate in tracking down copies. The bibliography follows the classified arrangement of the guide.

A publication pattern is discernible over the years. In spite of paper shortages and other problems, much was published during the war itself — 18% of the titles in this bibliography appeared between 1939 and 1945. In the decade after the war there was a flurry of publishing from government departments, local authorities and private firms, chronicling their own wartime activities and achievements. Many of the business histories, such as John Wadsworth's *Counter Offensive*, about the Midland Bank, were intended for circulation purely among their own staff, and so appeared only in limited editions. This period accounts for 18.1% of the references here. From the mid-1950s London's war began to seem 'old hat' from the book trade's point of view. Publications dwindled, and titles from the 1960s represent only 5% of this bibliography. Interest picked up during the 1970s (9.6%) and 1980s (17.9%), reaching a climax with the fiftieth anniversary of the end of the war, when sixty-one titles appeared in 1995 alone, that is 7.3% of the total bibliography in just one year; the average for the 1990s overall being 22.1%. Since then, the volume of published material has slowed somewhat, but is still flourishing.

The titles included here vary widely in their approach and amount of detail. Some are serious academic studies, others take a more popular approach. Many are personal accounts of wartime domestic or working lives written much later than the events they describe. All have something to offer the historian of London at this period.

'Surprisingly few places felt moved to compile a history of their experiences during the war and most of those that do exist tend to be a catalogue of air raids and Civil Defence activities with little, if any, reference to other aspects of civilian life', noted Norman Longmate in 1971 in *How We Lived Then* (p. 526). This gap has been remedied more recently in a spate of illustrated local histories like *Hackney at War, Southwark at War, Brent's War* and others, and articles such as 'Lewisham remembers 1945', and 'Paddle steamers and soldiers in Dockland'.

In compiling the list, the perennial problem facing the bibliographer of London has inevitably recurred. The capital is of such central importance in British life for so many reasons — social, political, economic — that most books about the country as a whole also contain material relevant to London specifically. This appears to be even more evident than usual for the years 1939–45. Some of the titles may therefore seem to be rather general to be included in a bibliography concentrating on London, but they do contain relevant information on the capital, sometimes in considerable quantity. Notable examples are the magisterial official *History of the Second World War: UK Civil Series*, dealing with the work of the government in wartime, like T.H. O'Brien's *Civil Defence*, and R.M. Titmuss' *Problems of Social Policy*. Far more readable than they might appear at first sight, and studded with detailed information about London, they are indispensable to those seriously interested in the subject. The War Cabinet had planned ahead from as early as October

1939 for these histories, asking departments, and eventually institutions like galleries and museums, for a full account of their wartime roles.

Not listed here, but containing essential evidence for London life in the war are newspapers at three levels: national — *The Times, Daily Telegraph* and many others, London-wide — *Evening Standard, Evening News* — and local — *The Kensington Post, Finsbury Weekly News, East London Advertiser* and dozens more. Regional papers, such as the *Yorkshire Post* and the *Manchester Guardian* also reported London events and can be useful for provincial reactions to news of raids, or the arrival of London evacuees. Files of all these papers, mostly now available on microfilm/fiche, are housed at the British Library's Newspaper Library at Colindale. Local history libraries usually have files of the most important titles for their area, and their staff have sometimes compiled an index to the run. Contemporary magazines of all kinds are valuable sources, too, from general interest periodicals like *Picture Post* to women's magazines such as *Vogue* and *Good Housekeeping*, which often carried articles about life in London. Specialist periodicals like *Theatre World*, 'The magazine for the playgoer', or the *Times Education Supplement* mention current problems and conditions in London, both in editorials and feature articles. The Library Association's annual *Subject Index to Periodicals* was maintained throughout the war, listing articles from a lengthy menu of English and American journals and a few Continental ones. Its 'London' heading is worth checking for contemporary preoccupations. *Whitaker's Almanack*, the *Annual Register* and *Keesing's Contemporary Archives* provide useful overviews of the year's events. Many wartime writers presented their own experiences in fictionalised form, and such novels can help the historian to appreciate the mood of the period. There are far too many to include in a bibliography like this, but the section on leisure and the arts contains more discussion of this additional source.

# BIBLIOGRAPHY

(Titles with national or international coverage all contain substantial material on London)

## FINDING AIDS AND BIBLIOGRAPHIES

1. BAYLISS, GWYN M. Bibliographical guide to the two World Wars: an annotated survey of English language reference materials. Bowker, 1977. xv, 658pp.

2. BLANC, BRIGITTE, and others (comps.). La Seconde Guerre Mondiale: guide des sources conservées en France, 1939–45. Paris: Archives Nationales, 1994. xxii, 1217pp.

3. BRIDGEMAN, IAN, and EMSLEY, CLIVE (eds.). A guide to the archives of the police forces of England and Wales. Leigh-on-Sea, Essex: Police History Soc., 1989. 241pp.

4. CANTWELL, JOHN D. The Second World War: a guide to documents in the Public Record Office. Rev. edn. *(PRO Handbooks, 15).* HMSO, 1993. 218pp. [First pubd. 1972, a new edition is due in November 1998.]

5. ENSER, A.G.S. A subject bibliography of the Second World War: books in English, 1939–74. Deutsch, 1977. 592pp.

6. ENSER, A.G.S. A subject bibliography of the Second World War and aftermath: books in English, 1975–87. 2nd ed. Aldershot, Hants.: Gower, 1990. xii, 287pp.

7. FOSTER, JANET, and SHEPPARD, JULIA (eds.). British archives. 3rd ed. Macmillan, 1995. lxiv, 627pp.

8. FUNK, ARTHUR L. The Second World War: a select bibliography of books in English published since 1975. Claremont, Calif.: Regina Books, 1985. xi, 210pp.

9. HEBBER, MICHAEL. London recent and present. *London Journal,* XX (1995) 91–101. [Recent writings, including material on war.]

10. JAMES, ANTHONY R. A bibliography of World War 2 HMSO paperbacks... dealing with contemporary aspects of World War Two and mostly published between 1941 and 1947, and including a price guide. Southwick, the compiler, 1993. 47pp.

11. MAYER, SYDNEY L., and KOENIG, WILLIAM J. The two World Wars: a guide to manuscript collections in the UK. New York: Bowker, 1976. xii, 317pp.

12. MILEWSKI, WACLAW, and others (comps.). Guide to the archives of the Polish Institute and Sikorski Museum. Vol. 1. Orbis, for Polish Institute, 1985. xxii, 372pp.

13. RICHMOND, LESLEY, and TURTON, ALISON. Directory of corporate archives. 4th ed. Business Archives Council, 1997. vii, 91pp.

14. SILVERTHORNE, ELIZABETH (ed.). London local archives: a directory of local authority record offices and libraries. 3rd ed. Guildhall Library, and GLAN, 1994. 44pp.

15. SOMERS, ERIK, and PIERS, MARK (comps.). Archievengids van de Tweede Wereldoorlog: Nederlands en Nederlands-Indie. Zutphen; Amsterdam: Walburg Inst.; Rijksinst. v. Oorlogsdoc., 1994. 407pp.

16. The wardens' post, 1939–45. Kensington Local Studies Dept., 1995. xiipp., illus. [Catalogue of Kensington war memorabilia.]

## WARTIME LONDON AND AREA: GENERAL

17. BATO, JOSEPH. Defiant city. Gollancz, 1942. 108pp.

18. Britain under fire, with a foreword by J.B. Priestley. Country Life, 1941. 96pp., illus. [Many London illustrations.]

19. BROMLEY, GORDON. London goes to war, 1939. Joseph, 1974. 128pp., illus.

20. CALDER, ANGUS. The people's war: Britain, 1939–45. Cape, 1969. 656pp., illus.

21. CHURCHILL, WINSTON S. The Second World War. Harmondsworth, Middx.: Penguin, 1989. xviii, 1011pp., illus.

22. DEAR, I.C.B. (ed.). The Oxford companion to the Second World War. OUP, 1995. xxii, 1343pp., illus. [Helpful UK section.]

23. FREEMAN, ROGER A. Britain at war. Arms & Armour P, for Daily Express, 1990. 96pp., illus.

24. HARDY, CLIVE, and ARTHUR, NIGEL. London at war. Quoin, Hulton-Deutsch, 1989. 176pp., illus. [Mainly photographs from the Hulton-Deutsch collection.]

25. HENNESSY, PETER. Never again: Britain, 1945–51. Cape, 1992. 544pp. [With historical introduction.]

26. HENREY, Mrs ROBERT. London under fire, 1940–5. Dent, 1969. 255pp., illus. [Comprises her three war-time books: A village in Piccadilly (1942);The incredible city (1944); The siege of London (1946).]

27. Historic London under fire. Ecclesiological Soc., 1942. iv, 87pp., illus.

28. HOGAN, J.P. Hair under a hat. Chaterson Ltd., 1949. viii, 160pp. [Essays on wartime London.]

29. HOOD, DOROTHY. London is invincible. Hutchinson, 1946. 192pp., illus.

30. KEE, ROBERT. The world we left behind, being a chronicle of the year 1939. Weidenfeld, 1984. x, 369pp., illus.

31. KEE, R., and SMITH, JOANNA. We'll meet again: photographs of daily life in Britain during the Second World War. Dent, 1984. 216pp., illus.

32    KENDALL, ALAN. Their finest hour: an evocative memoir of the British people in wartime, 1939–45. Wayland, 1972. 192pp., illus.

33    LEWIS, PETER. A people's war. Thames Methuen, 1986. vi, 250pp., illus. [Based on television series.]

34    LONGMATE, NORMAN. If Britain had fallen. BBC, Hutchinson, 1972. 276pp., illus. [Invasion fears and preparations.]

35    MACK, JOANNA, and HUMPHRIES, STEVE. The making of modern London: London at war. Sidgwick, 1985. 176pp., illus.

36    MCMILLAN, JAMES. The way it happened, 1939–50. Kimber, 1980. 269pp., illus. [Based on the files of the Daily Express.]

37    MARTIN, GEOFFREY, and others. Essex at war, 1939–45. Chelmsford: Essex R.O., 1995. 1 audio tape (45 mins.) + pamphlets. [Includes metropolitan areas.]

38    MORTON, H.V. I saw two Englands: the record of a journey before the war and after the outbreak of war in the year 1939. 2nd ed. Methuen, 1943. vii, 296pp. [First pubd. 1942.]

39    MOSLEY, LEONARD. Backs to the wall: London under fire, 1939–45. Weidenfeld, 1971. xiv, 397pp.

40    OGLEY, BOB. Kent at war: the unconquered county, 1939–45. Westerham, Kent: Froglets Pubns., 1994. 224pp., illus. [Includes metropolitan areas.]

41    OGLEY, B. Surrey at war, 1939–45. Westerham, Kent: Froglets Pubns., 1995. 200pp., illus. [Includes metropolitan areas.]

42    PALMER, ALAN. The East End: four centuries of London life. Murray, 1989. xiii, 197pp., illus. [Useful chapter on the East End in the war.]

43    PELLING, HENRY. Britain and the Second World War. Collins, 1970. 352pp., illus.

44    PHILLIPS, ANDREW. Essex at war: an oral history. Essex Jour., XXX (1995) 5–9. [Covers metropolitan Essex, and Londoners evacuated further out.]

45    POIRIER, FRANCOIS (ed.). Londres, 1939–45. Riches et pauvres dans le même élan patriotique: derrière la légende. Paris: Autrement, 1995. 300pp., illus.

46    PRIESTLEY, JOHN BOYNTON. Britain at war. New York: Harper, 1942. 118pp., illus.

47    RAMSEY, WINSTON G. The East End then and now. Battle of Britain Prints Internat., 1997. 528pp., illus.

48    ROOTES, ANDREW. Front line county. Hale, 1980. 223pp., illus. [Kent.]

49    SETH, RONALD. The day war broke out: the story of 3 September 1939. Spearman, 1963. 175pp., illus.

50    SMITH, GODFREY (ed.). How it was in the war: an anthology. Pavilion Books, 1989. 317pp., illus.

51    TAYLOR, A.J.P. English history, 1914–45, reprinted with revised bibliography. (Oxford History of England, 15). Clarendon P, 1976. xxvii,

718pp. [Substantial section on the war and its effect on civilians.]

52    THORPE, ANDREW. 'Britain'. In The civilian in war: the home front in Europe, Japan and the U.S.A. in World War II, ed. J. Noakes (Exeter: Exeter UP, 1992) pp. 14–34.

53    WHITING, CHARLES. Britain under fire: the bombing of Britain's cities, 1940–45. Century, 1986. 160pp., illus.

54    WHITNELL, LEWIS. Engines over London. Carroll & Nicolson, 1949. 164pp.

55    WOOLF, ARTHUR L. The battle of South London. Crystal Pubns., 1944. 20pp., illus.

56    ZIEGLER, PHILIP. London at war, 1939–45. Sinclair-Stevenson, 1995. x, 372pp., illus.

## NATIONAL GOVERNMENT, ADMINISTRATION, POLITICS

57    ADDISON, PAUL. The road to 1945: British politics and the Second World War. Rev. edn. Pimlico, 1994. 350pp., illus. [Previous edn. 1975.]

58    ADDISON, P. 'Journey to the Centre: Churchill and Labour in coalition, 1940–5.' In Crisis and controversy, ed. A. Sked and C. Cook (Macmillan, 1976) pp.165–93.

59    BROOKE, STEPHEN. Labour's war: the Labour Party during the Second World War. Oxford: OUP, 1992. xiii, 363pp., illus.

60    The Cabinet war rooms. New ed. Imperial War Museum, 1996. 36pp., illus. [Subterranean complex beneath Whitehall.]

61    CHARMAN, TERRY. 'A bit of campaign oratory': Wendell Willkie's visit to Britain, January 1941, and the fight for Lend Lease. Imperial War Museum Rev., IX (1994) 75–83.

62    CLEMENTS, SIBYL (ed.). A short history of the War Damage Commission, 1941 to 1962. The Commission, 1962. 98pp., illus.

63    FIELDING, STEVEN, and others. England arise! The Labour Party and popular politics in the 1940s. Manchester: Manchester UP, 1995. 244pp., illus.

64    HAY, IAN. The Post Office went to war. HMSO, 1946. 96pp., illus. [With chapter on London.]

65    HOWLETT, PETER (comp.). Fighting with figures. Central Statistical Office, 1995. vi, 298pp., illus. [A retitled and revised version of The statistical digest of the Second World War (HMSO, 1951).]

66    JAMES, ANTHONY R. Informing the people: how the government won hearts and minds to win World War Two. HMSO, 1996. iv, 141pp., illus.

67    KING, FRANCIS, and MATTHEWS, GEORGE (eds.). About turn: the British Communist Party and the Second World War: the verbatim record of the Central Committee meetings of 25 September and 2–3 October 1939. Lawrence & Wishart, 1990. 318pp.

68    LUDLOW, PETER W. Britain and Northern Europe, 1940–5. Scandinavian Jour. Hist., IV

(1979) 123–62.

69  MCCALLUM, RONALD B., and READMAN, ALISON. The British general election of 1945. Oxford: OUP, 1947. xv, 311pp. [Includes its wartime background.]

70  MCLAINE, IAN M. Ministry of morale: home front morale and the Ministry of Information in World War II. Allen & Unwin, 1979. 344pp. [Expanded from his Oxford DPhil thesis 'The Ministry of Information and British civilian morale during the Second World War' 1976.]

71  MASS-OBSERVATION. Home propaganda. *(Change, no.2)*. Advertising Service Guild, 1941. vi, 78pp.

72  RHODES, ANTHONY. Propaganda — the art of persuasion: World War II. Ed. V. Margolin. Angus & Robertson, 1976. 320pp., illus. [Chapter 3, Britain improvises, 1936–45, pp.107–36.]

73  RILEY, NORMAN. 999 and all that. Gollancz, 1940. 223pp. [Exposé of the Ministry of Information, said to have 999 employees.]

74  SREBNIK, HENRY F. London Jews and British Communism, 1935–45. Vallentine Mitchell, 1995. xiii, 258pp., illus.

75  TANFIELD, JENNIFER. In Parliament, 1939–50: the effect of the war on the Palace of Westminster. *(House of Commons Library Document, 20)*. HMSO, 1991. ix, 60pp.

76  TOMBS, ISABELLE S.L. Socialist politics and the future of Europe: the discussions between British Labour and continental socialists in London, 1939–45. *Cambridge Univ. PhD thesis*, 1988. iv, 436ff.

77  ULPH, COLIN. 150 not out: the story of the Paymaster General's Office, 1836–1986. Crawley, W. Sussex: HM Paymaster General's Office, 1985. viii, 163pp., illus.

78  WAGNER, IRENE. Socialist London at war. *Women's Research Committee Bull.*, no. 2 (1987) 3–5.

79  WATSON, SHEILA E.R. The Ministry of Information and the Home Front in Britain, 1939–42. *London Univ. PhD thesis*, 1984. 437ff.

80  WEBB, MARJORIE O. The government explains. Royal Inst. Public Admin., 1965. 229pp.

81  YASS, MARION. This is your war: Home Front propaganda in the Second World War. HMSO, 1983. vi, 62pp.

## *Political biographies, diaries, etc.*

82  BECKMAN, MORRIS. The 43 Group. Centerprise, 1992. 221pp., illus. [Fighting Fascism in the East End.]

83  BILAINKIN, GEORGE. Diary of a diplomatic correspondent. Allen & Unwin, 1942. 272pp., illus. [For Allied Newspapers.]

84  BRINITZER, CARL. Hier spricht London von einem, der dabei war. Hamburg: Hoffmann & Campe, 1969. 340pp., illus. [German diplomat, still in London in early stages of war.]

85  BROCKWAY, ARCHIBALD FENNER, Baron Brockway. Bermondsey story: the life of Alfred Salter. Allen & Unwin, 1951. xi, 246pp., illus. [MP and public health campaigner.]

86  BULLOCK, ALAN. The life and times of Ernest Bevin. Vol. 2, Minister of Labour, 1940–45. Heinemann, 1967. 407pp., illus.

87  CADOGAN, Sir ALEXANDER. The diaries, 1938–45, ed. D. Dilks. Cassell, 1971. 881pp., illus. [Permanent Under-Secretary, Foreign Office.]

88  CARANDINI ALBERTINI, ELENA. Passata la stagione: diari, 1944–7. Florence: Passigli, 1989. 379pp., illus. [Italian diplomat's wife.]

89  CHANNON, Sir HENRY. Chips: the diaries of Sir Henry Channon, ed. R.R. James. Weidenfeld, 1967. 495pp., illus. [MP. Covers 1934–58.]

90  COLVILLE, Sir JOHN. The fringes of power: Downing Street diaries, 1939–45. Hodder, 1985. 796pp., illus. [Assistant Private Secretary to Chamberlain and Churchill, and RAFVR pilot.]

91  COOPER, DUFF, Viscount Norwich. Old men forget. Hart-Davis, 1953. 399pp., illus. [Minister of Information 1940–1, Chancellor of Duchy of Lancaster 1941–3, chaired Cabinet Committee on Security.]

92  DALTON, HUGH. The Second World War diary of Hugh Dalton, 1940–45, ed. B. Pimlott. Cape, with LSE, 1986. xliii, 913pp., illus. [Labour politician, President of Board of Trade 1942.]

93  DALTON, H. The fateful years: memoirs, 1931–45. Muller, 1957. 493pp., illus.

94  DUGDALE, BLANCHE. Baffy: the diaries of Blanche Dugdale, 1936–47. Vallentine, Mitchell, 1973. xxiv, 262pp., illus. [Active in Zionist Organisation.]

95  FARRER, DAVID. The sky's the limit. Hutchinson, 1943. 95pp. [Beaverbrook at the Ministry of Aircraft Production.]

96  GALLACHER, WILLIAM. The rolling of the thunder. Lawrence & Wishart, 1947. 229pp., illus. [Communist MP's autobiography.]

97  GORMAN, JOHN. Knocking down Ginger. Caliban, 1995. 260pp., illus. [Communist.]

98  HARVEY, OLIVER, Baron Tasburgh. War diaries, ed. J. Harvey. Collins, 1978. 399pp. [Diplomat, Eden's Private Secretary 1941–3.]

99  HARRISON, STANLEY. Good to be alive: the story of Jack Brent. Lawrence & Wishart, 1954. 96pp., illus. [Communist, Hon. Secretary of the International Brigades Association, London.]

100  HERBERT, DENNIS, Baron Hemingford. Backbencher and chairman: some parliamentary reminiscences. Murray, 1946. viii, 248pp., illus.

101  LANCUM, F. HOWARD. 'Press officer please!' Crosby Lockwood, 1946. 144pp., illus. [Press Officer for the Ministry of Agriculture and Fisheries.]

102  LEE, RAYMOND E. The London observer: the journal of General Raymond E. Lee, 1940–1, ed. J. Leutze. Hutchinson, 1972. xxi, 489pp. [First pubd. Boston, Mass.: Little, Brown, 1971.]

103 LOCKHART, Sir ROBERT B.H. Comes the reckoning. Putnam, 1947. 384pp. [Diplomat, in charge of Political Warfare Executive 1941–5.]

104 MacDONALD, MALCOLM. People and places: random reminiscences... Collins, 1969. 254pp., illus. [Minister of Health, 1940–1.]

105 MACMILLAN, HAROLD. The blast of war, 1939–45. Macmillan, 1967. 765pp., illus. [Conservative politician's autobiography. Approach of war is covered in his Winds of Change, 1914–39 (Macmillan, 1966).]

106 MARQUIS, FREDERICK J., 1st Earl of Woolton. Memoirs. Cassell, 1959. xii, 452pp., illus. [Minister of Food, and later of Reconstruction.]

107 MARTIN, Sir JOHN. Downing Street: the war years. Bloomsbury, 1991. 200pp., illus. [Churchill's Private Secretary.]

108 MENZIES, Sir ROBERT. Dark and hurrying days, ed. A.W. Martin and P. Hardy. Canberra: National Lib. Australia, 1993. 187pp. [1941 diaries of Australian Prime Minister, covering visit to England.]

109 MORRISON, HERBERT, Lord Morrison of Lambeth. An autobiography. Odhams, 1960. 336pp. [Home Secretary, Minister of Home Security.]

110 NICOLSON, HAROLD. Diaries and letters, 1939–45, ed. N. Nicolson. Collins, 1967. 511pp., illus. [MP, Parliamentary Secretary to Ministry of Information, 1940–1.]

111 REITH, JOHN C.W., Baron Reith. The Reith diaries, ed. C. Stuart. Collins, 1975. 541pp., illus. [Minister of Information, 1940.]

112 RITCHIE, CHARLES. The siren years: undiplomatic diaries, 1937–45. Macmillan, 1974. 216pp. [Canadian diplomat.]

113 ROOSEVELT, ELEANOR. This I remember. Hutchinson, 1950. 304pp., illus. [Wife of US President.]

114 WILLIAMS, FRANCIS, Baron Francis-Williams. Nothing so strange: an autobiography. Cassell, 1970. ix, 354pp. [Ministry of Information Controller of Press and Censorship.]

115 WINANT, JOHN G. A letter from Grosvenor Square: an account of a stewardship. Hodder, 1947. 200pp. [American ambassador, 1941–6.]

## LOCAL GOVERNMENT AND ADMINISTRATION

### London region in general

116 Kent: the county administration in war, 1939–45. Maidstone, Kent: Kent County Council, 1946. vii, 170pp., illus.

117 KNOWLES, C.C., and PITT, P.H. The history of building regulation in London, 1189–1972. Archit. P, 1972. 164pp., illus. ['The Second World War', pp. 118–32.]

118 LONDON COUNTY COUNCIL. A short account of the services of the Council during the war of

1939–45. The Council, 1949. 8pp. [Accompanied by a volume of photographs.]

119 LONDON COUNTY COUNCIL. London statistics. New ser. vol. 1, 1945–54, with comparative figures for 1938. The Council, 1957. x, 242pp. [Data not published during war.]

120 SAINT, ANDREW (ed.). Politics and the people of London: the London County Council, 1889–1965. Hambledon P, 1989. xvii, 278pp., illus.

121 YOUNG, KEN, and GARSIDE, PATRICIA. Metropolitan London: politics and urban change, 1837–1981. Edward Arnold, 1982. xiv, 401pp., illus.

### By locality, A–Z

**Barking**

122 CLIFFORD, TONY, and others (comps.). On the Home Front: Barking and Dagenham in Word War II. Barking and Dagenham Libs. Dept., 1991. 94pp., illus.

**Barnet**

123 REBOUL, PERCY, and HEATHFIELD, JOHN. Barnet at war. Stroud, Glos.: Sutton, 1995. x, 107pp., illus.

**Bermondsey**

124 STEWART, JAMES D. Bermondsey in war, 1939–45. The author, 1980. 92pp., illus.

**Bethnal Green**

125 VALE, GEORGE F. Bethnal Green's ordeal, 1939–45. Bethnal Green Council, c. 1945. 16pp., illus.

**Bexley**

126 SCOTT, MICK. Home fires: a borough at war. Bexley Borough Council, 1986. 40pp., illus.

**Brent**

127 LONG, JANET. Brent's war: wartime memories of the people of Brent. Brent Council, 1995. 44pp., illus.

**Bromley**

128 BLAKE, LEWIS. Bromley in the front line. Rev. edn. The author, 1983. 96pp., illus.

129 RASON, PAUL (comp.). Memories of the many: 50 years on, a collection of memories of people from the London Borough of Bromley reflecting on their war. Environment Bromley, 1996. v, 66pp., illus.

130 REEVES, GRAHAM. Undaunted: the story of Bromley in the Second World War. Bromley Leisure Services, 1990. v, 105pp., illus.

**Camden**

131 HART, VALERIE, and MARSHALL, LESLEY. Wartime Camden: life in Camden during the First and Second World Wars. Camden Public Libraries, 1983. 36pp., illus.

**City of London**

132 GRANT, IAN, and MADDREN, NICHOLAS. The City at war. Joseph, 1975. 128pp., illus.

**Croydon**

133 CROYDON TIMES. Croydon courageous: the story of Croydon's ordeal and triumph, 1939–45. 3rd edn. Croydon Times, 1946. 90pp., illus.

134 SAYERS, W.C. BERWICK (ed.). Croydon and the Second World War: the official history of the war work of the borough... Croydon Corporation, 1949. xxi, 581pp., illus.

**Dagenham**

135 O'LEARY, JOHN. Danger over Dagenham, 1939–45. Dagenham Corporation, 1947. 88pp.

**Deptford**

136 BLAKE, LEWIS. Red alert: South East London, 1939–45: told for the first time, the story of the former metropolitan boroughs of Deptford, Greenwich, Lewisham and Woolwich under air attack... Whitstable, Kent.: the author, 1982. 106pp., illus.

137 BLAKE, L. How we went to war: Deptford and Lewisham, 1939–45. The people's story, reminiscences contributed by the Age Exchange Reminiscence Centre. Lewisham Arts and Library Service, 1995. 74pp., illus.

**Dulwich**

138 GREEN, BRIAN. Dulwich home front, 1939–45. Dulwich Soc., 1995. 36pp., illus.

**Ealing**

139 UPTON, DENNIS. The dangerous years: life in Ealing, Acton and Southall in the Second World War, 1939–45. The author, 1993. 38pp., illus.

**Enfield**

140 GILLAM, GEOFFREY. Enfield at war, 1939–45: events in Edmonton, Enfield and Southgate during the Second World War. Enfield Archaeol.Soc., 1985. 58pp., illus.

**Fulham**

141 HASKER, LESLIE. Fulham in the Second World War. Fulham and Hammersmith Hist. Soc., 1984. 89pp., illus.

**Hackney**

142 GOLDEN, JENNIFER. Hackney at war. Hackney Archives Dept., 1995. 154pp., illus.

143 MERNICK, PHILLIP, and KENDALL, DOREEN. A pictorial history of Victoria Park. East London Hist. Soc., 1997. 72pp., illus. [Useful coverage of war years.]

**Hampstead**

144 Hampstead at war, 1939–45. Hampstead Borough Council, 1947. 40pp., illus. [Reprinted 1995.]

**Hornsey**

145 TRAVERS, BEN (ed.). Home fires: a north London suburb at war. Hornsey Hist. Soc., 1992. 48pp. [Includes map of bomb damage.]

**Isle of Dogs**

146 HOSTETTLER, EVE (ed.). The Island at war: memories of war time life on the Isle of Dogs, East London. Island Hist. Trust, 1989. 61pp., illus.

**Kensington**

147 BARTLETT, ELIZABETH, and SENIOR, DIANA. All pulling together: North Kensington at war, 1939–45. North Kensington Memories Group, 1990. 32pp., illus.

148 FERGUSON, RACHEL. Royal borough. Cape, 1950. 320pp., illus.

**Lambeth**

149 GIBBERD, GRAHAM. On Lambeth Marsh: the South Bank and Waterloo. Jane Gibberd, 1992. xiv, 175pp., illus.

150 ROTHWELL, STANLEY. Lambeth at war. S.E.1 People's Hist. project, 1981. 36pp., illus.

**Lewisham**

151 BYRNE, STEPHEN. The changing face of Lewisham. Lewisham Borough Council, 1965. 76pp., illus.

**Pinner**

152 The villager at war: a diary of home front Pinner, 1939–45. Pinner Association, 1995. 120pp., illus.

**St Pancras**

153 HALDANE, CHARLOTTE. Truth will out. Weidenfeld, 1949. 339pp. [Experiences with St Pancras Emergency Committee.]

**Shepherds Bush**

154 Around the Bush: the war years, 1914–18, 1939–45. Shepherds Bush Local Hist. Soc., 1987. 71pp., illus.

**Southwark**

155 DAVIS, REBECCA, and SCHWEITZER, PAMELA (eds.). Southwark at war: a book of memories and photographs. Southwark Local Studies Lib., 1996. 38pp., illus.

**Streatham**

156 SALMON, D.M. To, for and about you: the people of Streatham. St Leonard's Church, 1945. 92pp., illus.

**Tottenham**

157 GOUGH, T.W. Wartime letters from Tottenham Home Front. (*Edmonton Hundred Hist. Soc. Occas. Papers, 54*). The Society, 1994. 52pp., illus.

**Tower Hamlets**

158 LLOYD, CHRISTOPHER. Tower Hamlets at war. Tower Hamlets Borough Council, 1985. 30pp., illus. [Covers First World War as well as Second.]

159 NEECH, DAPHNE. Cable Street as it used to be in 1940. *Cockney Ancestor,* No. 64 (1994) 49.

**Uxbridge**

160 PEARCE, K.R. Uxbridge at war, 1939–45. Uxbridge Local Hist. & Archives Soc., 1989. 20pp., illus.

**Waltham Forest**

161 WALTHAM FOREST ORAL HISTORY GROUP. Boats, billets and letters home. The Group, n.d. 31pp., illus.

**Wandsworth**

162 LOOBEY, PATRICK, and MILLS, JOHN (comps.). The boroughs of Wandsworth and Battersea at war. (*Britain in Old Photographs*). Stroud, Glos.: Sutton, 1996. 128pp., illus.

163 SHAW, ANTHONY, and MILLS, JOHN. 'We served': war time Wandsworth and Battersea, 1939–45. Wandsworth Borough Council, 1989. 64pp., illus.

**West Ham**

164 IDLE, EMILY D. War over West Ham: a study of community adjustment. Faber, 1943. 136pp.

*West Wickham*

165   WALKER, JOYCE. West Wickham in the Second World War. Hollies Pubns., 1990. 144pp., illus.

*Willesden*

166   VALENTINE, K.J. Willesden at war. The author, 1994–5. 2 pts.

*Wimbledon*

167   PLASTOW, NORMAN. Safe as houses: Wimbledon at war, 1939–45. 2nd edn. Wimbledon Soc., 1990. 92pp. [Contains incident map of borough.]

## PERSONAL EXPERIENCE

168   ALLEN, JAMES A. The Allen chronicle: a family in war and peace. Braunton, Devon: Merlin, 1988. 199pp., illus. [New Malden.]

169   ANDERSON, VERILY. Spam tomorrow. Hart-Davis, 1956. 264pp.

170   ARMSTRONG, ANTHONY. We keep going. Collins, 1946. 192pp., illus. [Writer.]

171   BASE, EDITH. Dearest Phylabe: letters from wartime England, ed. B.F. and C.R. Byerly. Niwot, Colorado: Colorado UP, 1996. vii, 193pp., illus.

172   BEARDMORE, GEORGE. Civilians at war: journals, 1938–46. Murray, 1984. 203pp., illus. [Harrow and central London.]

173   BEATON, CECIL. The years between: diaries, 1939–45. Weidenfeld, 1965. 352pp., illus. [Society photographer.]

174   BENSON, THEODORA. Sweethearts and wives: their part in war. Faber, 1942. 114pp. [Ambulance driver, Chelsea area.]

175   BENTLEY, NICOLAS. A version of the truth. Deutsch, 1960. 208pp., illus. [Writer and illustrator.]

176   BLOOM, URSULA. War isn't wonderful. Hutchinson, 1961. 222pp., illus. [Novelist.]

177   BOLITHO, HECTOR. War in the Strand: a notebook of the first two and a half years in London. Eyre & Spottiswoode, 1942. v, 185pp. [Writer.]

178   BRITTAIN, VERA. Wartime chronicle: diary, 1939–45, ed. A. Bishop and Y.A. Bennett. Gollancz, 1989. 352pp., illus. [Writer.]

179   BROWN, IRENE. One woman's war: recollections of a Cockney kid. Excalibur, 1991. 85pp., illus.

180   BRYHER [pseud.], ie ELLERMAN, ANNE WINIFRED. The days of Mars: a memoir, 1940–6. Calder & Boyars, 1972. xii, 190pp. [Novelist.]

181   BYROM, JAMES. The unfinished man. Chatto, 1957. 252pp., illus. [Novelist.]

182   CABLE, MARY (ed.). It happened to us: East Enders remember the Second World War. Ragged School Museum Trust, 1990. 36pp., illus.

183   CALDER, ANGUS, and SHERIDAN, DOROTHY (eds.). Speak for yourself: a Mass-Observation anthology, 1937–49. Cape, 1984. xii, 259pp., illus.

184   CAMPBELL, BEATRICE, Baroness Glenavy. Today we will only gossip. Constable, 1964. 206pp., illus.

185   CHERNOW, RON. The Warburgs: a family saga. Chatto, 1993 xvii, 820pp., illus. [Banking family.]

186   COOPER, DIANA, Viscountess Norwich. Trumpets from the steep. Hart-Davis, 1960. 253pp., illus. [Society life, including war work and evacuees.]

187   CRISP, QUENTIN. The naked civil servant. Cape, 1968. 217pp. [Homosexual life.]

188   CROALL, JONATHAN (ed.). Don't you know there's a war on? The people's voice, 1939–45. Hutchinson, 1988. 232pp., illus.

189   DAVISON, PETER. 'Fragments of shrapnel'. In War culture: social change and changing experience in World War Two, ed. P. Kirkham and D. Thoms (Lawrence & Wishart, 1995) pp. 231–40. [Author's memories of North London in early war years.]

190   DELMER, SEFTON. Black boomerang. Secker, 1962. 320pp. [Novelist.]

191   DICKINSON, PATRIC. The good minute: an autobiographical study. Gollancz, 1965. 238pp., illus. [Writer.]

192   EAST ENDER. East Enders at war. Published weekly as supplement to the East Ender, March 5–April 23 1976. East Ender, 1976. 8 pts., each 4pp.

193   EAST LONDON ADVERTISER. Families at war. Published weekly as supplement to the East London Advertiser, March 5–June 4 1976. East London Advertiser, 1976. 14 pts., each 4pp.

194   EDWARDS, HAZEL. War among the ruins. Oxford: Phoenix, 1996. 162pp., illus. [Children's author.]

195   FITZGIBBON, THEODORA. With love. Century, 1982. 186pp., illus. [Cookery writer.]

196   FOREST HILL SCHOOL. South East London in the Second World War: reminiscences of residents gathered by the boys at Forest Hill School. The School, 1987. 26pp., illus.

197   FYFE, HAMILTON. Britain's wartime revolution. Gollancz, 1944. 248pp., illus. [Diary, Sept. 1939–Dec. 1942.]

198   GORDON, JANE. Married to Charles. Heinemann, 1950. 282pp., illus. [Autobiography of Mrs Charles Graves.]

199   GRAVES, CHARLES P.R. Off the record. A Londoner's life. Great days. Pride of the morning. Hutchinson, 1941–1945. 4 vols. [Writer's war diaries.]

200   GRENFELL, JOYCE. Darling Ma: letters to her mother, 1932–44, ed. J. Roose-Evans. Coronet, 1988. xxvi, 484pp., illus. [Life in London, theatrical engagements.]

201   HAMBURGER, MICHAEL. Strings of beginnings: intermittent memoirs, 1924–54. Skoob, 1991. 338pp. [Poet and translator. First pubd. Carcanet, 1973, as A Mug's Game.]

202   HEARD, PERCY A. An octogenarian's memoirs. Ilfracombe, Devon: Stockwell, 1974. 144pp., illus. [Teacher.]

203   HODGSON, VERE. Few eggs and no oranges: a

diary showing how unimportant people in London and Birmingham lived through the war years, 1940–45. Dobson, 1976. 480pp., illus. [Notting Hill.]

204 HUGHES, MARIAN. No cakes, no jam. Heinemann, 1994. 248pp.

205 JESSE, F. TENNYSON, and HARWOOD, H.M. London front: letters written to America, 1939–40. While London burns: letters written to America July 1940–June 1941. Constable, 1940, 1942. 2 vols. [Writer.]

206 JORDAN, MABEL. Mabel Jordan: an autobiography. Osbaldeston, Lancs.: Malcolm Jordan, 1986. 53pp., illus.

207 KOPS, BERNARD. The world is a wedding. Macgibbon & Kee, 1963. 261pp. [First half mainly about Stepney Green and Bethnal Green in the 1930s and the war.]

208 LAMBERT, DEREK. The sheltered days: growing up in the war. Deutsch, 1965. 191pp.

209 LEES-MILNE, JAMES. Ancestral voices. Prophesying peace. Chatto, 1975, 1977. 2 vols. [Diaries, 1942–3, 1944–5, while working for the National Trust.]

210 LEHMANN, JOHN. I am my brother. Longmans, 1960. viii, 326pp. [Poet and writer.]

211 LONGHURST, HENRY. My life and soft times. Cassell, 1971. vii, 366pp., illus. [Golf writer.]

212 LONGMATE, NORMAN (ed.). The Home Front: an anthology of personal experience, 1938–45. Chatto, 1981. xiii, 242pp., illus.

213 LOWE, ROSE. Daddy Burtt's for dinner. Centerprise, 1976. 35pp., illus. [Hoxton before and during the war.]

214 LOWNDES, MARIE BELLOC. Diaries and letters, 1911–47, ed. S. Lowndes. Chatto, 1971. xi, 291pp., illus. [Writer. Wimbledon and Westminster.]

215 MACAULAY, ROSE. Letters to a sister, ed. C. Babington Smith. Collins, 1964. 352pp., illus. [Writer. She was bombed out.]

216 MCKENNA, ELAINE. Better than dancing: the wandering years of a young Australian, Mary Brennan. Richmond, Victoria: Greenhouse, 1987. 231pp., illus. [Wartime Plumstead.]

217 MACLAREN-ROSS, JULIAN. Memoirs of the Forties. Cardinal, 1991. xiv, 348pp. [Fitzrovia and Soho.]

218 MAJOR-BALL, TERRY. Major major: memories of an older brother. Duckworth, 1994. 167pp., illus. [Suburban south west London, including the war years.]

219 MAYHEW, PATRICK. One family's war. Hutchinson, 1985. xi, 237pp., illus. [Correspondence between the Mayhew and Howarth families.]

220 MITCHISON, NAOMI. Among you taking notes: the wartime diary of Naomi Mitchison, 1939–45, ed. D. Sheridan. Gollancz, 1985. 384pp., illus. [Writer. Based in Argyllshire during the war, but made occasional visits to London and described the situation there.]

221 MOGGS, DON. Dad's war. Edinburgh: Pentland P, 1994. 213pp., illus.

222 MORDAUNT, ELINOR. This was our life. Hutchinson, 1942. 174pp.

223 PARTRIDGE, FRANCES. A pacifist's war. Hogarth P, 1978. 223pp., illus. [Much on Bloomsbury.]

224 PENN-BULL, BETTY. War letters. Windsor, Berks.: the author, 1991. viii, 248pp., illus.

225 PHELAN, NANCY. The swift foot of time: an Australian in England, 1938–45. Melbourne: Quartet, 1983. 232pp.

226 PICKLES, WILFRED. Between you and me. Werner Laurie, 1949. 223pp., illus. [Popular broadcaster.]

227 PIERCE, DORIS V. Memories of the civilians' war, 1939–45. Temple Pubg., 1996. 137pp., illus.

228 PLUCKWELL, GEORGE. Children of the war: an autobiography. Regency P, 1966. 130pp., illus. [Poet.]

229 PRICHARD, KATHARINE S. Child of the hurricane: an autobiography. Angus & Robertson, 1964. 266pp., illus. [Writer.]

230 PULLEN, DORIS E. (ed.). Wartime memories: a collection of personal memories of the Second World War. Merlin, 1989. 162pp., illus.

231 PYM, BARBARA. A very private eye: an autobiography in letters and diaries, ed. H. Holt and H. Pym. Panther, 1985. xvii, 492pp., illus. [Novelist.]

232 QUENNELL, PETER. The wanton chase: an autobiography from 1939. Collins, 1980. 192pp., illus. [Writer and historian.]

233 RAYMOND, ERNEST. Please you, draw near: autobiography, 1922–68. Cassell, 1969. 179pp., illus. [Writer.]

234 REED, FRANCES. All my teenage years: wartime recollections of events in Oban and London. Oban: the author, 1994. 40pp., illus.

235 Respectfully yours, Annie: letters from a London cook. New York: Dutton, 1942. 230pp.

236 RICHARDS, Sir JAMES M. Memoirs of an unjust fella. Weidenfeld, 1980. 279pp., illus. [Architect.]

237 ROYDE-SMITH, NAOMI. Outside information: a diary of rumours. Macmillan, 1941. vii, 190pp. [Novelist. Diaries, September– October 1940.]

238 SCHIMANSKI, STEFAN K., and TREECE, HENRY (eds.). Leaves in the storm. Lindsay Drummond, 1947. 299pp. [Diaries.]

239 SCHWITZER, JOAN, and THOMPSON, KATHERINE. Children and young people in wartime. Oral Hist., XV (1987) 32–7. [North Londoners in the Second World War.]

240 SHERIDAN, DOROTHY (ed.). Wartime women: an anthology of women's wartime writing for Mass-Observation, 1937–45. Heinemann, 1990. xiv, 267pp. [Contains several contributions from London and suburbs.]

241 SIDDALL, MARGARET. Safe as houses: childhood through the forties. Christow, Devon: Devonshire House, 1995. 192pp., illus. [Dulwich and Peckham.]

242 STAMMER, OLIVE W.(ed.). George, 1940–6: a collection of letters from George Stammer to his sister. Brighton: the editor, 1986. 80pp., illus. [Richmond.]

243 STARK, FREYA. Letters, ed. L. Moorehead. Vol.5, New worlds for old, 1943–6. Salisbury: Russell, 1978. 310pp. [Travel writer.]

244 TIMOLEON [pseud.], ie DARLING, Sir WILLIAM. King's Cross to Waverley. Glasgow: Hodge, 1944. 168pp. [Civil Servant's 'discursive diary'.]

245 VALERY, ANNE. Talking about the war. M. Joseph, 1991. x, 166pp., illus.

246 WALTON, SYDNEY. From the white cottage: letters in war time. Epworth P, 1942. 156pp. [Writer.]

247 WATSON, ELIZABETH. Don't wait for it; or, impressions of war, 1939–41, ed. Felicia France. Imperial War Museum, 1994. iii, 57pp., illus. [Accompanied exhibition of the artist's work, and contains autobiographical account of her ambulance driving experience.]

248 WAUGH, ALEC. The best wine last: an autobiography through the years 1932–69. Allen, 1978. v, 319pp., illus. [Writer.]

249 WESTALL, ROBERT (comp.). Children of the Blitz: memories of wartime childhood. Oxford: Clio, 1989. 241pp., illus.

250 WEYMOUTH, ANTHONY. Journal of the war years, 1939–45, and one year later. Worcester: Littlebury, 1948. 2 vols. [Real name Ivo Cobb. BBC talks editor, and Harley Street specialist.]

251 WEYMOUTH, A. A psychologist's war-time diary. Longmans, 1940. 300pp.

252 WEYMOUTH, A. Plague year, March 1940–February 1941. Harrap, 1942. 251pp.

253 WHITEING, EILEEN. Some sunny day ... reminiscences of a young wife in the Second World War. Sutton Pub. Libs., 1983. 84pp., illus.

254 WILLMOTT, PHYLLIS. Coming of age in wartime. Peter Owen, 1988. 154pp.

255 WYNDHAM, JOAN. Love lessons: a wartime diary. Love is blue: a wartime diary. Heinemann, 1985, 1986. 2 vols.

# CIVIL DEFENCE

## General

256 CLAXTON, ERIC C. More ways than one of fighting a war: the story of a battle school for Civil Defence and the creation of Casualties Union. Lewes, Sussex: Book Guild, 1990. 128pp., illus.

257 ESSEX COUNTY COUNCIL. A report of the ARP Committee on the organisation and administration of the Civil Defence services with a brief account

of the operations in which they were engaged, 1939–45. Essex County Council, 1947. 29pp. [Includes metropolitan Essex.]

258 EYRE, A.H. Perpetual target: a tribute to the air raid wardens, the firefighters and rescue parties... and ... the ordinary people of South and East London and North West Kent, 1940–45. Welling, Kent: the author, 1946. 42pp.

259 HALDANE, JOHN B.S. ARP. Gollancz, 1938. 296pp.

260 LLOYDS OF LONDON. Lloyds under fire: a tribute to the Civil Defence services of Lloyds, 1938–45. The firm, 1946. 126pp., illus.

261 MINISTRY OF HOME SECURITY. Front line, 1940–1: the official story of the Civil Defence of Britain. HMSO, 1942. 160pp., illus.

262 O'BRIEN, TERENCE H. Civil Defence. (History of the Second World War. UK Civil Ser.). HMSO, 1955. xvii, 729pp., illus.

263 SCOTT, Sir HAROLD. Your obedient servant. Deutsch, 1959. 192pp. [CD Regional Commissioner for the Metropolis.]

264 SHEAD, HERBERT. How to protect your borough against air attacks. Communist Party (Woolwich Branch), 1938. 41pp., illus.

265 SIMEY, T.S., and WILLIAMS, MARY L. The Civil Defence Acts, 1937 and 1939, with a chapter on Civil Defence and financial notes by F.E. Price. Knight, 1939. lii, 384pp.

266 SWANWICK, F.W. ARP (Civil Defence) in the borough of Heston and Isleworth, 1938–45. The author, 1961. 64pp., illus.

267 TICHELAR, MICHAEL. A plan for Lambeth: Labour and Civil Defence, 1938–9. *South London Record,* I (1985) 41–7.

268 TIQUET, STANLEY (comp.). It happened here: the story of Civil Defence in Wanstead and Woodford, 1939–45. Wanstead & Woodford Borough Council, 1948. iv, 83pp., illus.

269 The war in Westminster: a summary report of the work of the city council's Civil Defence and related services, compiled by the city librarian. Westminster City Council, 1945. 16pp.

270 WARBURTON, S. Chingford at war, 1939–45: a record of the Civil Defence and allied services and incidents which occurred in the borough. Chingford Borough Council, 1946. 172pp., illus.

271 WYLD, ROSS. The war over Walthamstow: the story of Civil Defence, 1939–45. Walthamstow Borough Council, 1945. 29pp., illus.

## *Bombing and bomb damage generally*

272 BOARD, CHRISTOPHER. The secret map of the County of London, 1926, and its sequels. *London Topog. Record,* XXVII (1995) 157–80. [Military map later issued as Ordnance Survey street map in 1933 and adapted by German Military Intelligence for aerial attacks.]

273 The bombed buildings of London. *London and*

*Middx. Archaeol. Soc. Trans.*, n.s. IX (1948) 66–80, 100–2.

274 BONE, JAMES. London echoing, with pictures by Muirhead Bone. Cape, 1948. 173pp., illus.

275 DILLON, MARTIN. The enemy within. Doubleday, 1994. xxii, 298pp., illus. [IRA bombs, 1939–94, especially in London.]

276 EAST LONDON ADVERTISER. The roll of honour: civilians from the old Borough of Bethnal Green (and Stepney and Poplar) who gave their lives in the East End between 1939 and 1945. East London Advertiser, 1995. 3 parts. [Reprinted from issues of 4, 11 and 18 May 1995.]

277 EVENING NEWS. Hitler passed this way: four years of bombs. 170 pictures from the London Evening News. Text by W. Crawford Snowden. Assoc. Newspapers, 1945. 96pp., illus.

278 FERRY, JOHN W. (comp.). Panorama of Pinner Village, Middlesex. Pinner Assoc., 1947. 60pp., illus. [Contains map showing bomb sites.]

279 FITZGIBBON, CONSTANTINE. London's burning. Macdonald, 1971. 160pp., illus. [First pubd. New York: Ballantine, 1970.]

280 FREEMAN, LESLIE. The Blitz, 1940–4. *Barnes and Mortlake Hist. Soc. Newsletter,* no.114 (1990) 2–13. [Effects of bombing in Barnes and Mortlake.]

281 HARRISON, ROY. Blitz over Westminster: City of Westminster Civil Defence bomb incident photographs, 1940–4. Westminster Pub. Libs., 1990. 36pp., illus.

282 HILL, WILLIAM T. Buried London. Phoenix House, 1955. 192pp., illus. [Chapters 9–14 deal with bomb damage to London.]

283 HOLDEN, C.H., and HOLFORD, W.G. The City of London: a record of destruction and survival. Archit. P, 1951. 341pp., illus.

284 HOOK, JOHN. The beating of his wings: the air raids on the county borough of Bromley, 1940–45. The author, 1995. 99pp. [Lists incidents, fatalities and their addresses. Coverage of other boroughs follows; further volumes are in preparation.]

285 HOOK, J. Dawn was theirs: London Borough of Camden; the air raids on the former metropolitan boroughs of Hampstead, Holborn and St Pancras, 1940–5. The author, 1997. 121pp.

286 HOOK, J. 'Blow out, you bugles!' Civilian casualties in the City of London 1940–5: a brief history of the raids... The author, 1996. 53pp., illus.

287 HOOK, J. 'The glorious dead': the air raids on the London Borough of Islington, 1940–5. The author, 1996. 100pp., illus.

288 HOOK, J. 'Nor the years condemn': the air raids on the London Metropolitan Borough of Lambeth, 1940–5. 2nd ed. The author, 1997. 113pp., illus.

289 HOOK, J. 'Weep not, ye mourners': the air raids on the London Borough of Tower Hamlets, 1940–5. Chronological listing of the fatal casualties. The author, 1996. 186pp., illus.

290 HOOK, J. 'The angel of death has been abroad': the air raids on the London Borough of Wandsworth. The author, 1997. 2 vols. [Covers Battersea and Wandsworth casualties.]

291 HOOK, J. 'Resolute and undismayed': a listing of the fatal casualties in the City of Westminster... The author, 1997. 3 vols. [Also covers Paddington and St Marylebone.]

292 IMPERIAL WAR GRAVES COMMISSION. 1939–45: civilian war dead in the United Kingdom. Vols. 3–4, London. The Commission, 1957. 2 vols.

293 KENT, WILLIAM. The lost treasures of London. Phoenix House, 1947. x, 150pp., illus.

294 KEVIN, DICK, and POPE, H.G.C. (eds.). Complete guide to London. Devereaux Pubns., 1948. 119pp., illus. [Pp. 66–81: list of important bomb damaged buildings.]

295 LORD MAYOR'S NATIONAL AIR RAID DISTRESS FUND. A survey of the work of the Fund, September 1940–June 1946. The Fund, 1946. 88pp., illus.

296 PERRETT, BRYAN. A history of Blitzkrieg. Hale, 1983. 296pp., illus.

297 PRICE, ALFRED. Blitz on Britain: the bomber attacks on the United Kingdom, 1939–45. Shepperton, Middx.: Allan, 1977. 192pp., illus.

298 Report of the repair of war damage in Battersea caused during the years 1940–5. Battersea Metropolitan Borough Council, 1948. 11pp., illus.

299 RICHARDS, JAMES M. (ed.). The bombed buildings of Britain: a record of architectural casualties, 1940–5. 2nd edn. Archit. P, 1947. 202pp., illus. [First pubd. 1942.]

300 THE TIMES. The City of London after the air raids. Times Pubg. Co., 1945. 4pp., illus. [Reprinted from The Times August 7 1945.]

301 TRENCH, RICHARD. London before the Blitz. Weidenfeld, 1989. 190pp., illus. [With descriptions and photographs of war damage.]

302 WALLER, JANE, and VAUGHAN-REES, MICHAEL. Blitz: the civilian war, 1940–5. Optima, 1990. xii, 339pp., illus.

## The 1940–41 blitz

303 ABBOTT, CHRISTINE. The Blitz: September 7 1940, 4.30 p.m. *East London Hist. Soc. Newsletter,* No. 6 (1994) 4–5. [In Poplar.]

304 AGAR, HERBERT. Britain alone: June 1940–June 1941. Bodley Head, 1972. 227pp.

305 BELL, REGINALD W. The bull's eye: a tale of the London target. Cassell, 1943. 94pp. [Air attacks on East End, 1940–1.]

306 BERMANT, CHAIM. Point of arrival: a study of London's East End. Methuen, 1975. 292pp., illus. [Useful chapter on the Blitz.]

307 BIRCH, R.T.W. The family row. *Woolwich and District F.H.S.,* No. 60 (1995) 8–11. [Brockley in the Blitz.]

308 The Blitz. *Images of War,* I no.3 (1994) 57–84.

309 BLOCH, HOWARD (ed.). Black Saturday: the first day of the Blitz. East London memories of September 7th 1940. THAP Books, 1984. 35pp., illus.

310 BOWEN, ELIZABETH. 'London, 1940'. In Collected Impressions (Longmans, 1950) pp. 217–20. [Oxford Street on the morning after a raid.]

311 BRAMLEY, EDWARD T. Bombers over London. Communist Party of G.B., 1940. 14pp., illus.

312 BRITTAIN, VERA. England's hour: an impression of civilian life under fire. Macmillan, 1941. xvi, 301pp. [Writer.]

313 BUGGINS, JOANNE. 1940: Londoners underground. MHQ: Quarterly Jour. of Milit. Hist., VI (1994) 54–61.

314 CALDER, ANGUS. The myth of the Blitz. Cape, 1991. xvi, 302pp., illus.

315 CARTER, ERNESTINE (ed.). Grim glory: pictures of Britain under fire. Lund Humpries, 1941. 109pp., illus.

316 CHISNALL, CHARLES. Beyond the High-Bob. East London Record, no.16 (1993) 2–8. [Poplar High Street during the Blitz.]

317 CHRISP, PETER. The Blitz. Brighton, Sussex: Mass-Observation Archive, 1987. 26pp., illus. [For schools.]

318 COLLIER, RICHARD. The city that wouldn't die: London, May 10–11 1941. Collins, 1959. 256pp., illus.

319 CROSS, ARTHUR, and TIBBS, FRED. The London Blitz, ed. M. Seaborne. Nishen, 1987. 31pp.

320 CROSSLAND, JOHN F. 1940: the scars of war. Illus. London News, CCLXXVIII (1990) 28–31.

321 FARSON, NEGLEY. Bomber's moon. Gollancz, 1941. 160pp.

322 FAVIELL, FRANCES. A Chelsea concerto. Cassell, 1959. ix, 259pp. [Chelsea during the Blitz. Author was a nurse.]

323 FISK, NICHOLAS. Pig ignorant. Walker Books, 1992. 117pp. [The Blitz in London.]

324 FITZGIBBON, CONSTANTINE. The Blitz, with drawings by Henry Moore. Wingate, 1957. xv, 272pp., illus.

325 FORBES-ROBERTSON, DIANA, and CAPA, ROBERT. The battle of Waterloo Road. New York: Random House, 1941. 124pp. [The Blitz in Lambeth.]

326 GREEN, MICHAEL (ed.). On the Home Front: shelling of London memories, 1940s. Wymondham, Norfolk: Stylus P, 1994. 55pp., illus.

327 GREER, DAY (ed.). London's burning: the Blitz, memories. Stylus Pubns., 1991. 36pp., illus.

328 HAISMAN, MERVYN, and SNELLGROVE, WILLIAM E. 'Dear Merv....Dear Bill'. Llandysul, Cardigs.: Gomer P, 1992. 173pp., illus. [Letters on the Blitz between two schoolboys in South East London, 1939–41.]

329 HARRISSON, TOM. Living through the Blitz. Collins, 1976. 372pp. [Much from Mass-Observation archives.]

330 HARVEY, A.D. Local authorities and the Blitz. Contemporary Rev., CCLVII (1990) 197–201. [London boroughs.]

331 HEWITT, KENNETH. The physical and cultural devastation of 'The Blitz'. Geog. Mag., LXII (May 1990) 10–13.

332 HILL, MAUREEN. The London Blitz, September 1940–May 1941. Chapmans, 1990. 234pp., illus.

333 HOUGH, CHRISTINE. Killed in the Blitz. Hackney Terrier, no.32 (1993) 5–6. [Coronation Avenue, Stoke Newington.]

334 JACKSON, ROBERT. The London blitz. Museum of London, 1990. 16pp., illus.

335 JOHNSON, DAVID. The City ablaze: the second great fire of London, 29th December 1940. Kimber, 1980. 217pp., illus.

336 JONES, SYDNEY R. London triumphant. Studio, 1942. 278pp.

337 LEE, ASHER. Blitz on Britain. Four Square Books, 1960. 159pp.

338 LEWEY, FRANK R. Cockney campaign. Paul, 1944. 144pp. [Stepney, 1940–1, by the mayor.]

339 MILLER, ALEXANDER. Inquest on bombardment: a pacifist account of the bombing of East London. Grindlay & Smith, 1940. 4pp. [Reprinted from Peace Commentary no. 53 (12 December 1940).]

340 MURROW, EDWARD R. This is London. Cassell, 1941. 278pp. [Reporter for CBS. Served as fire-watcher.]

341 NEVILLE, JOHN. The Blitz: London then and now, intro. by T. Hopkinson. Hodder, 1990. 128pp., illus.

342 PARK, KEITH R. Background to the Blitz. Hawker Siddeley Rev., IV no.4 (1951) 100–2.

343 PARSONS, FREDERICK. One boy's heroes. Longfield, Kent: Blue Bird Pubns., 1995. 184pp., illus. [The Blitz in South London.]

344 PASMORE, STEPHEN. Memories of the Blitz in Kensington. Kensington Soc. Annual Rept. (1990–1) 32–3.

345 PERRY, COLIN. Boy in the Blitz: the 1940 diary of Colin Perry. Farnham Common, Surrey: the author, 1980. 222pp., illus.

346 PONTING, CLIVE. 1940: myth and reality. Hamilton, 1990. 263pp., illus.

347 POPE-HENNESSY, JAMES. History under fire: fifty-two photographs of air raid damage to London buildings, 1940–1. Batsford, 1941. viii, 117pp., illus. [Photographs by Cecil Beaton.]

348 POSTGATE, RAYMOND W. Glimpses of the Blitz, ed. J. Postgate. Hist. Today, XLIII (1993) 21–8. [Postgate's wartime correspondence with U.S. publisher Alfred Knopf.]

349 RAMSEY, WINSTON (ed.). The Blitz — then and now. Battle of Britain Prints Internat., 1987–90. 3 vols., illus.

350 RAY, JOHN. The night blitz, 1940–1. Arms &

Armour, 1996. 288pp., illus.

351 RECKITT, BEATRICE. Stepney letters: extracts from letters written from Stepney during the Blitz of 1940–1. Milnthorpe: the author, for private circulation, 1991. 46pp., illus.

352 REYNOLDS, QUENTIN J. A London diary. New York: Angus & Robertson, 1941. 249pp. [Originally pubd. New York: Random House, 1941.]

353 REYNOLDS, Q. J. The wounded don't cry. Only the stars are neutral. Cassell, 1941, 1942. 2 vols. [War correspondent in 1940–1.]

354 ROBBINS, GORDON. Fleet Street Blitzkrieg diary. Benn, 1944. 64pp.

355 RODGER, GEORGE. The Blitz: the photography of George Rodger, intro. by T. Hopkinson. Viking, 1990. 176pp., illus.

356 ROGERS, JOAN A. Memories of Homerton recalled. *Cockney Ancestor,* No.62 (1994) 50–2. [Sutton Place and the author's memories of the Blitz.]

357 ROTHNIE, NIALL. The Baedeker Blitz: Hitler's attack on Britain's historic cities. Shepperton, Middx.: Allan, 1992. 144pp., illus.

358 SANSOM, WILLIAM. The Blitz: Westminster at war. Oxford: OUP, 1990. xv, 213pp., illus. [First pubd. Faber, 1947 as Westminster in War.]

359 SAVA, GEORGE. They stayed in London. Faber, 1941. xv, 231pp.

360 SCHALL, GABRIELLE. Bombed out in Wandsworth. *Wandsworth Historian,* no. 57 (1989) 21–2.

361 SCHWEITZER, PAMELA (ed.). Londoners remember living through the Blitz. Age Exchange, 1991. 56pp., illus.

362 STEELE, JESS (ed.). A working class war: tales from two families. Deptford Forum Pubg., 1995. iv, 116pp., illus. [The Welch and Shingler families in the South London Blitz.]

363 THOMAS, CAMERON. Remembering the Blitz. *Nat. Geographic,* CLXXX (July 1991) 60–77 [Author was 16 in 1940.]

364 THOMPSON, LAURENCE. 1940: year of legend, year of history. Collins, 1966. 254pp.

365 VINCENT, SAM. Memories of the Blitz. *Cockney Ancestor,* no. 31 (1986) 18–21.

366 WICKS, BEN. Waiting for the All Clear: true stories from survivors of the Blitz. Bloomsbury, 1990. 209pp., illus.

367 WILSON, HERBERT A. Death over Haggerston: an account of the adventures that befell some East Londoners, 1940–1... Mowbray, 1941. 157pp.

368 WOON, BASIL. Hell came to London: a reportage of the Blitz during 14 days. Davies, 1941. ix, 211pp.

## The 'little blitz' and V-weapons, 1944–5

369 BAKER, RICHARD B. The year of the buzz bomb: a journal of London, 1944. New York: Exposition, 1952. 118pp.

370 BATES, HERBERT E. Flying bombs over England, ed. B. Ogley. Westerham, Kent: Froglets Pubns., 1994. 160pp., illus. [Written in 1944 but censored.]

371 BLAKE, LEWIS. Bolts from the blue: South East London and Kent under V2 rocket attack. The author, 1990. ii, 90pp., illus.

372 CALVERT, PETER W. (comp.). Tottenham Grammar School V2, 15 March 1945. The compiler, 1995. 16pp., illus.

373 COLLIER, BASIL. The battle of the V-weapons, 1944–5. Hodder, 1964. 191pp.

374 COLLYER, D.G. (comp.). Buzz bomb diary. Deal, Kent: Kent Aviation Hist. Research Soc., 1994. x, 182pp., illus. [In Kent.]

375 COOKSLEY, PETER G. Flying bomb. Hale, 1979. 208pp., illus.

376 DORNBERGER, WALTER. V2. Hurst & Blackett, 1954. 264pp.

377 FLINT, PETER, and FLINT, IRIS. Bourne doodlebugs. Bourne Soc., 1994. 24pp., illus. [V1 offensive in South East Surrey.]

378 HOME OFFICE. CIVIL DEFENCE DEPARTMENT. INSPECTOR GENERAL'S BRANCH. Flying bomb incident at Lewisham on 28th July 1944: a complete report on the conduct of Civil Defence operations. Home Office, 1946. 93pp., illus. [With photographs of damage.]

379 IRVING, DAVID. The mare's nest. Kimber, 1964. 320pp. [Flying bombs.]

380 JOHNSON, DAVID. V for vengeance: the second battle of London. Kimber, 1981. 203pp., illus.

381 LONGMATE, NORMAN. The doodlebugs: the story of the flying bombs. Hutchinson, 1981. 549pp., illus.

382 LONGMATE, N. Hitler's rockets: the story of the V2s. Hutchinson, 1985. 422pp., illus.

383 MUNDAY, RAYMOND. The summer of the doodlebugs. *Lewisham Hist. Jour.,* No.2 (1994) 47–53. [V1 rockets over Lewisham.]

384 NEWMAN, BERNARD. They saved London. Laurie, 1952. 192pp. [From flying bombs.]

385 OGLEY, BOB. Doodlebugs and rockets. Westerham, Kent: Froglets Pubns., 1992. 208pp., illus. [London and the South East.]

386 STEELE, JESS (ed.). Rations and rubble: remembering Woolworth's, Britain's worst V2 disaster, New Cross Road, 25 November 1944. Deptford Forum Pubg., 1994. 55pp., illus. [Cassette of interviews '50 years on: remembering Woolworth's' produced by Deptford Community Radio Project, also available from same publisher.]

387 Streatham's 41, with an introduction by Sir Ernest Gowers. South London Motors, 1945. 50pp., illus. [Civil Defence service's work in flying bomb incidents.]

388 YOUNG, RICHARD A. The flying bomb. Shepperton, Middx.: Allan, 1978. 160pp., illus.

## ARP work

389 BOURNE, DOROTHEA ST H. They also serve. Winchester Pubns., 1947. viii, 226pp., illus. [Pp. 156–75: the rescue dogs of London.]

390 BURY, ADRIAN. Dusk to dawn: letters by a warden. Constable, 1941. xi, 216pp.

391 DEAR, NORA. Some wartime ARP memories. *Pinner Local Hist. Soc. Newsletter,* No. 68 (1995) 6–7.

392 EKPENYON, E.I. Some experiences of an African air raid warden. Sheldon P, 1943. 14pp.

393 GREENE, GRAHAM. Ways of escape. Penguin, 1980. 237pp. [Pp. 79–88 describe his experiences as an Air Raid Warden in Bloomsbury, 1940–1.]

394 HULL, W.E. Diary extracts. In Private words: letters and diaries from the Second World War, ed. R. Blythe (Viking, 1991) pp. 254–7. [He was Chief Air Raid Officer for Paddington. The full diary in in the IWM Department of Documents.]

395 KNOWLDEN, PATRICIA. The long alert. The author, 1988. 46pp., illus. [ARP service in Bromley.]

396 NIXON, BARBARA. Raiders overhead: a diary of the London Blitz. Scolar, Gulliver, 1980. 176pp., illus. [Air raid warden's diary. First pubd. Lindsay Drummond, 1943.]

397 STRACHEY, JOHN. Post D: some experiences of an air raid warden. Gollancz, 1941. 135pp. [Author's experiences, but fictionalised. Also pubd. New York: Random House, 1941 as Digging for Mrs Miller.]

398 THE TIMES. When the sirens sounded: an account of Air Raid Precautions in Printing House Square. The newspaper, 1949. 99pp., illus. [The Times' headquarters.]

399 WALKER, DOUGLAS. At war with Alice. Ilfracombe, Devon: Stockwell, 1993. 100pp., illus. [Air raid wardens' anecdotes.]

400 WOOLVEN, ROBIN. Air raid precautions in St Pancras, 1935–45: the borough against the German Air Force. *Camden Hist. Rev.,* XVI (1989) 20–5.

401 WOOLVEN, R. Air raid precautions and London government, 1935–45. *MA (London Studies) dissertation,* The author, 1988. 72ff. [For Birkbeck College.]

## Firefighting

402 BETTS, BEN. Heroes with grimy faces: authentic cartoons of life in the Fire Service and the lighter side of the Blitz. Pearson, 1941. 32pp.

403 BLACK, TOM. The bells go down: the diary of a London AFS man, ed. S. Black. Methuen, 1942. 175pp., illus. [The Auxiliary Fire Service in the East End, formed basis for film of same name.]

404 BLACKSTONE, GEOFFREY V. A history of the British fire service. Routledge, 1957. 483pp., illus.

405 DEMARNE, CYRIL. The London Blitz: a fireman's tale. Battle of Britain Prints Internat., 1991. 156pp., illus.

406 FIREBRACE, Sir AYLMER. Fire service memories. Andrew Melrose, 1949. xiv, 299pp., illus. [Including wartime London.]

407 HOLLISS, BARRY R. 37 Fire Force: fire and rescue, South East London. Enthusiasts Pubns., 1988. 186pp. [Fire service in South East London, 1941–5.]

408 HOLLISS, B. R. The forgotten front line: Station 40, New Cross. Enthusiasts Pubns., 1989. xv, 294pp., illus. [Auxiliary Fire Service and National Fire Service in South London.]

409 INGHAM, H.S. (ed.). Fire and water: the London firefighters' Blitz, 1940–2, remembered. 1992. 220pp., illus. [Reminiscences of London Auxiliary Fire Service.]

410 LONDON COUNTY COUNCIL. Fire over London: the story of the London fire service, 1940–1. Hutchinson, for LCC, 1941. 32pp., illus. [A facsimile reprint was published by the Imperial War Museum in 1995.]

411 LONDON FIRE BRIGADE. Firefighters of London in action. New York: Garden City, 1941. ix, 49pp.

412 LONDON FIRE AND CIVIL DEFENCE AUTHORITY. On the waterfront: the work of the London Fire Brigade River Service. The authority, 1989. 23pp., illus.

413 LONDON FIRE AND CIVIL DEFENCE AUTHORITY. Under fire: the Blitz remembered. The authority, 1990. 40pp., illus. [Fire Brigade.]

414 RADFORD, FREDERICK H. 'Fetch the engine': the official history of the Fire Brigades' Union. The Union, 1951. 192pp., illus.

415 RICHARDSON, MAURICE L. London's burning. Hale, 1941. vii, 184pp. [A fireman in the Blitz.]

416 SANDALL, ALAN G. Are you 17? Frome, Som.: the author, 1993. 173pp., illus. [Firefighting during the Blitz in London and Reading.]

417 SANSOM, WILLIAM, and others. Jim Braidy: the story of Britain's firemen, illustrated by the work of fireman artists. Drummond, 1943. 64pp., illus. [Features London.]

418 STEDMAN, HENRY W. The battle of the flames: the personal story of the London bombing as seen by one Auxiliary Fireman. Jarrolds, 1942. 80pp.

419 WALLINGTON, NEIL. Firemen at war: the work of London's firefighters in the Second World War. Newton Abbot, Devon: David & Charles, 1981. 222pp., illus.

420 WASSEY, MICHAEL. Ordeal by fire: the story and lesson of fire over Britain and the battle of the flames. Secker, 1941. 192pp., illus.

421 WHILE, JACK. Fire! Fire! A story of firefighting in peace and war. Muller, 1944. 168pp., illus.

## Air raid shelters

422 BANCROFT, PETER. The railway to King William Street and Southwark deep tunnel air-raid shelter. Woking, Surrey: the author, 1981. 29pp., illus.

423 BUGGINS, JOANNE. An appreciation of the shelter photographs taken by Bill Brandt in 1940. *Imperial War Museum Rev.,* IV (1989) 32–42.

424 COMMUNIST PARTY OF GB. LONDON DISTRICT COMMITTEE. ARP for Londoners: in the opinion of the experts only the tunnel scheme can give real protection. Communist Party London District, 1939. 16pp.

425 CONWAY, PETER. Living tapestry. Staples P, 1946. 214pp. [Shelter life during the air raids.]

426 DARBY, MADGE (ed.). The Hermitage shelter minutes, December 1940. Hist. of Wapping Trust, 1990. 16pp., illus. [Minutes kept by shelter committee at Hermitage Steam Wharf shelter.]

427 DUNNE, LAURENCE R. Report of an enquiry into the accident at Bethnal Green Tube Station shelter on 3 March 1943. HMSO, 1945. 34pp. [Cmd. 6583. Contains table of shelter accommodation available in Bethnal Green area in January 1943.]

428 HORDER, THOMAS J., Baron Horder. Recommendations of Lord Horder's committee regarding the conditions in air raid shelters with special reference to health. HMSO, 1940. 7pp. [Cmd. 6234.]

429 HORDER, T.J., Baron Horder. The modern troglodyte. *Roy. Soc. Arts Jour.,* LXXXIX (1940–1) 365–76. [Public air raid shelters.]

430 KENDALL, DOREEN. The Bethnal Green tube disaster. *East London Record,* no.15 (1992) 27–35. [March 1943.]

431 MASS-OBSERVATION. 'The tube-dwellers'. In The Saturday Book vol.3 (Hutchinson, 1943) pp. 102–12.

432 MEISEL, JOSEPH S. Air raid shelter policy and its critics in Britain before the Second World War. *Twentieth Century British Hist.,* V (1994) 300–19.

433 Ministry of Home Security deep tunnel air raid shelters. The Engineer, (Nov. 27, Dec.4 and 11 1942) 12pp.

434 PENNICK, NIGEL. Bunkers under London. 2nd edn. Cambridge: Electric Traction, 1985. 32pp., illus. [The tubes as air raid shelters.]

435 PIRATIN, PHIL. Our flag stays red. Rev. ed. Lawrence & Wishart, 1978. xvi, 91pp. [Pp. 70–8: Stepney in the war, including protest at the Savoy Hotel as East Enders demanded access to safer air raid shelters.]

436 SEABORNE, MIKE (ed.). Shelters: living underground in the Blitz. Nishen, 1988. 32pp., illus. [Photographs by Bill Brandt.]

437 TRENCH, RICHARD, and HILLMAN, ELLIS. London under London. Murray, 1985. 224pp., illus. [Includes underground shelters.]

## *Welfare services*

438 CHAMBERS, ROSALIND C. 'A study of three voluntary organisations'. In Social mobility in Britain, ed. D.V. Glass (Routledge, 1954) pp. 383–46. [Including WVS]

439 CHASE, MARGARET. Never too late. San Francisco, Calif.: Ausonia, 1983. 224pp., illus. [American Red Cross work.]

440 FREUD, ANNA. Infants without families, and, Reports on the Hampstead nurseries, 1939–45. Hogarth P, 1974. xxx, 681pp.

441 Friends in need: the story of the the British War Relief Society of America, 1939–45. HMSO, 1947. 75pp., illus.

442 GRAVES, CHARLES P.R. Women in green: the story of the Women's Voluntary Service. Heinemann, 1948. x, 284pp., illus.

443 LEWIS, LORNA. Tea and hot bombs. Oxford: OUP, 1943. 192pp., illus. [A canteen volunteer.]

444 RIDGE, ALAN D. The County of London's rest centre service, 1939–45, and its archives. *Jour. Soc. Archivists,* I no.4 (1956) 104–8.

445 SEGAL, CHARLES S. Backward children in the making. Muller, 1949. xi, 172pp., illus.

446 STREATFEILD, NOEL. 'Tea on a mobile'. In Tea on service (Tea Centre, 1947) pp. 53–62. [Author's experiences on WVS mobile canteens in London.]

447 WILSON, ROGER C. Quaker relief: an account of the relief work of the Society of Friends, 1940–8. Allen & Unwin, 1952. 373pp., illus. [Includes the work of the Friends' Relief Service's evacuation and hostel work.]

## EVACUATION OF CIVILIANS

448 BARBER, PHYLLIS, and others. 'Where's your horns': people of Spitalfields talk about the evacuation. Spitalfields Books, 1979. 56pp., illus.

449 BARNETT HOUSE. London children in war time Oxford: a survey of social and educational results of evacuation. Oxford: OUP, for Barnett House, 1947. xi, 113pp.

450 BAUM, JEFFREY, and BAUM, BARBARA. Never before, never again: evacuation, 1939. *Heritage,* no.4 (1992) 58–96.

451 BODY, ALFRED H. Children in flight: some pictures of the evacuation. London UP, 1940. 95pp., illus.

452 BREED, BRYAN. I know a rotten place. Arlington, 1975. vi, 117pp. [Memories of evacuation.]

453 BROWN, R. DOUGLAS. East Anglia, 1939. Lavenham, Suffolk: Dalton, 1980. viii, 200pp., illus. [Pp. 164–175 on London evacuees. Later volumes by same author on East Anglia 1940–5 (pubd. 1981–94) also contain material on evacuees in the area.]

454 CHARLTON, CONSTANCE. Goodbye home: an account of the evacuation of the Stubbs family from 12 De Beauvoir Square, N.1, on 1 September 1939. The author, 1989. 30pp.

455 CHRISP, PETER. Evacuation. Brighton, Sussex: Mass-Observation Archive, 1987. 20pp., illus. [For schools.]

456 CROSBY, TRAVIS L. The impact of civilian evacuation in the Second World War. Croom Helm, 1986. 176pp. [Concentrates on London cases.]

457   HOLMAN, BOB. The evacuation: a very British revolution. Oxford: Lion, 1995. 192pp., illus.

458   INGLIS, RUTH. The children's war: evacuation, 1939–45. Collins, 1989. x, 178pp., illus.

459   ISAACS, SUSAN (ed.). The Cambridge evacuation survey. Methuen, 1941. x, 235pp. [Includes case histories of London evacuees.]

460   JACKSON, CARLTON. Who will take our children? The story of the evacuation in Britain, 1939–45. Methuen, 1985. xxi, 217pp., illus.

461   JOHNSON, BRIAN S.(ed.). The evacuees. Gollancz, 1968. 288pp., illus.

462   KOBRIN, JANET S. Please, teacher, may we go on with the air raid? London children during the Blitz and evacuation of the Second World War. *Pennsylvania Univ. MA thesis,* 1989. 106ff.

463   NATIONAL FEDERATION OF WOMEN'S INSTITUTES. Town children through country eyes: a survey of evacuation. Dorking, Surrey: the Federation, 1940. 23pp.

464   PADLEY, RICHARD, and COLE, MARGARET (eds.). Evacuation survey: a report to the Fabian Society. The Society, 1940. viii, 296pp.

465   POOLEY, RICHARD P. The evacuee. Hull: Anglo-American Pub. Services, 1972. 54pp. [Experiences.]

466   RICHARDSON, JOY (ed.). Children in retreat: an anthology of evacuee stories. Sittingbourne, Kent: SAWD, 1990. 131pp., illus.

467   RILEY, DENISE. War in the nursery: theories of the child and mother. Virago, 1983. vi, 250pp., illus.

468   SAMWAYS RICHARD (ed.). We think you ought to go: an account of the evacuation of children from London during the Second World War, based on the original records of the London County Council. GLRO, 1995. 56pp., illus.

469   SCHWEITZER, PAMELA, and others (eds.). Goodnight children everywhere: memories of evacuation in the Second World War. Age Exchange, 1990. 256pp., illus.

470   STRACHEY, AMY. Borrowed children: a popular account of some evacuation problems and their remedies. Murray, 1940. xiv, 134pp.

471   TACK, DORA K. From bombs to buckets: Brixton to Papworth St Agnes, 1940–8. Wyton, Hunts.: King's Music, 1989. 147pp., illus.

472   WICKS, BEN. No time to wave goodbye. Bloomsbury, 1988. 288pp., illus.

473   WICKS, B. The day they took the children. Bloomsbury, 1989. 176pp., illus.

474   WOLF, KATHERINE M. Evacuation of children in wartime. *Psychoanalytic Study of the Child,* I (1945) 389–404. [Bibliography of psychological studies.]

475   WOMEN'S GROUP ON PUBLIC WELFARE. Our towns: a close-up. A study made in 1939–42. Oxford: OUP, 1943. xx, 143pp. [Evacuation.]

## The Military Presence

### Regular troops

476   BALY, MONICA E. A ringside view of the Battle of Britain, 15th September 1940. *Hist. Nursing Soc. Jour.,* III (1990) 58–9.

477   BATES, LEONARD M. When Wrens defended the Thames. *Port of London,* LXX (1995) 12–13.

478   CLUETT, DOUGLAS, and others. Croydon airport and the Battle for Britain, 1939–40. Sutton Libraries & Arts Service, 1984. x, 166pp., illus.

479   COLLIER, BASIL. The defence of the United Kingdom. *(History of the Second World War. UK Milit. Ser.).* HMSO, 1957. xix, 557pp., illus.

480   COOKSLEY, PETER G. Croydon airport flypast. Sutton Libs. and Arts Service, 1984. 44pp., illus.

481   CORBELL, PETER. RAF Hornchurch. *Air Britain Digest,* III no. 9 (1951) 1–4, no. 10 (1951) 6–8.

482   DYSON, STEPHEN W. Twins in tanks: East End brothers in arms, 1943–5. Leo Cooper, with Imperial War Museum, 1994. 207pp., illus.

483   HALPENNY, BRUCE B. Action stations. 8, Military airfields of Greater London. Cambridge: Stephens, 1984. 248pp., illus.

484   HOCKIN, JOHN. The air defence of the Port of London: number one target for the Luftwaffe. *P.L.A. Monthly,* XX no.235 (1945) 59–61; no.236 (1945) 76–8; no.237 (1945) 90–2; no. 238 (1945) 110–11.

485   HOGBEN, ARTHUR. Design to kill: a history of bomb disposal in Britain. Wellingborough, Northants.: Stephens, 1987. 256pp., illus. [Royal Engineers.]

486   HUNT, H.J. Bombs and booby traps, ed. P. Swadling. Romsey, Hants.: Romsey Medal Centre, 1986. viii, 148pp., illus. [Experiences of a bomb disposal officer.]

487   JONES, R.V. Most secret war. H. Hamilton, 1978. xx, 556pp., illus. [Scientific intelligence work.]

488   LEWIS, J.H. London diary — 1940. *Air Britain Digest,* V no.5 (1953) 7–10.

489   LOWRY, BERNARD (ed.). Twentieth century defences in Britain. Council for British Archaeol., 1995. xii, 145pp., illus.

490   MARCHANT, HILDE. Women and children last: a woman reporter's account of the Battle of Britain. Gollancz, 1941. 190pp.

491   PILE, Sir FREDERICK. Ack-Ack: Britain's defence against air attack during the Second World War. Harrap, 1949. 410pp., illus.

492   PRESTON, DIANA. D-Day and the Thames. *Port of London,* LIX (1984) 97–9.

493   ROYAL AIR FORCE COMFORTS COMMITTEE. Farewell Berkeley Square: a survey of the work of the Royal Air Force Comforts Committee, October 1939 to June 1946. Air Ministry, 1946. 28pp., illus.

494   SAUNDERS, HILARY A.ST G. The Battle of Britain. Wingate-Butler, 1969. 144pp., illus. [Official history pubd. HMSO, 1941, Saunders later

identified as author. This compilation also includes selections from Luftwaffe war diaries.]

495 SMITH, GRAHAM. Essex airfields in the Second World War. Newbury, Berks.: Countryside Books, 1996. 287pp., illus.

496 SUTTON, H.T. Raiders approach! The fighting tradition of RAF Station Hornchurch and Sutton's Farm. Aldershot, Hants.: Gale & Polden, 1956. 181pp., illus.

497 TAYLOR, GORDON. London's Navy: a story of the Royal Naval Volunteer Reserve. Quiller P, 1983. 176pp., illus.

498 TOWNSEND, PETER. Duel of eagles. Weidenfeld, 1970. xvii, 455pp., illus. [Battle of Britain. Sequel, Duel in the dark, pubd. Harrap, 1986.]

499 WAR OFFICE AND AIR MINISTRY. Roof over Britain: the official story of Britain's anti-aircraft defences, 1939–42. HMSO, 1943. 88pp., illus. [Pp. 48–54: the great London barrage.]

500 WILSON, EUNICE. Dangerous sky: resource guide to the Battle of Britain. Westport, Conn.: Greenwood P, 1995. xxvii, 128pp., illus.

501 WILTON, ERIC. Crew Centre: a memory of the Royal Observer Corps. Royal Observer Corps Centre, Bromley, 1946. 84pp., illus.

502 WINSLOW, T.E. Forewarned is forearmed: a history of the Royal Observer Corps. Hodge, 1948. 290pp., illus.

## The Home Guard

503 BRUMBY, A.F. (ed.). The book of Number 2 Platoon A Company 1st City of London Home Guard. Causton, 1945. 47pp., illus. [Responsible for the Temple area.]

504 FINE, SIMON. With the Home Guard. Alliance P, 1943. 78pp.

505 GRAVES, CHARLES P.R. The Home Guard of Britain. Hutchinson, 1943. 364pp. [Includes much on London battalions.]

506 HOPKINS, A.W. Home Guard 'Utility': a history of the 22nd (5th G.P.O.) City of London Battalion, Home Guard. Flint & Co. (printer), 1944. 96pp.

507 LDV (pseud.). The Bromley Home Guard: a history of the 51st Kent Battalion. n.p., 1945(?). v, 80pp., illus.

508 LONDON PASSENGER TRANSPORT BOARD. Seven battalions: the story of London Transport's Home Guard, 1940–6. The Board, 1947. 128pp., illus.

509 LONDON TRANSPORT BOARD. A history of the 44th London (London Transport) Battalion of the Home Guard, 1940–6. The Board, 1948. 36pp., illus.

510 LONGMATE, NORMAN. The real Dad's Army: the story of the Home Guard. Hutchinson, 1974. 128pp., illus.

511 MACKENZIE, COMPTON. Keep the Home Guard turning. Chatto, 1943. 214pp.

512 MACKENZIE, S.P. The Home Guard: a military and political history. Oxford: OUP, 1995. xiv, 262pp., illus.

513 SADLER, STEPHEN. With the Home Guard in East London. East London Hist. Soc. Newsletter, no. 10 (1996) 5–7.

514 STREET, A.G. From dusk till dawn. Oxford: OUP, 1989. 138pp. [Life in the Home Guard. First pubd. Blandford P., 1942.]

515 THOMAS, GARTH. Records of the militia from 1757, including ... Territorials and the Home Guard. (P.R.O. Reader's Guide, 3). P.R.O. Pubns., 1993. 59pp.

516 THOMAS, SAMUEL E. (comp.). Laughs with the Home Guard. Harrap, 1942. 47pp., illus.

517 WHITTAKER, L.B. Stand down! Orders of battle for the units of the Home Guard of the UK, November 1944. Newport, Gwent: Ray Westlake Milit. Books, 1990. 153pp. [Identifies whereabouts of all the units.]

518 YELTON, D.K. British public opinion, the Home Guard, and the defense of Great Britain, 1940–4. Jour. Milit. Hist., LVIII (1994) 461–80.

## Allied forces

519 GARDINER, JULIET. 'Over here': the GIs in wartime Britain. Collins & Brown, 1992. 224pp., illus.

520 KAYE, PATRICIA. Under an English heaven. Pen & Ink Graphics (printers), 1993. 10pp., illus. [No.1 Auxiliary Hospital, Australian Imperial Forces, at Harefield, Middx.]

521 LONGMATE, NORMAN. The GIs: Americans in Britain, 1942–5. Hutchinson, 1975. xv, 416pp., illus.

522 McELHERAN, BROCK. V-bombs and weathermaps: reminiscences of World War II. Montreal: McGill-Queen's UP, 1995. xvii, 199pp., illus. [With Canadian Forces.]

523 REYNOLDS, DAVID. Rich relations: the American occupation of Britain, 1942–5. HarperCollins, 1995. xiii, 555pp., illus.

524 SIMPICH, FREDERICK. When GI Joe took London. National Geographic, LXXXVI (1944) 337–54.

525 SMITH, GRAHAM. When Jim Crow met John Bull: Black American soldiers in World War Two Britain. Tauris, 1987. 265pp., illus.

526 STACEY, CHARLES P., and WILSON, BARBARA A. The half-million: Canadians in Britain, 1939–46. Toronto: Toronto UP, 1987. xii, 198pp., illus.

527 What a celebration! Correspondence from New Zealand servicemen and servicewomen relating to the New Zealand Forces Club, 4–6 Charing Cross Road. Westminster City Libs., Charing Cross Lib., 1995. 12pp., illus. [Now the Charing Cross Library.]

## Enemy forces

528 BLOEMERTZ, GUNTHER. Heaven next stop: a Luftwaffe fighter pilot at war. Stroud, Glos.: Sutton, 1998. 192pp., illus. [First pubd. Bonn: Europaischer V, 1952 as Der Himmel am nächsten.]

529    BOOG, HORST. 'The Luftwaffe and indiscriminate bombing up to 1942'. In The conduct of the air war in the Second World War: an international comparison, ed. H. Boog (New York: Berg, 1992) pp. 373–404. [Discusses London raids.]

530    CLARKE, NIGEL J. Adolf Hitler's holiday snaps: German aerial reconnaissance photography of London and the Home Counties, 1939–42. Lyme Regis, Dorset: N.J. Clarke Pubns., 1996. 111pp., illus.

531    MURRAY, WILLIAMSON. Luftwaffe. Allen & Unwin, 1985. xii, 324pp., illus.

532    PHILPOTT, BRYAN. German bombers over England: a selection of German wartime photographs. 2nd ed. Wellingborough, Northants.: P. Stephens, 1988. 95pp., illus.

533    WHEATLEY, R. Operation Sea Lion: German plans for the invasion of England, 1939–42. Oxford: Clarendon P, 1958. viii, 201pp., illus.

## OVERSEAS VISITORS

### General

534    BALTHAZAR, HERMAN. L'internationale socialiste: les débats de Londres en 1940–1. Cahiers d'Hist. de la Seconde Guerre Mondiale, V (1973) 191–210.

535    GILLMAN, PETER, and GILLMAN, LENI. 'Collar the lot!' How Britain interned and expelled its wartime refugees. Quartet, 1980. xvi, 334pp., illus.

536    HOOPER, ALEX. Wimbledon's forgotten residents: a Second World War internment camp at Wimbledon. Local Hist., no.19 (1988) 19–20.

537    KOCHAN, MIRIAM. Britain's internees in the Second World War. Macmillan, 1983. xiii, 182pp., illus.

538    MADOL, HANS R. The league of London: a book of interviews with Allied sovereigns and statesmen. Hutchinson, 1942. 141pp., illus.

539    PANAYI, PANIKOS. 'Immigrants, refugees, the British state and public opinion during World War Two'. In War culture: social change and changing experience in World War Two, ed. P. Kirkham and D. Thoms (Lawrence & Wishart, 1995) pp. 201–8.

540    STENT, RONALD. A bespattered page? The internment of His Majesty's 'Most Loyal Enemy Aliens'. Deutsch, 1980. 282pp., illus.

### By nationality, A–Z

#### Belgian

541    BALTHAZAR, HERMAN, and GOTOVITCH, JOSE. Camille Huysmans: documenten. Huysmans in London. Antwerp, Amsterdam: Standaard Wetensch. Uitgeverij, 1978. 268pp.

542    COOLSAET, RIK. Buitenlandse zaken. Leuven: Kritak, 1987. 264pp. [Foreign affairs: Belgian government in London.]

543    GOTOVITCH, JOSE. 'Camille Huysmans et la seconde guerre mondiale: Londres 1940.' In Bijdragen tot het Camille Huysmans-onderzoek (Antwerp: Stichting C. Huysmans, 1971) pp.123–69.

544    GOTOVITCH, J. Camille Huysmans. Gescriften en documenten, 8: De Belgische socialisten en Londen. Antwerp: Standaard Wetersch. Uitgeverij, 1981. ix, 227pp.

545    JONES, ISABELLE. La mission économique belge à Londres (20 juillet–31 décembre 1940): le Baron Boel et l'engagement de la flotte belge dans l'effort de guerre allié. Cahiers d'Hist. de la Seconde Guerre Mondiale, XI (1989) 187–206.

546    LAUREYS, VERONIQUE. The Belgian government in exile in London and the Jewish question during the Second World War. Historical Research, LXVII (1994) 212–23.

547    LOVINFOSSE, GEORGE DE. Au service de Leurs Majestés: histoire secrète des Belges à Londres. Strombeek-Bever: Byblos, 1974. 278pp., illus.

548    SCHEPENS, LUC. De Belgen in Groot-Brittannie, 1940–4. Nijmegen: Gottmer, 1980. 238pp., illus. [Belgian government in exile in London, and other refugees.]

549    SMETS, DORE, and RENS, JEF. Historique du Centre Syndical Belge à Londres, 1941–4. Brussels: F.G.T.B., 1976. 209pp.

#### Chinese

550    CHIANG YEE. The silent traveller in war time. Country Life, 1939. 132pp., illus.

#### Dutch

551    BRAVE-MAKS, MONIKA H. De Koningin in Londen. Zutphen, De Walburg Pers, 1980. 117pp., illus. [London exile of Queen Wilhelmina, 1940–5.]

552    Eenige hoofdpunten van het regeringsbeleid in Londen gedurende de oorlogsjaren, 1940–5. The Hague: Rijksuitgeverij, 1946. 251pp.

553    JONG, L. DE. Koningin Wilhelmina in Londen, 1940–5. Amsterdam: Noord-Hollandsche, 1966. 25pp.

554    NEUMAN, H.J. Impasse te Londen: Nederlands veiligheidsbeleid, 1940–5. Utrecht: Veen, 1990. 302pp.

555    VRIES, LEONARD DE. De Londense Vrij Nederland, een fascinerende selectie uit de jaargangen 1940–5. Laren: Sharabee, 1973. 160pp., illus.

#### French

556    ACCOCE, PIERRE. Les Français à Londres, 1940–1. Paris: Balland, 1989. 342pp.

557    COINTET, MICHELE, and COINTET, JEAN-PAUL. La France à Londres: renaissance d'un état, 1940–3. Brussels: Edns. Complexe, 1990. 271pp.

558    ECK, HELENE (ed.). La guerre des ondes: histoire des radios de langue française pendant la Deuxième Guerre Mondiale. Paris, etc.: Collin, 1985. 382pp. [Including French and Belgian radio stations

operating from London.]

559 MAGUIRE, G.E. Anglo-American policy towards the Free French. Macmillan, 1995. x, 210pp. [Ch. 1, pp. 1–17: De Gaulle in London and the formation of Free France, 1940–2.]

### German

560 GLEES, ANTHONY. Exile politics during the Second World War: the German Social Democrats in Britain. Oxford: Clarendon, 1982. 263pp. [Expanded from his Oxford University DPhil thesis 'The SPD, the Labour party and the Foreign Office: a study of exile politics in London, 1939–45'.]

561 GLEES, A. 'The German political exile in London, 1939–45'. In Exile in Great Britain: refugees from Hitler's Germany, ed. G. Hirschfeld (Leamington Spa, Warwicks.: Berg, for German Hist. Inst., 1984) pp. 83–99. [The SPD and the British Labour Party.]

562 SHERMAN, A.J. Island refuge: Britain and refugees from the Third Reich, 1933–9. 2nd ed. Cass, 1994. 293pp., illus.

563 SPIER, EUGEN. The protecting power. Skeffington, 1951. 252pp. [Anti-Nazi German's experiences of England, including internment.]

564 WOLFF, HELGA. No longer strangers. World of Books, 1995. 168pp., illus. [Student teacher, Jewish refugee.]

### Hungarian

565 TABORI, PAUL. Londoni napls. Sylvan P, 1945. 124pp. [Hungarian refugee, in London during Blitz.]

### Italian

566 COLPI, TERRI. 'The impact of the Second World War on the British Italian community'. In The internment of aliens in 20th century Britain, ed. D. Cesarani and T. Kushner (Cass, 1993) pp. 167–87. [Also in Immigrants and Minorities, XI (1992).]

567 SPONZA, LUCIO. 'The anti-Italian riots, June 1940'. In Racial violence in England, ed. P. Panayi (Leicester: Leicester UP, 1993) pp. 130–48.

### Norwegian

568 KROSBY, VIVIEN. Host to exiles: the Foreign Office and the Norwegian government in London, 1940–5. London Univ. PhD thesis, 1979. 167ff.

569 LEHMKUHL, DIK. Journey to London: the story of the Norwegian government at war. Hutchinson, 1945. 152pp., illus.

570 NYGAARDSVOLD, JOHAN. Norge i krig: London, 1940–5. Oslo: Tiden, 1983. 276pp., illus.

571 RISTE, OLAV. 'London regjeringa': Norge i krigsalliansen, 1940–5. Oslo: Samlaget, 1995. 2 vols. [First pubd. 1973, 1979.]

### Polish

572 DYDYMSKI, LEON. Wplyw jezyka angielskiego na wymowe polska mlodziezy w Londynie. Polski Uniwersytet na Obczyznie, 1970. 44pp. [Poles in London.]

573 KYRIACOU, SAV, and POLISH REMINISCENCE GROUP (eds.). Passport to exile: the Polish way to London. Ethnic Communities Oral Hist. Project, 1988. 40pp., illus. [Text also in Polish: Paszport

na wygnanie.]

574 POLONSKY, ANTHONY B. Polish failure in wartime London: attempts to forge a European alliance, 1940–4. Internat. Hist. Rev., VII (1985) 576–91.

575 RACZYNSKI, EDWARD. In Allied London. Weidenfeld, 1962. xiv, 381pp. [Polish ambassador's memoirs.]

576 SWORD, KEITH, and others. The formation of the Polish community in Great Britain, 1939–50. Schl. of Slavonic & E. European Studies, 1989. 498pp., illus. [Many settled in West London.]

### Portuguese

577 CORTESAO, ARMANDO. Cartas de Londres, 1941–9. Coimbra: Biblioteca general da universidade, 1974. xii, 409pp.

### Spanish

578 CAMBA, JULIO. Londres: impresiones de un espanol. 2nd ed. Madrid: Espasa-Calpe, 1943. 154pp.

### Yugoslav

579 JEVTOVIC, MIROLJUB. Sta kase Radio-London. Beograd: A-S Delo, 1989. 490pp. [BBC's Yugoslav service.]

## THE HOME FRONT: SOCIETY AND MORALE

580 ADAMSON, JOHN, and HUDSON, LEN (eds.). The London Town miscellany. Vol.2, 1939–90. Alexius P, 1993. 283pp., illus. [Selected articles from the LCC Staff Gazette/London Town, including material on evacuation, the Home Guard, rationing, etc.]

581 ALLEN, ELEANOR. Wartime children, 1939–45. Black, 1945. 64pp., illus.

582 BEVERIDGE, Sir WILLIAM. Voluntary action: a report on methods of social advance. Allen & Unwin, 1948. 420pp., illus.

583 BRAYLEY, MARTIN, and INGRAM, RICHARD. World War II British women's uniforms. Windrow & Greene, 1995. 95pp., illus. [Captioned colour photographs.]

584 BRIGGS, SUSAN. The Home Front: war years in Britain, 1939–45. New York: Amer. Heritage Pubg. Co., 1975. 256pp., illus.

585 BRIGGS, S. Keep smiling though. Weidenfeld, 1977. 256pp., illus.

586 BUGGINS, JOANNE. West Indians in Britain during the Second World War. Imperial War Museum Rev., V (1990) 86–97. [Including London.]

587 CARTER, GEORGE G. The Battle of Britain: the Home Front. New York: Mason & Lipscomb, 1974. viii, 279pp.

588 CASSANDRA. The English at war. Secker, 1941. 127pp.

589 CASSIN-SCOTT, JACK. Women at war, 1939–45. Osprey, 1980. 40pp.

590 CHAMBERLIN, E.R. Life in wartime Britain. Batsford, 1972. 190pp., illus.

591   COLE, GEORGE D.H. The war on the Home Front. Fabian Soc., 1941. 15pp.

592   COSTELLO, JOHN. Love, sex and war: changing values, 1939–45. Collins, 1985. 384pp., illus.

593   DOUIE, VERA. Daughters of Britain. Oxford: Ronald, 1950. 159pp., illus. [Women and the war effort.]

594   FERGUSON, SHEILA. Studies in the social services. *(History of the Second World War. UK Civil Ser. gen. ser.).* HMSO, Longmans, 1954. 367pp., illus. [Successor to Titmuss' Problems of Social Policy.]

595   FUSSELL, PAUL. Wartime: understanding and behaviour in the Second World War. New York, London: OUP, 1989. x, 330pp., illus. [Psychological effects in US and UK.]

596   GIBBS, RICHARD. Children at war. Brighton, Sussex: Mass-Observation Archive, 1987. 30pp., illus. [For schools.]

597   GLASS, D.V. Social mobility in Britain. Routledge, 1954. viii, 412pp. [Including effects of the war.]

598   GRAFTON, PETE. You, you and you: the people out of step with World War II. Pluto, 1981. 169pp., illus. [Conscientious objectors, etc.]

599   GREEN, MICHAEL (ed.). Blackouts and rationing and London memories. Wymondham, Norfolk: Stylus P, 1995. 60pp., illus. [From contemporary newspapers, as are following items.]

600   GREEN, M. (ed.). Eleven o'clock Sept. 3 1939: shelters and blackout and London. Wymondham, Norfolk: Stylus P, 1996. 78pp., illus.

601   GREEN, M. (ed.). Families at war and London memories. Wymondham, Norfolk: Stylus P, 1995. 50pp., illus.

602   GREEN, M. (ed.). A London's [sic] childhood and wartime experiences. Wymondham, Norfolk: Stylus P, 1996. 23pp., illus.

603   GREEN, M. (ed.). On the domestic front: London. Wymondham, Norfolk: Stylus P, 1996. 98pp., illus.

604   GREEN, M. (ed.). A thirties childhood. London, the war years. Wymondham, Norfolk: Stylus P, 1996. 66pp., illus.

605   GREEN, M. (ed.). Women at war and London's memories. Wymondham, Norfolk: Stylus P, 1994. 44pp., illus.

606   HARRIS, JOSE. War and social history: Britain and the Home Front during the Second World War. *Contemporary European Hist.,* I (1992) 17–35.

607   HARRISSON, TOM, and MADGE, CHARLES. War begins at home. Chatto, 1940. viii, 425pp. [Mass Observation social surveys to December 1939.]

608   HAYES, DENIS. The challenge of conscience: the COs' story, 1939–49. Allen & Unwin, for Central Board of COs ., 1949. xvi, 406pp. [Conscientious objectors.]

609   ISAACS, SUSAN, and others. Children in wartime. New Education Fellowship, 1940. 80pp.

610   KUSHNER, TONY. The persistence of prejudice: anti-semitism in British society during the Second World War. Manchester: Manchester UP, 1989. ix, 257pp., illus.

611   KUSHNER, T. The Heymishe Front: Jews in wartime Britain. *(Research Papers, 3).* London Museum of Jewish Life, 1992. 16pp.

612   KUSHNER, T. 'Sex and semitism, Jewish women in Britain in war and peace'. In Minorities in wartime, ed. P. Panayi (Leamington Spa, Warwicks.: Berg, 1993) pp. 118–49. [Including wartime London.]

613   LANG, CAROLINE. Keep smiling through: women in the Second World War. Cambridge: CUP, 1989. 48pp.

614   LONGMATE, NORMAN. How we lived then: a history of everyday life during the Second World War. Arrow, 1973. xvi, 568pp., illus.

615   MCDOWELL, COLIN. Forties fashion and the New Look. Bloomsbury, 1997. 192pp., illus. [Includes London fashion world in wartime.]

616   MARSHALL, OLIVER (ed.). The Caribbean at war: 'British' West Indians in World War II. *(North Kensington Community Ser., 5).* North Kensington Archive, 1993. 30pp., illus.

617   MARWICK, ARTHUR. The Home Front: the British and the Second World War. Thames & Hudson, 1976. 192pp., illus.

618   MARWICK, A. 'People's war and top people's peace? British society and the second World War.' In Crisis and controversy, ed. A. Sked and C. Cook (Macmillan, 1976) pp. 148–64.

619   MASS-OBSERVATION. An enquiry into people's homes... *(Change, no.4).* Murray, for Advertising Service Guild, 1943. xxiv, 228pp.

620   MINNS, RAYNES. Bombers and mash: the domestic front, 1939–45. Virago, 1980. 236pp., illus.

621   MOORHEAD, CAROLINE. Troublesome people: enemies of war, 1916–86. Hamilton, 1987. xx, 344pp., illus. [Based on interviews with pacifists and conscientious objectors.]

622   MORDAUNT, ELINOR. Blitz kids. Oxford: OUP, 1941. 160pp., illus.

623   Ourselves in wartime: an illustrated survey of the Home Front in the Second World War. Odhams, 1944. 256pp., illus.

624   PANETH, MARIE. Branch Street: a sociological study. Allen & Unwin, 1944. 128pp., illus. [Social worker's experience in Paddington.]

625   PARKES, JAMES. An enemy of the people: anti-semitism. Harmondsworth, Middx.: Penguin, 1945. 150pp.

626   PARKIN, DIANA J. Contested sources of identity: nation, class and gender in Second World War Britain. *London University PhD thesis,* 1988. 348ff.

627   ROSS, ALAN. The Forties: a period piece. Weidenfeld, 1950. unpagd., illus.

628   SMITH, HAROLD L. (ed.). War and social change:

British society in the Second World War. Manchester: Manchester UP, 1986. xi, 271pp.

629   SMITH, H.L. (ed.). Britain in the Second World War: a social history. Manchester: Manchester UP, 1996. viii, 189pp. [Extracts from contemporary documents, with useful introduction.]

630   SPENDER, STEPHEN. Citizens in war and after. Harrap, 1945. 112pp., illus.

631   SREBRNIK, HENRY. Class, ethnicity and gender intertwined: Jewish women and the East London rent strikes, 1935–40. *Women's History Review,* IV no.3 (1995) 283–99.

632   STAMMERS, NEIL E. Civil liberties in Britain during the Second World War. Croom Helm, 1984. vi, 250pp. [Expanded from his Sussex University DPhil thesis 'Civil liberties in Britain during the Second World War' 1980.]

633   SUMMERFIELD, PENNY. Reconstructing women's wartime lives: discourse and subjectivity in oral histories of the Second World War. Manchester: Manchester UP, 1998. 224pp., illus.

634   SUMMERFIELD, P. 'Approaches to women and social change in the Second World War'. In What difference did the war make? ed. B. Brivati and H. Jones (Leicester: Leicester UP, 1993) pp. 63–79.

635   TITMUSS, RICHARD M. Problems of social policy. Rev. edn. *(History of the Second World War. UK Civil Ser.).* HMSO, 1976. xi, 632pp., illus. [First pubd. 1950.]

636   TITMUSS, R.M., and TITMUSS, KATHLEEN. Parents' revolt. Secker, 1942. 128pp. [Declining birthrate.]

637   TURNER, ERNEST S. The Phoney War on the Home Front. Joseph, 1961. 311pp.

638   What Britain has done, 1939–45. Ministry of Information, 1945. 49pp., illus. [Civilian life.]

## THE ECONOMY

### *General, and labour supply*

639   BRULEY, SUSAN. 'Very happy crows': women in industry in South London in World War Two. *History Workshop,* XLIV (1997) 58–76. [The Old Kent Road.]

640   HANCOCK, WILLIAM K., and GOWING, MARGARET M. British war economy. Rev. edn. *(History of the Second World War. UK Civil Ser.).* HMSO, 1975. xvii, 634pp. [First pubd. 1949.]

641   HARGREAVES, ERIC L., and GOWING, MARGARET M. Civil industry and trade. *(History of the Second World War. UK Civil Ser. gen. ser.).* HMSO, 1952. xii, 678pp.

642   HARRISSON, TOM (ed.). War factory: a report by Mass-Observation. Gollancz, 1943. 127pp.

643   HORNBY, WILLIAM. Factories and plant. *(History of the Second World War. UK Civil Ser. War Production ser.).* HMSO, Longmans, 1958. 421pp.

644   HURSTFIELD, JOEL. The control of raw materials. *(History of the Second World War. UK Civil Ser. War Production ser.).* HMSO, 1953. xv, 530pp.

645   KOHAN, C.M. Works and buildings. *(History of the Second World War. UK Civil Ser.).* HMSO, 1952. xvi, 540pp.

646   MASS-OBSERVATION. People in production: an enquiry into British war production. Murray, 1942. 280pp.

647   MILWARD, ALAN S. War, economy and society 1939–45. Allen Lane, 1977. xiv, 395pp., illus.

648   MINISTRY OF LABOUR AND NATIONAL SERVICE. Manpower, by J.B. Priestley. HMSO, 1944. 60pp., illus. [The mobilisation of civilians.]

649   NICHOLSON, MAVIS (ed.). What did you do in the war, Mummy? Women in World War II. Chatto, 1995. 264pp., illus. [Including a soubrette from the Windmill Theatre, and a Home Intelligence officer.]

650   PARKER, HENRY M.D. Manpower: a study of wartime policy and administration. *(History of the Second World War. UK Civil Ser. gen. ser.).* HMSO, Longmans, 1957. 535pp., illus.

651   POSTAN, MICHAEL M. British war production. *(History of the Second World War. UK Civil Ser.).* HMSO, 1952. xvi, 512pp.

652   ROBB, NESCA. An Ulsterwoman in England, 1924–41. CUP, 1942. viii, 175pp. [Describes attempts to find war work.]

653   SCHWEITZER, PAMELA (ed.). What did you do in the war, mum? Women recall their wartime work. Age Exchange, 1985. 72pp., illus.

654   SCOTT, JOHN D., and HUGHES, RICHARD. The administration of war production. *(History of the Second World War. UK Civil Ser. War Production ser.)* HMSO, Longmans, 1956. 544pp., illus.

655   SUMMERFIELD, PENNY. Women workers in the Second World War. 2nd edn. Routledge, 1989. ix, 214pp., illus. [First pubd. Croom Helm, 1984.]

656   THOMAS, GEOFFREY. Women at work: the attitudes of working women toward postwar employment. Wartime Social Survey, 1944. 37pp.

657   WILLIAMS-ELLIS, AMABEL. Women in war factories. Gollancz, 1943. 312pp.

### *Transport*

658   BANCROFT, PETER (comp.). London Transport records at the Public Record Office. Pt. 1. Alton, Hants.: Nebulous Books, 1996. 96pp.

659   BARKER, T.C., and ROBBINS, MICHAEL. A history of London Transport: passenger transport and the development of the metropolis. Vol. 2, The 20th century to 1970. Allen & Unwin, 1974. xx, 554pp., illus.

660   BELL, ROBERT. History of British Railways during the war. Railway Gazette, 1946. 291pp.

661   BRUCE, J. GRAEME, and CROOME, DESMOND F. The twopenny tube. Capital Transport Pubg., 1996. 80pp., illus. [The Central Line. Includes war use as shelters and for munitions work.]

662   CARTER, ERNEST F. Railways in wartime. Muller, 1964. 221pp., illus.

663   CROOME, DESMOND F., and JACKSON, ALAN A.C. Rails through the clay: a history of London's tube railways. 2nd edn. Capital Transport, 1993. 574pp., illus. [Two chapters deal with the tube in wartime, including use as air raid shelters.]

664   CRUMP, NORMAN E. By rail to victory: the story of the LNER in wartime. London & North Eastern Railway, 1947. xii, 196pp., illus.

665   DARWIN, BERNARD. War on the line: the story of the Southern Railway in wartime. Midhurst, Sussex: Middleton, 1984. iv, 215pp., illus.

666   GLAZIER, KEN. London buses and the Second World War. Capital Transport, 1986. 192pp., illus.

667   GRAVES, CHARLES P.R. London Transport at war. 3rd edn. Harpenden, Middx.: Oldcastle, with London Transport Museum, 1989. 95pp., illus. [First pubd. 1947 as London Transport carried on.]

668   HAMBLEY, JOHN A.S. London Transport buses and coaches, 1939–45. Upton-on-Severn, Worcs.: Images, 1995. 160pp., illus.

669   HAMBLEY, J.A.S. London Transport buses and coaches 1946, including a supplement of photographs covering the years 1939–45 and 1948–55. Upton-on-Severn, Worcs.: Images, 1996. 160pp., illus.

670   NEWMAN, ANTHONY G. London's wartime gas buses. Capital Transport, 1997. 64pp., illus.

671   ROBERTSON, R. Steaming through the war years: reminiscences of the ex-GER in London. Oxford: Oakwood P, 1996. 152pp., illus. [Great Eastern Railway.]

672   SAVAGE, CHRISTOPHER I. Inland transport. (History of the Second World War. UK Civil Ser. gen ser.). HMSO, Longmans, 1957. 678pp., illus.

673   TAYLOR, SHEILA. A journey through time: London Transport photographs, 1880–1965. Laurence King, 1992. 160pp., illus. [Pp. 110–27: A city at war.]

## Munitions and aircraft production

674   BENNEY, MARK. Over to bombers. Allen & Unwin, 1943. 236pp. [Work in an aircraft factory.]

675   BROWN BROTHERS LTD. BBL in the 'Blitz': a record of events at the premises of Brown Brothers Limited, Great Eastern Street, London EC2, 1939–45. The firm, 1946. 56pp., illus. [Aeroplane fittings.]

676   INMAN, PEGGY. Labour in the munitions industries. (History of the Second World War. UK Civil Ser. War Production ser.). HMSO, Longmans, 1957. 461pp.

677   LONDON ELECTRIC WIRE CO. AND SMITHS, LTD. Every kind of bomb... The firm, 1945. 16pp., illus. [The company's wartime years.]

678   MINISTRY OF AIRCRAFT PRODUCTION. The aircraft builders: an account of British aircraft production, 1935–45, by Nigel Balchin. HMSO, 1947. 96pp., illus.

679   MINISTRY OF SUPPLY. ROF: the story of the Royal Ordnance Factories, 1939–48, by Ian Hay. HMSO, 1949. 104pp., illus. [Three were in the London area, at Woolwich, Enfield and Waltham.]

680   MORGAN CRUCIBLE CO. LTD. Morgan's at war: a story of achievement under fire, 1939–45. The firm, 1946. 76pp., illus. [Headquarters in Battersea.]

681   MURPHY, JOHN T. Victory production. Lane, 1942. 164pp. [Author's 17 months in engineering and aircraft factory.]

682   PUTNAM, TIM, and WEINBREN, DAN. A short history of the Royal Small Arms Factory, Enfield. Middlesex U., 1992. 160pp., illus.

## The river and docks

683   BATES, LEONARD M. The Thames on fire: the battle of London river, 1939–45. Lavenham, Suffolk: Dalton, 1985. ix, 189pp., illus.

684   COUPAR, ANNE R. War service of the Women's Legion at the Docks. PLA Monthly, XX no. 236 (1945) 82–4. [Mobile canteens.]

685   FOX, LEONARD. Docker goes to war. Worcester: Square One Pubns., 1992. 138pp., illus.

686   HERBERT, ALAN P. The Thames. Weidenfeld, 1966. 256pp., illus. [Including war period.]

687   HOVEY, JOHN. A tale of two ports: London and Southampton. Industrial Society, 1990. xi, 180pp., illus. [In the Second World War.]

688   PEMBERTON, MURRAY. Barge ahoy! A tale of the Thames in wartime. Meridian, 1946. 127pp., illus.

689   Port maintenance and new works during the war. P.L.A. Monthly, XX no. 239 (1945) 115–18.

690   ROYALL, ARTHUR. Paddle steamers and soldiers in Dockland, winter 1939–40. Cockney Ancestor, No. 74 (1997) 32–3.

691   TINTON, BEN T. War comes to the docks. Marshall, Morgan & Scott, 1942. ix, 124pp.

## Finance and banking

692   ASHWORTH, WILLIAM. Contracts and finance. (History of the Second World War. UK Civil Ser. War Production ser.). HMSO, 1953. x, 309pp.

693   HENNESSY, ELIZABETH. A domestic history of the Bank of England, 1930–60. Cambridge: CUP, 1992. 449pp., illus. [Contains a chapter on the Bank's wartime activities and problems.]

694   NATIONAL PROVIDENT INSTITUTION. Some war reminiscences of the NPI staff. The firm, 1947. 77pp.

695   WADSWORTH, JOHN. Counter defensive: being the story of a bank in battle. Hodder, 1946. 106pp., illus. [The Midland Bank.]

## Miscellaneous

696   COMMUNIST PARTY OF GB. LONDON DISTRICT COMMITTEE. London clothing

industry: Communist policy for victory and peace-time production. Communist Party London District, 1944. 8pp.

697  East Ham Electricity Undertaking at war, 1939–45. Dray (printers), 1946. 30pp., illus.

698  EDGSON, W. STANLEY. Effects of the war and government policy on urban real property. Auctioneers' & Estate Agents' Inst., 1946. 32pp. [Reprint from Auctioneers' and Estate Agents' Institute Journal.]

699  FELTMAKERS' COMPANY. The Feltmakers' Company of London: a record of this worshipful company's proceedings and experiences in the Second World War... The Company, 1946. 35pp. [Reproduced from ms. Goldsmiths Library GL C8 c.1]

700  KAYE, BARBARA. The company we kept. New Castle, Del.: Oak Knoll P, 1995. 234pp., illus. [Struggles to keep the antiquarian book firm Elkin Matthews afloat during the war.]

701  RUDD, W.J. Liberty print works: wartime remembrances. Merton Hist. Soc., 1997. 16pp., illus. [Author worked for Liberty & Co., silk printers, in Merton from 1939, and was also a CD bicycle messenger.]

702  STONE, J., & CO. By singleness of purpose. J. Stone & Co., 1945. 112pp., illus. [Wartime activities of Deptford engineering firm.]

703  WALDEN, H.A. 'Operation textiles': a City warehouse in wartime London. Hitchcock, Williams & Co., 1946. 89pp., illus. [Hitchcock, Williams & Co., St Paul's Churchyard.]

## FOOD AND RATIONING

704  DRAKE, BARBARA. Community feeding in wartime. Gollancz, with Fabian Soc., 1942. 29pp.

705  GLOVER, BRIAN. Brewing for victory: brewers, beer and pubs in World War II. Cambridge: Lutterworth P, 1995. ix, 179pp., illus.

706  HAMMOND, R.J. Food. 1, The growth of policy. 2, Studies in administration and control. 3, Studies in administration and control, contd. *(History of the Second World War. UK Civil Ser.)*. HMSO, Longmans, 1951–62. 3 vols.

707  IMPRESARIO [pseud.]. The market square: the story of the Food Ration Book, 1940–44. HMSO, for Ministry of Food, 1944. 62pp., illus. [Facsimile ed. pubd. by Imperial War Museum, 1997.]

708  JOSEPH, SHIRLEY. If their mothers only knew: an unofficial account of life in the Women's Land Army. Faber, 1946. 157pp. [Many were Londoners, in the countryside for first time.]

709  LONDON COUNTY COUNCIL. Important: Blitz feeding. London County Council, 1941. 7pp. [Arrangements for the London boroughs.]

710  MASS-OBSERVATION. Clothes rationing survey. *(Change, no.1)*. Advertising Service Guild, 1941. vi, 85pp.

711  MINISTRY OF FOOD. How Britain was fed in war time: food control, 1939–45. HMSO, for Ministry

of Food, 1946. ii, 65pp.

712  ORR, Sir JOHN, and LUBBOCK, DAVID. Feeding the people in war-time. Macmillan, 1940. vii, 88pp.

## LAW AND ORDER
### Crime and policing

713  APPLEBY, PAULINE. A force on the move: the story of the British Transport Police, 1825–1995. Malvern, Worcs.: Images Pubg., 1995. 286pp., illus. [An amalgamation of the railway, docks, canal and London Transport Police. A section covers the Second World War.]

714  BAILEY, VICTOR. Delinquency and citizenship: reclaiming the young offender, 1914–48. Oxford: Clarendon, 1987. viii, 352pp. [Good section on wartime delinquency.]

715  FIELDING, STEVE. Antonio Mancini: the life and death of a London gangster. *Criminologist,* XIX (1995) 231–4. [Gangs in 1941.]

716  GOSLING, JOHN. Ghost squad. Allen, 1959. 206pp., illus. [CID, including war years.]

717  HILL, WILLIAM C. Boss of Britain's underworld. Naldrett P, 1955. 231pp., illus. ['Billy' Hill led a criminal gang, active in wartime black market.]

718  HOWGRAVE-GRAHAM, HAMILTON M. The Metropolitan Police at war. HMSO, 1947. vii, 89pp., illus.

719  INGLETON, ROY. The gentlemen at war: policing Britain, 1939–45. Maidstone, Kent: Cranborne Pubns., 1994. viii, 392pp., illus.

720  JONES, STEPHEN. When the lights went down: crime in wartime London. Nottingham: Wicked Pubns., 1995. 88pp., illus.

721  LEFEBURE, MOLLY. Evidence for the Crown. Murder on the Home Front: experiences of a pathologist's secretary in World War II. Grafton, 1990. 299pp., illus. [Based in London, with Dr Keith Simpson.]

722  LEON, CLARE. Special constables in the First and Second World Wars. *Police Hist. Soc. Jour.,* VII (1992) 1–41.

723  MANNHEIM, HERMANN. Crime in wartime England. *Amer. Acad. Polit. and Social Science Annals,* CCXVII (1941) 134–6.

724  MURPHY, ROBERT. Smash and grab: gangsters in the London underworld, 1920–60. Faber, 1993. x, 182pp., illus. [Contains chapter on 'The underworld at war'.]

725  PLEYDELL, PETER J.E. The Special Constabulary in Walthamstow, 1940–3. *Police Hist. Soc. Jour.,* No.8 (1993) 71–80. [A wartime Occurrence Book.]

726  ROLPH, CECIL H. Living twice: an autobiography. Gollancz, 1974. 287pp., illus. [Chief Inspector, City of London Police during war.]

727  SMITHIES, EDWARD. Crime in wartime: a social history of crime in World War II. Allen & Unwin, 1982. 219pp. ['London was the crime capital of the country...']

728  WEINBERGER, BARBARA. The best police in the world: an oral history of English policing from the 1930s to the 1960s. Aldershot, Hants.: Scolar, 1995. 224pp. [Chapter 7 deals with policing in wartime.]

## Prisons

729  COMMISSIONERS OF PRISONS. Reports, 1939–41, 1942–4, 1945. HMSO, 1946–7. 3 vols. [Cmd 6820, 7010, 7146.]

730  MOSLEY, DIANA, Lady Mosley. A life of contrasts. Hamilton, 1977. 296pp., illus. [Covers wartime internment in Holloway Prison.]

731  ST JOHN, STELLA. A prisoner's log: Holloway Prison in.1943. Howard League for Penal Reform, 1944. 22pp. [Pacifist, refused to do war work.]

732  SIMPSON, ALFRED W. In the highest degree odious: detention without trial in wartime Britain. Oxford: Clarendon P, 1992. x, 453pp., illus.

## The legal profession

733  BAKER, GEOFFREY, and COMYN, Sir JAMES. Fifty years ago: the Temple in ruins, and, The Temple and my war. Inner Temple Historical Section, 1994. Unpagd. [Wartime life and bomb damage at the Temple.]

734  DODSON, Sir GERALD. Consider your verdict: memoirs. Hutchinson, 1967. 268pp., illus. [Recorder of London, 1937–59.]

735  MACKINNON, Sir FRANK D. The ravages of war in the Inner Temple. Colchester, Essex: Spottiswoode, Ballantyne, 1945. 43pp., illus.

736  Middle Temple ordeal, being an account of what the Second World War meant to the Inn ... Hon. Soc. Middle Temple, 1948. 55pp., illus.

## EDUCATION

737  BOARD OF EDUCATION. The schools in wartime. HMSO, 1941. 26pp., illus. [As affected by evacuation.]

738  BRAY, W.R. The country should be grateful: the wartime history of the South West Essex Technical College and School of Art. The College, 1947. 132pp., illus. [In Walthamstow.]

739  CARDEN, JOAN (ed.). City of London School for Girls' Old Girls' Association: memories of evacuation, 1939–43. The School, 1994. 51pp., illus.

740  COBBAN, Sir JAMES. Dulwich goes to war — and from it. Dulwich College, 1995. 8pp., illus. [Dulwich College.]

741  DAVIS, O.L., and DAVIS, MATTHEW D. From city to countryside: London schools in Kent, 1939–40. *Bygone Kent,* XVI (1995) 329–33.

742  DENT, HAROLD C. Education in transition: a sociological study of the impact of war on English education, 1939–43. Kegan Paul, 1944. xi, 244pp.

743  DOULTON, A.J.F. Highgate School, 1938–44: the story of a wartime evacuation. The author, 1977.

34pp.

744  GOSDEN, P.H.J.H. Education in the Second World War: a study in policy and administration. Methuen, 1976. 527pp.

745  GRUNFELD, JUDITH. Shefford: the story of a Jewish school community in evacuation, 1939–45. Soncino P, 1980. xvii, 125pp., illus. [Jewish Secondary School evacuated to Bedfordshire.]

746  HASSELL, GEOFFREY. Camberwell School of Arts and Crafts: its students and teachers, 1943–60. Woodbridge, Suffolk: Antique Collectors' Club, 1995. 239pp., illus.

747  LEAKEY, J.H. School errant: the story of the wartime adventures of Dulwich College Prep. School. The School, 1951. 91pp., illus.

748  LEINSTER-MACKAY, DONALD. Alleyn's and Rossall Schools: the Second World War, experience and status. Leeds: Univ. Museum of Hist. of Education, 1990. 51pp.

749  LONDON COUNTY COUNCIL. London school plan: development plan for primary and secondary education adopted by the London County Council under the Education Act 1944. LCC, 1974. 274pp.

750  LONDON COUNTY COUNCIL. Replanning London schools: a short account of the development plan... LCC, 1947. 64pp., illus.

751  LONDON COUNTY COUNCIL SCHOOL OF PHOTO-ENGRAVING. The London County Council School of Photo-engraving and Lithography: report by the Principal on the war work of the School. LCC, 1945. iii, 32pp.

752  OBA, SADAO. The 'Japanese' war: London University's World War II secret teaching programme and the experts sent to help beat Japan. Transl. A. Kaneko. Folkestone, Kent: Japan Library, 1995. viii, 171pp., illus.

753  PEARSE, RACHEL N. (comp.). The story of the Mary Datchelor Girls' School, 1877–1977. New ed. Hodder, 1977. 267pp., illus. [Camberwell. Contains: 'An unusual happening' by M.D. Brock, about wartime evacuation. First pubd. 1957.]

754  PRESSWELL, DOROTHY. A sparrow in the meadow. Merlin, 1985. 64pp., illus. [Author's evacuation with Sandringham Road School, East Ham, to Suffolk.]

755  TODD, LES. Caps and gymslips: children at school in inner London in the twenties, thirties and war time. ILEA, 1983. 48pp., illus.

756  WARMINGTON, ERIC H. A history of Birkbeck College, University of London, during the Second World War, 1939–45. Birkbeck College, 1954. 206pp., illus.

## HEALTH CARE

757  ALEXANDRA, Princess Arthur of Connaught and Duchess of Fife. A nurse's story. Bumpus, 1955. 160pp., illus. [Nursed at University College Hospital, Sister in charge of casualty clearing station.]

758 ANDREWS, LUCILLA. No time for romance: an autobiographical account of a few moments in British and personal history. Corgi, 1988. 239pp., illus. [Nurse at St Thomas's Hospital during the war.]

759 BARDELL, EUNICE B. Dame Agatha's dispensary. *Pharmacy in History,* XXVI (1984) 13–19. [Agatha Christie was a VAD dispenser at University College Hospital during the war.]

760 BISHOP, P.M.F. Guy's and the German War. *Guy's Hospital Gazette,* n.s. LIX (1945) 172–9, 211. [Includes map of area from which Guy's bomb casualties were drawn.]

761 COCKETT, FRANK, and COCKETT, DOROTHEA (eds.). The war diary of St Thomas's Hospital, 1939–45. Starling P, 1991. 80pp., illus. [St Thomas's Hospital published its War Diary, 1940–4 in 1946.]

762 COCKETT, F. The bombing of St Thomas's. *Brit. Medical Jour.,* CCCI (1990) 1464–6.

763 CURNOCK, GEORGE C. (ed.). Hospitals under fire: but the lamp still burns. Allen & Unwin, 1941. 148pp., illus.

764 DAVIES, ARFOR T. Friends' Ambulance Unit: the story of the FAU in the Second World War, 1939–46. Allen & Unwin, 1947. xi, 494pp., illus.

765 JOINT WAR ORGANISATION. Humanity keeps an appointment: the story of the war organisation of the British Red Cross Society and Order of St John of Jerusalem. Joint War Organisation, 1944. 44pp., illus.

766 JONES, HELEN. Health and society in 20th century Britain. Longman, 1994. x, 204pp. [Ch. 5, The people's health, 1939–45, pp. 88–116.]

767 KERNAGHAN, PAMELA. St John Ambulance in World War Two. Order of St John, 1995. 39pp., illus.

768 LAIRD, SYDNEY M. Venereal disease in Britain. Harmondsworth, Middx.: Penguin, 1943. 80pp.

769 LINDSAY, DONALD. A form of gratitude: the life of Angela Limerick. East Grinstead: Chid P, 1992. 302pp., illus. [President of County of London British Red Cross Society during war, and LCC member.]

770 MACKINTOSH, JAMES M. The nation's health. Pilot P, 1944. 64pp., illus.

771 MACNALTY, ARTHUR S., and others (eds.) Medical services in war: the principal medical lessons of the Second World War. *(History of the Second World War. UK Medical Ser.).* HMSO, 1968. xviii, 781pp.

772 MELLOR, WILLIAM F.(ed.). Casualties and medical statistics. *(History of the Second World War. UK Medical Ser.).* HMSO, 1972. xvi, 893pp., illus.

773 MINISTRY OF HEALTH. On the state of the public health during six years of war... report of the Chief Officer of the Ministry of Health, 1939–45. HMSO, 1946. iv, 280pp. [With chapters on the Emergency Medical Services and the Civil Defence casualty service.]

774 MORGAN, JANET. Edwina Mountbatten: a life of her own. Harper Collins, 1991. 509pp., illus. [County President for London of St John Ambulance Brigade from 1939, and active in Civil Defence.]

775 OCKRIM, MOIRA. The bombing of St Thomas's Hospital. *St Thomas's Hospital Gazette,* LXXXVIII (1990) 76–90.

776 O'DONNELL, I., and FARMER, R.D.T. Epidemiology of suicide on the London underground. *Social Science and Medicine,* XXXVIII (1994) 409–18. [From 1940–90.]

777 RAVEN, Dame KATHLEEN. London, 1940. *Hist. Nursing Soc. Jour.,* III (1990) 37–50.

778 RAVEN, Dame K. Nursing history: waiting for the bombs to fall. *Nursing Standard,* V no. 6 (1990) 16–19.

779 REID, HILDA. The story of the County of London Branch [of the Red Cross]. British Red Cross Soc., 1948. 96pp., illus.

780 SAUNDERS, HILARY A.ST G. The Middlesex Hospital, 1845–1948. Parrish, 1949. 100pp., illus. [Including war.]

781 SCOTT, GEORGE R. Sex problems and dangers in war-time: a book of practical advice for men and women on the fighting home fronts. Laurie, 1940. x, 85pp.

782 STANTON, MONA E. Four glorious years. Pen P, 1996. 173pp., illus. [New Zealander, trained as VAD at the Middlesex Hospital from 1942.]

783 WALKER, A.H.C. Fifty years on: a survivor remembers. *St Thomas's Hospital Gazette,* LXXXVIII (1990) 91–3. [St Thomas's Hospital.]

784 WILLIAMS, BERNARD. Fifty years on: a survivor remembers. *St Thomas's Hospital Gazette,* LXXXVIII (1991) 168–70. [A wartime registrar at St Thomas'.]

# RELIGIOUS OBSERVANCE

785 ABBOTT, HARRY. Singing through the war. *Westminster Abbey Chorister* (Winter 1989–90) 17–18. [The choir's arrangements.]

786 BAPTIST UNION. Our bombed churches. Kingsgate P, 1945. 41pp., illus.

787 BARRY, FRANK R. Period of my life. Hodder, 1970. 224pp., illus. [Memoirs of Rector of St John's, Smith Square and Sub-dean of Westminster to 1941.]

788 CASSON, HUGH, and others. Bombed churches as war memorials. Archit. P, 1945. 43pp., illus.

789 CHURCH OF ENGLAND. BISHOP OF LONDON'S COMMISSION. The City churches: final report of the Bishop of London's commission. Church Assembly, 1946. 20pp.

790 CHURCH OF ENGLAND CENTRAL COUNCIL FOR THE CARE OF CHURCHES. Saving the art treasures of the church, 1941–5. Church Assembly P, 1945. 59pp.

791 COMMISSION OF THE CHURCHES FOR INTERNATIONAL FRIENDSHIP AND SOCIAL RESPONSIBILITY. Evacuation and the churches: a report of the Survey Committee... Student Christian Movement P, 1941. 63pp. [Concern that no official role being allocated to churches, nor provision made for religious education of evacuees.]

792 FIRKINS, ROGER. Sulphur and black treacle at Christ's Hospital. *Westminster Abbey Chorister* (Winter 1989–90) 15–16. [Westminster choristers evacuated to Horsham.]

793 HART, LIONEL W. The stoning of St Stephen: 20th century. Crystal Pubns., 1945. 36pp., illus. [Bomb damage to St Stephen's Dulwich.]

794 HENSON, HERBERT H. Retrospect of an unimportant life! Vol. 3, 1939–46, the years of retirement. OUP, 1950. x, 394pp., illus. [Bishop of Durham, Canon of Westminster Abbey, 1940–1.]

795 LONDON MISSION. The battle of London. London Mission, 1941. 52pp., illus. [Methodist missions in the Blitz.]

796 MASS-OBSERVATION. Puzzled people: a study in popular attitudes to religion, ethics, progress and politics in a London borough. Gollancz, 1947. 159pp., illus. [Based on 'a 1944 survey of attitudes to religion in a typical London borough', probably Fulham.]

797 MATHEW, DAVID. Catholicism in England: the portrait of a minority, its culture and tradition. 3rd edn. Eyre & Spottiswoode, 1955. x, 295pp. [Including war years.]

798 MATTHEWS, LESLIE, and BELL, MOBERLY. Chelsea Old Church: bombing and rebuilding. Industrial Arts, 1957. 46pp., illus.

799 MATTHEWS, WALTER R. St Paul's Cathedral in wartime, 1939–45. Hutchinson, 1946. 104pp., illus.

800 MOBERLEY, ROBERT H. East London in wartime: what is the church doing? *East and West Rev.,* (April 1941) 67–74. [Moberley was Bishop of Stepney.]

801 MOREHOUSE, CLIFFORD P. An American churchman's view of Britain in 1942. New York: Morehouse-Graham, 1942. 237pp., illus.

802 NIXON, ENID. How the abbey coped with war. *Westminster Abbey Chorister* (Winter 1989–90) 10–14.

803 PARKER, PERCY G. The life story of the tin-hat pastor (Pastor BE Peake, of Fulham). 2nd edn. Shelter Evangelism, 1941. 80pp., illus.

804 RICHARDS, JAMES M. Night watch at St Paul's. *Country Life,* CLXX (1981) 363–7. [Fire-watching at St Paul's Cathedral.]

805 St Mary Magdalene's. *Woolwich and District Family Hist. Soc.,* no.52 (1993) 13–17, no.53 (1994) 12–15. [Register entries, 1939–40.]

806 St Paul's in war and peace, 1939–58. Times, 1960. xii, 76pp., illus. [Cathedral.]

807 SMART, WILLIAM J. London, its tragedy and triumph. London Mission, 1945. 51pp. [Methodist London Mission, 1940–5.]

808 SPINKS, G. STEPHENS. Religion in Britain since 1900. Dakers, 1952. 256pp. [Including war years.]

809 THOMPSON, DOUGLAS. Donald Soper: a biography. Nutfield, Surrey: Denholm House, 1971. 222pp., illus. [West London Mission, Kingsway Hall.]

810 TUBBS, RALPH. Memories of 'The Watch'. *Dome,* No. 30 (Winter 1992–3) 10–11. [Fire-watching at St Paul's Cathedral.]

811 WILSON, HERBERT A. East window. Mowbray, 1946. 146pp. [Church life in Haggerston.]

## LEISURE AND THE ARTS

### Literature: general

812 CADOGAN, MARY, and CRAIG, PATRICIA. Women and children first: the fiction of two World Wars. Gollancz, 1978. 301pp., illus.

813 CHIBNALL, STEVE. 'Pulp versus Penguins: paperbacks go to war'. In War culture: social change and changing experience in World War Two, ed. P. Kirkham and D. Thoms (Lawrence & Wishart, 1995) pp. 131–49.

814 HARTLEY, JENNY (ed.). Hearts undefeated: women's writing of the Second World War. Virago, 1994. xv, 302pp. [Many extracts relate to London.]

815 HARTLEY, J. Millions like us: British women's fiction of the Second World War. Virago, 1997. ix, 265pp., illus.

816 HEWISON, ROBERT. Under siege: literary life in London, 1939–45. Weidenfeld, 1977. x, 219pp., illus.

817 KNIGHT, STEPHEN. 'Murder in wartime'. In War culture: social change and changing experience in World War Two, ed. P. Kirkham and D. Thoms (Lawrence & Wishart, 1995) pp. 161–71. [Crime fiction.]

818 KLEIN, HOLGER, and others (eds.). The Second World War in fiction. Macmillan, 1984. ix, 249pp.

819 MUNTON, ALAN. English fiction of the Second World War. Faber, 1989. x, 118pp.

820 SINCLAIR, ANDREW. War like a wasp: the lost decade of the forties. Hamilton, 1989. 321pp., illus.

821 WALLER, JANE, and VAUGHAN-REES, MICHAEL. Women in wartime: the role of women's magazines, 1939–45. Optima, 1987. 128pp., illus.

### Literature and journalism

822 BLYTHE, RONALD. 'Writing in a Blitz'. In Private words: letters and diaries from the Second World War, ed. R. Blythe (Viking, 1991) pp. 250–62.

823 BRITTAIN, VERA. Testament of experience. Gollancz, 1957. 480pp.

824 CALDER, RITCHIE. Carry on London. EUP, 1941.

xv, 163pp. [Journalist.]

825  CALDER, R. The lesson of London. Secker, 1941. 127pp.

826  CHRISTIANSEN, ARTHUR. Headlines all my life. Heinemann, 1961. xi, 295pp., illus. [Journalist.]

827  CUDLIPP, HUGH. Publish and be damned! The astonishing story of the Daily Mirror. Dakers, 1953. xi, 292pp., illus.

828  DAVIDSON, MICHAEL. The world, the flesh and myself. Bruce & Watson, 1973. 354pp., illus. [Journalist.]

829  DRIBERG, TOM. Ruling passions. Cape, 1977. x, 271pp., illus. [Journalist with Daily Express.]

830  DRIBERG, T. Colonnade. Pilot P, 1949. 384pp. [Selections of his journalism, 1937–47.]

831  FISHER, JOHN (ed.). Eye-witness: an anthology of British reporting. Cassell, 1960. xv, 284pp., illus. [Includes Café de Paris bomb.]

832  HODSON, JAMES L. Through the dark night. Towards the morning. Before daybreak. Home Front. The sea and the land. Gollancz, 1941–45. 5 vols. [War correspondent's experiences, 1939–45.]

833  HOPKINSON, TOM. Of this our time: a journalist's story, 1905–50. Hutchinson, 1982. 316pp., illus.

834  HOPKINSON, T. (ed.). Picture Post, 1938–50. Allen Lane, 1970. 288pp., illus. [Selections from the influential magazine.]

835  INGERSOLL, RALPH. Report on England. Lane, 1941. 247pp. [American journalist.]

836  KENDRICK, ALEXANDER. Prime time: the life of Edward R. Murrow. Dent, 1970. viii, 548pp., illus. [First pubd. Boston, Mass.: Brown, Little, 1969.]

837  KING, CECIL H. With malice towards none: a war diary, ed. W. Armstrong. Sidgwick, 1970. vii, 343pp., illus. [The Daily Mirror.]

838  MCDONALD, IVERACH. The history of The Times. Vol.5, Struggles in peace and war, 1939–66. Times Books, 1984. ii, 514pp., illus.

839  MARTIN, KINGSLEY. Editor: a second volume of autobiography, 1931–45. Hutchinson, 1968. 340pp., illus. [Editor of the New Statesman.]

840  ORWELL, GEORGE. Collected essays, journalism and letters, ed. S. Orwell and I. Angus. Vols. 2, 3. Secker, 1968. 2 vols. [Covers the wartime period.]

841  PANTER-DOWNES, MOLLIE. London war notes, 1939–45, ed. W. Shawn. Longmans, 1972. 378pp. [Journalist.]

842  POCOCK, TOM. 1945: the dawn came up like thunder. Collins, 1983. 288pp. [Journalist's memories.]

843  PRIESTLEY, JOHN B. Margin released. Heinemann, 1962. viii, 236pp. [Writer.]

844  RECHNITZER, F.E. War correspondent: the story of Quentin Reynolds. New York: Messner, 1943. 214pp., illus.

845  RESTON, JAMES. Prelude to victory. Heinemann, 1942. vi, 151pp. [Journalist with London bureau of New York Times, 1939–41.]

846  ROBERTSON, BEN. I saw England. Jarrolds, 1941. 190pp. [American journalist.]

847  SPENDER, STEPHEN. World within world: the autobiography of Stephen Spender. Hamilton, 1951. ix, 349pp. [Poet.]

848  SPENDER, S. The thirties and after: poetry, politics and people. Macmillan, 1978. 286pp., illus.

849  STANFORD, DEREK. Inside the forties: literary memoirs, 1937–57. Sidgwick, 1977. viii, 242pp., illus. [Writer.]

850  UNWIN, STANLEY. The truth about a publisher: an autobiographical record. Allen & Unwin, 1960. 455pp., illus.

851  WARD, ALFRED C. A literary journey through wartime Britain. Oxford: OUP, 1943. 95pp., illus. [Mainly London.]

852  WILLIS, JEROME. It stopped at London. Hurst & Blackett, 1944. 144pp. [Reporter's account of London, 1938–41, contrasted with Barcelona and Paris.]

853  WOOLF, LEONARD. The journey not the arrival matters: an autobiography of the years 1939–69. Hogarth P, 1969. 217pp., illus. [Editor, publisher.]

854  WYATT, WOODROW. Confessions of an optimist. Collins, 1985. 364pp., illus. [Journalist.]

## Art and music

855  BARKER, SYBIL. Sybil Barker's war: the wartime diary of a Director of Music and organist at the Royal Holloway College, ed. L. Pike. Woking, Surrey: Churchman, 1989. ix, 84pp., illus.

856  BATHURST, RALPH H. Eight London churches in war: paintings made in 1945. Melland, 1969. 19pp., illus.

857  BROWSE, LILLIAN. The National Gallery in wartime and other memories. Apollo, CXLV (1997) 3–14.

858  BUTLER, ARTHUR S.G. Recording ruin. Constable, 1942. 146pp., illus. [Author was artist, and surveyor of bomb damage for Chelsea Borough Council.]

859  CLARK, KENNETH. The other half: a self-portrait. Hamilton, 1986. xii, 261pp., illus. [Director of the National Gallery.]

860  ECKSTEIN, JEREMY, and HARRIS, ROBERTA. The art market in the Second World War. Art Quart., no.21 (1995) 49–52. [In London.]

861  FLETCHER, HANSLIP. Bombed London: ...drawings of historic buildings damaged during the bombing of London in the Second World War. Cassell, 1947. 43pp., illus.

862  FOOT, MICHAEL R.D. Art and war: 20th century warfare as depicted by war artists. Headline, 1990. 240pp., illus. [With many London examples.]

863  FOSS, BRIAN F. British artists and the Second World War, with particular reference to the War Artists' Advisory Committee of the Ministry of Information. London Univ. PhD thesis, 1991. 624ff.

864　LASSIMONNE, DENISE (comp.). Myra Hess by her friends, ed. H. Ferguson. Hamilton, 1966. x, 119pp., illus. [Covers the famous National Gallery concerts during the war.]

865　LEWIS, ADRIAN. 'Henry Moore's 'Shelter Drawings': memory and myth'. In War culture: social change and changing experience in World War Two, ed. P. Kirkham and D. Thoms (Lawrence & Wishart, 1995) pp. 113–27.

866　London's hour as seen through the eyes of the firefighters. Staples Books Ltd., 1942. 51pp., illus. [Paintings by serving firemen.]

867　MCCORMICK. KEN, and PERRY, HAMILTON D. (eds.). Images of war: the artist's vision of World War II. Cassell, 1991. xvi, 453pp., illus. [Includes several paintings of London.]

868　MOORE, HENRY. A shelter sketchbook. British Museum Pubns., 1988. 22pp., illus. [Facsimile of notebook drawn in 1941, first pubd. 1945.]

869　OSTROWSKA, WANDA. London's glory: twenty paintings of the city's ruins, text by Viola Garvin. Allen & Unwin, 1945. 55pp., illus.

870　RICHARDSON, ROBERT. 'Closings and openings: leading public art galleries during the Second World War'. In War culture: social change and changing experience in World War Two, ed. P. Kirkham and D. Thoms (Lawrence & Wishart, 1995) pp. 87–97.

871　ROSS, ALAN. Colours of war: war art, 1939–45. Cape, 1983. 192pp., illus. [British artists.]

872　ROTHENSTEIN, Sir JOHN. Brave day, hideous night: autobiography, 1939–65. Hamilton, 1966. xii, 386pp., illus. [Director of the Tate Gallery.]

873　SPALDING, FRANCES. Dance till the stars come down: a biography of John Minton. Hodder, 1991. xi, 271pp., illus. [Artist.]

874　STANSKY, PETER, and ABRAHAMS, WILLIAM. London's burning: life, death and art in the Second World War. Constable, 1994. xiii, 201pp., illus.

875　SUMMERFIELD, ANGELA. The artist at war: Second World War paintings and drawings from the Walker Art Gallery's collection. Liverpool: Nat. Museums & Galleries on Merseyside, 1989. 27pp., illus. [Includes John Piper's 'Ruined House of Commons' and Sir Francis Cook's 'London ARP.']

876　TOPOLSKI, FELIKS. Britain in peace and war. Methuen, 1941. 128pp., illus. [Drawings, including London.]

877　VAUGHAN, KEITH. Journals, 1939–77. Murray, 1989. xviii, 217pp. [Painter.]

## Museums, galleries, libraries

878　ABBOTT, G. The Tower of London during World War II. Kendal: the author, 1997. 2pp.

879　CANTWELL, JOHN D. The Public Record Office, 1838–1958. HMSO, 1991. x, 631pp., illus. [Ch. 14, pp. 397–444 covers evacuation of documents and other wartime arrangements.]

880　JAGODZINSKI, Z., and others (eds.). Biblioteka Polska w Londynie, 1942–92. Biblioteka Polska, 1993. 129pp., illus. [Polish Library in London.]

881　KEELING, C.H. They all came into the ark: a record of the Zoological Society of London in two world wars. Guildford: Clam Pubns., 1988. 200pp., illus. [Reproduced from typescript.]

882　LINGARD, J.R. 'Cyril A. Farey: a personal tribute to St Paul's Cathedral and the City of London, 1940–4'. In English architecture public and private, ed. J. Bold and E. Chaney (Hambledon P, 1993) pp. 311–27. [Architectural draughtsman, and a fire-watcher at St Paul's.]

883　MILLER, EDWARD. That noble cabinet: a history of the British Museum. Deutsch, 1973. 400pp., illus. [Pp.321–59 cover wartime arrangements.]

884　MINISTRY OF WORKS. War and archaeology in Britain: the excavation of ancient sites and the preservation of historic buildings. HMSO, 1949. 56pp., illus. [Bombing and wartime construction projects revealed many previously unknown sites.]

885　O'NEIL, B.H. ST J. War and archaeology in Britain. Antiq. Jour., XXVIII (1948) 20–44.

886　ROWELL, PHYLLIS. Dr Johnson's house during the war. Four Oaks Lib., 1987. 32pp., illus.

887　RUSSELL, DALE C. A social history of public libraries in London, 1939–45. University of North London MA dissertation, 1995. 114ff.

888　WILSON, ALYSON. Buried treasure. Art Quart., no.21 (1995) 29–33. [London museums and galleries during the war.]

## Theatre

889　AGATE, JAMES. Ego: the autobiography of James Agate. Harrap, 1944–5. 9 vols. [Theatre critic. Vols, 6–7 cover the war period.]

890　BRAHMS, CARYL, and SHERRIN, NED. Too dirty for the Windmill: a memoir of Caryl Brahms. Constable, 1986. xvii, 286pp.

891　CHAMBERS, COLIN. The story of the Unity Theatre. Lawrence & Wishart, 1989. 446pp., illus.

892　DEAN, BASIL. The theatre at war. Harrap, 1956. 573pp., illus. [ENSA, the Entertainments National Services Association.]

893　HARGREAVES, BRENDA. Wartime playtimes: reminiscences of amateur dramatic groups in wartime Streatham. Streatham Soc., 1989. 25pp., illus.

894　HEMBRY, JEAN. My wartime travels with ENSA. Streatham Soc., 1991. 40pp., illus.

895　HUGHES, JOHN G. The greasepaint war: show business, 1939–45. New English Lib., 1976. 216pp., illus. [ENSA.]

896　KEULS, H.A. Het Londensche tooneel in oorlogstijd. Amsterdam: Republiek der Letteren, 1945. 96pp., illus. [The London stage in wartime.]

897　NINETEEN HUNDRED AND THIRTY-NINE. Since 1939. Vol.1, Ballet, Film, Music, Painting.

Vol.2, Drama, The novel, Poetry, Prose literature. Phoenix House, 1948, 1949. 2 vols., illus.

898 TREWIN, WENDY, and TREWIN, J.C. The Arts Theatre, London, 1927–81. Soc. Theatre Research, 1986. vi, 123pp., illus.

899 WEARING, J.P. The London stage, 1940–9: a calendar of plays and players. Metuchen, N.J.: Scarecrow P, 1991. 2 vols.

## Cinema

900 ALDGATE, ANTHONY, and RICHARDS, JEFFREY. Britain can take it: British cinema in the Second World War. New edn. Edinburgh: Edinburgh UP, 1994. 362pp., illus. [First pubd. 1986.]

901 BARR, CHARLES. War record. *Sight and Sound,* (Autumn 1989) 260–5. [British cinema in the war.]

902 COULTASS, CLIVE. Images for battle: British film and the Second World War, 1939–45. Assoc. Univ. Presses, 1989. 217pp., illus.

903 DRAZIN, CHARLES. The finest years: British cinema in the 1940s. Deutsch, 1998. xiv, 281pp., illus.

904 JENNINGS, MARY LOU. Humphrey Jennings: film-maker, painter, poet. British Film Inst., Riverside Studios, 1982. 75pp., illus. [Accompanied an exhibition.]

905 MORGAN, GUY. Red roses every night: an account of London cinemas under fire. Quality P, 1948. 127pp., illus. [Includes list of British film releases, month by month.]

906 NELSON, JAMES. Survival of a fleapit: how the Electric, Portobello Road, survived the hazards of fire, bombing and modernisation in the war years. *Picture House,* No. 20 (1994–5) 13–15.

907 NEWMAN, ROSIE. England at war. Chiswick P, 1942. xii, 51pp., illus. [Film making in wartime London and nearby.]

908 RANK ORGANISATION. Twenty-first anniversary, 1937–58; Gaumont State, Kilburn. Magnet Advertising Co., 1958. 16pp., illus.

909 RICHARDS, JEFFREY. Fires were started. *History Today,* XLV (1995) 29–34. [Analysis of Humphrey Jennings' film about the AFS (1943).]

910 ROBINSON, ALAN J. An assessment of British non-newsreel films as used to influence the attitudes and activities of domestic audiences during World War II. *Lancaster Univ. MA thesis,* 1985. 147ff.

911 SORENSEN, COLIN. London on film: 100 years of filmmaking in London. Museum of London, 1996. 176pp., illus. [Bombed London features as background in many postwar films.]

912 TAYLOR, PHILIP M. (ed.). Britain and the cinema in the Second World War. New York: St Martin's P, 1988. x, 210pp.

913 THORPE, FRANCES, and PRONAY, NICHOLAS. British official films in the Second World War: a descriptive catalogue. Oxford: Clio P, 1980. x, 321pp., illus. [Many filmed in London.]

## Broadcasting

914 BELFRAGE, BRUCE. One man in his time. Hodder, 1951. 255pp. [Belfrage continued to read the news calmly while time-bomb hit Broadcasting House.]

915 BRIGGS, ASA. The history of broadcasting in the United Kingdom. Vol. 3, The war of words. Oxford: OUP, 1970. xviii, 766pp., illus.

916 ECKERSLEY, ROGER H. The BBC and all that. Sampson Low, 1946. 216pp.

917 GORHAM, MAURICE. Sound and fury: 21 years at the BBC. Percival Marshall, 1948. 248pp.

918 HIBBERD, STUART. This is London. Macdonald & Evans, 1950. 322pp. [BBC announcer's diary.]

919 HICKMAN, TOM. What did you do in the war, Auntie? The BBC at war, 1939–45. BBC, 1995. 224pp., illus.

920 KAVANAGH, HENRY E. Tommy Handley. Hodder, 1949. 255pp., illus. [Handley's ITMA radio comedy programme was an important morale-booster.]

921 MACLEOD, JOSEPH. A job at the BBC. Glasgow: Maclellan, 1947. 255pp. [Announcer.]

922 MURROW, EDWARD R. In search of light: the broadcasts of E.R. Murrow, 1938–61, ed. E. Bliss. Macmillan. 1968. 304pp., illus.

923 NICHOLAS, SIAN. The echo of war: Home Front propaganda and the wartime BBC, 1939–45. Manchester: Manchester UP, 1996. x, 307pp., illus.

924 O'SULLIVAN, TIM. 'Listening through: the wireless and World War Two'. In War culture: social change and changing experience in World War Two, ed. P. Kirkham and D. Thoms (Lawrence & Wishart, 1995) pp. 173–85.

925 WHITE, ANTONIA. The BBC at war. BBC, 1941. 48pp., illus.

926 WORSLEY, FRANCIS. ITMA, 1939–48. Vox Mundi, 1948. viii, 102pp., illus. [Worsley was ITMA producer.]

## Sport

927 ALLISON, GEORGE F. Allison calling: a galaxy of football and other memories. Staples P, 1948. 240pp., illus.

928 COMPTON, DENIS. Playing for England. New edn. Sampson Low, 1949. xi, 241pp., illus. [First pubd. 1948.]

929 COX, RICHARD W. Sport in Britain: a bibliography of historical publications, 1800–1988. Manchester: Manchester UP, 1991. xxxi, 285pp. [London section contains many general histories of London sports clubs also covering war years.]

930 MCCARTHY, TONY. War games: the story of sport in World War Two. Macdonald, 1989. 192pp., illus. [Some London cricket and football coverage.]

931 MIDWINTER, ERIC. The lost seasons: cricket in wartime. Methuen, 1987. 176pp., illus.

932 PROLE, D. Football in London. Soccer Book Club, 1965. 212pp. [Including war years.]

**933** ROLLIN, JACK. Soccer at war, 1939–45. Collins, 1985. 308pp., illus.

**934** SIMMONS, G.W. Tottenham Hotspur Football Club: its birth and progress, 1882–1946. The Club, 1947. viii, 224pp., illus.

**935** WALVIN, JAMES. The people's game: the history of football revisited. Rev. ed. Edinburgh: Mainstream, 1994. 224pp., illus. [Includes wartime.]

**936** WARNER, Sir PELHAM. Lord's, 1787–1945. Pavilion, 1986. 328pp., illus. [First pubd. 1946.]

## Miscellaneous

**937** FLYNN, KEITH. Freemasonry at war: an account of English freemasonry in the Second World War. *(Prestonian Lecture for 1991)*. United Grand Lodge, 1990. 42pp. [Includes roll of honour.]

**938** ROWNTREE, B. SEEBOHM, and LAVERS, G.R. English life and leisure: a social study. Longmans, 1951. xvi, 482pp., illus. [Research done in 1947, but relevant to war years. Several London case histories.]

**939** SAUNDERS, HILARY A.ST G. The left handshake: the Boy Scout movement during the war. Collins, 1949. 256pp.

## THE FUTURE: POSTWAR NEEDS AND PLANS

**940** ABERCROMBIE, Sir PATRICK. The Greater London Plan, 1944: a report prepared on behalf of the Standing Conference on London Regional Planning. The Standing Conference, 1945. x, 220pp.

**941** BARKER, FELIX, and HYDE, RALPH. London as it might have been. Murray, 1982. 223pp., illus. [Ch. 15, pp. 177–95, includes wartime plans for postwar period.]

**942** BENDIT, PHOEBE D., and BENDIT, LAURENCE J. Living together again. Gramol Pubns., 1946. 80pp. [Advice for families separated during War.]

**943** BRETT-JAMES, NORMAN. Postwar London. *London and Middx. Archaeol. Soc. Trans.,* n.s. IX (1944) 42–66. [Planning.]

**944** CARTER, E.J., and GOLDFINGER, ERNO. The County of London Plan explained. Penguin, 1945. 80pp., illus.

**945** CLUNN, HAROLD P. London marches on: a record of the changes which have taken place in the metropolis of the British Empire between the two World Wars and much that is schedled for reconstruction. Caen P, 1947. 247pp., illus.

**946** CORPORATION OF LONDON. IMPROVEMENTS AND TOWN PLANNING COMMITTEE. Report of the Committee... on the preliminary draft proposals for postwar reconstruction in the City of London, 1944. Batsford, for the Corporation, 1944. 77pp., illus.

**947** CORPORATION OF LONDON. IMPROVEMENTS AND TOWN PLANNING COMMITTEE. The City of London. Archit. P, 1951. 341pp., illus. [The damage suffered 1940–5, and proposals for reconstruction.]

**948** FORSHAW, JOHN H., and ABERCROMBIE, PATRICK. County of London plan. Macmillan, 1943. xii, 188pp., illus. [LCC's post-war plans, especially for slum redevelopment.]

**949** FORSHAW, J.H., and ABERCROMBIE, P. Replanning the County of London: a brief account of the County of London Plan. LCC, 1944. 24pp.

**950** LAMBETH. METROPOLITAN BOROUGH. Report of Special Committee on the County of London Plan, 1943. Borough of Lambeth, 1943. 30pp., illus. [Cover title: The County of London Plan as it affects Lambeth.]

**951** MASS-OBSERVATION. The journey home. *(Change, no.5)*. Murray, for Advertising Service Guild, 1944. 123pp. [Public opinion on postwar needs.]

**952** MILLER, M. The elusive green background: Raymond Unwin and the Greater London Regional Plan. *Planning Perspectives,* IV (1989) 15–44.

**953** PURDOM, C.B. How should we rebuild London? Dent, 1946. xi, 308pp., illus.

**954** ROYAL ACADEMY. PLANNING COMMITTEE. London replanned. Country Life, 1942. 32pp., illus. [Ideas for postwar planning.]

## VICTORY CELEBRATIONS

**955** CHILDS, MARQUIS W. London wins the battle. *National Geographic,* LXXXVIII (1945) 129–52.

**956** CONNAUGHTON, RICHARD. Celebration of Victory: VE Day, 1945. Brassey's, 1995. 175pp., illus.

**957** DERRICK, JONATHAN. Lewisham remembers 1945. *Lewisham Hist. Jour.,* No. 3 (1995) 12–25.

**958** GILBERT, MARTIN. The day the war ended. HarperCollins, 1995. xxii, 472pp., illus.

**959** GREEN, MICHAEL (ed.). When the bunting came down, and postwar London. Wymondham, Norfolk: Stylus P, 1995. 60pp., illus.

**960** GREEN, M. (ed.). VE Day and London memories. Wymondham, Norfolk: Stylus P, 1994. 51pp., illus.

**961** NEVIN, PATRICK. Put your right leg out... VE Day and memories, ed. M. Green. Wymondham, Norfolk: Stylus P, 1996. 86pp., illus.

**962** RIDGE, TOM (comp.). From VE Day to VJ Day: a chronology of street parties and events in the East End during the ending of World War II. Ragged School Museum Trust, 1995. 18pp.

**963** SCHWEITZER, PAMELA, and DAVIS, REBECCA (comps.). When the lights go on again: memories of VE Day and after. Age Exchange, 1995. 52pp., illus.

# AUTHOR INDEX TO BIBLIOGRAPHY

(Figures refer to entry numbers)

*1944: a London Record*

*For dwellers in London, it was the year of the "Doodle Bug" or Flying Bomb & of the Rocket or Gas main.*

*For the outer world, it was the year of "D Day" The Normandy Landing.*

Percy Home, of Onslow Gardens, Kensington, begins his diary and scrapbook for 1944
with a picture of a V1 passing his window
*(Guildhall Library Ms 21,599)*

# 8. Index to the Guide and Bibliography

(for authors see previous index)

Figures in light type refer to page references in the Guide; figures in **heavy** type to Bibliography entries.

# 9. Useful Addresses

## General

Business Archives Council,
3rd and 4th Floor,
101 Whitechapel High Street,
London E1 7RE
Tel. 0171 247 0024

Centre for Metropolitan History,
Institute of Historical Research,
University of London,
Senate House,
Malet Street,
London WC1E 7HU
Tel. 0171 862 8790
www.ihr.sas.ac.uk/cmh/cmh.main.html

Greater London Archives Network
(GLAN),
c/o Hackney Archives,
43 De Beauvoir Road,
London N1 5SQ
Tel. 0171 241 2886

London Archive Users' Forum (LAUF),
29 Stepney Green,
London E1 3JX

London at War Study Group,
81 Harrowdene Gardens,
Teddington, Middx.
Tel. 0181 977 6559

National Register of Archives,
Quality House,
Quality Court,
Chancery Lane,
London WC2A 1HP
Tel. 0171 242 1198
www.hmc.gov.uk/main.htm

## Repositories with very wide coverage

Public Record Office,
Ruskin Avenue,
Kew,
Richmond, Surrey TW9 4DU
Tel. 0181 876 3444
www.pro.gov.uk

London Metropolitan Archives (formerly
GLRO),
40 Northampton Road,
London EC1R 0HB
Tel. 0171 332 3820

Guildhall Library,
Aldermanbury,
London EC2P 2EJ
Tel. 0171 332 1863
www.ihr.sas.ac.uk/ihr/ghmnu.html

Imperial War Museum,
Lambeth Road,
London SE1 6HZ
Tel. 0171 416 5000
www.iwm.org.uk

Museum of London,
150 London Wall,
London EC2Y 5HN
Tel. 0171 600 3699
www.museum-london.org.uk

Mass-Observation Archive,
University of Sussex,
Falmer, Brighton,
E. Sussex BN 1 9QL
Tel. 01273 678157
www.susx.ac.uk/units/library/massobs/
homearch.html

## Special interest collections

Where they survive, the records of almost
every institution which functioned in
London during the war, or evacuated its
staff early on, will contain some material of
potential interest. It would be impossible to
list them all, those that follow are examples
whose collections the editor has consulted
in compiling this guide. Others will be
found in the London section of *British
Archives* by Janet Foster and Julia Sheppard
(3rd ed. London: Macmillan, 1995, 4th ed.
now in preparation), and in the *Directory of
Corporate Archives* by Lesley Richmond
and Alison Turton (3rd ed. London:
Business Archives Council, 1992).

Ballet Rambert,
94 Chiswick High Road,
London W4 1SH
Tel. 0181 995 4246

Barclays Bank plc,
Archives and Records Management,
Secretary's Office,
Johnson Smirke Building,
4 Royal Mint Court,
London EC3N 4HJ
Tel. 0171 626 1567

Baptist Union,
Regent's Park College,
Pusey Street,
Oxford OX1 2LB
Tel. 01865 288120

Bishopsgate Institute,
230 Bishopsgate,
London EC2M 4QH
Tel. 0171 247 6198

Bodleian Library,
Department of Western Manuscripts,
University of Oxford,
Broad Street,
Oxford OX1 3BG

Tel. 01865 277158
www.bodley.ox.ac.uk

The Boys' Brigade,
National Training Centre,
Felden Lodge,
Hemel Hempstead,
Herts. HP3 0BL
Tel. 01442 231681

British Broadcasting Corporation
BBC Written Archives Centre,
Caversham Park,
Reading,
Berks.
RG4 8TZ
Tel. 01734 472742
www.bbc.co.uk

British Film Institute,
National Film & Television Archive,
21 Stephen Street,
London W1P 1PL
Tel. 0171 255 1444
www.bfi.org.uk

British Institute for Cartoon Research,
University of Kent,
Canterbury CT2 7NU
Tel. 01227 764000
www.ukc.ac.uk/cartoons

British Library National Sound Archive,
96 Euston Road,
London NW1 2DB
Tel. 0171 412 7440
www.portico.bl.uk

British Library Newspaper Library,
Colindale Avenue,
London NW9 5HE
Tel. 0171 412 7353

British Red Cross Society,
9 Grosvenor Crescent,
London SW1
Tel. 0171 235 5454

Haringey,
Bruce Castle Museum,
Lordship Lane,
London N17 8NU
Tel. 0181 808 8772
[Tottenham, Hornsey and Wood Green.]

Harrow Local History Collection,
Civic Centre Library,
Box 4, Civic Centre,
Station Road, Harrow HA1 2UU
Tel. 0181 424 1056
[Harrow.]

Havering Refence Library,
Central Library,
St Edward's Way, Romford RM1 3AR
Tel. 01708 46040
[Romford, Hornchurch.]

Hillingdon Heritage Service,
Central Library, High Street,
Uxbridge, Middx. UB8 1HD
Tel. 01895 250702
[Hayes and Harligton, Ruislip, Northwood,
    Yiewsley and West Drayton, Uxbridge.]

Hounslow Heritage and Tourism
    Department,
Hounslow Library,
24 Treaty Centre,
High Street, Hounslow TW3 1ES
Tel. 0181 570 0622
[Brentford and Chiswick, Heston and
  Isleworth, Feltham.]

Islington Local History Collection,
Central Reference Library,
2 Fieldway Crescent,
London N5 1PF
Tel. 0171 609 3051
[Islington, Finsbury.]

Kensington and Chelsea Local Studies,
Central Library,
Hornton Street,
London W8 7RX

Tel. 0171 937 2542
[Kensington, Chelsea.]

Kingston Museum and Heritage Service,
North Kingston Centre,
Richmond Road,
Kingston-upon-Thames KT2 5PE
Tel. 0181 547 6738
[Kingston, Malden and Coombe, Surbiton.]

Lambeth Archives Department,
Minet Library,
52 Knatchbull Road,
London SE5 9QY
Tel. 0171 926 6076
[Lambeth, Streatham, Clapham.]

Lewisham Local History Centre,
The Manor House,
Old Road, Lee
London SE13 5SY
Tel. 0181 852 5050
[Lewisham, Deptford.]

Merton Local Studies,
Wimbledon Reference Library,
Wimbledon Hill Road,
London SW19 7NB
Tel. 0181 946 1136
[Mitcham, Wimbledon, Merton and
  Morden.]

Newham Local Studies Library,
Stratford Reference Library,
Water Lane,
London E15 4NJ
Tel. 0181 557 8856
[East Ham, West Ham, parts of Barking and
  Woolwich.]

Redbridge Local History Room,
Central Library,
Clements Road,
Ilford, Essex IG1 1EA
Tel. 0181 478 7145
[Ilford, Wanstead and Woodford, parts of
  Dagenham and Chigwell.]

Richmond Local Collections,
Central Reference Library,
Old Town Hall,
Whittaker Avenue,
Richmond-upon-Thames, Surrey
TW9 1TP
Tel. 0181 940 5529
[Richmond and Barnes, Twickenham.]

Southwark Local Studies Library,
211 Borough High Street,
London SE1 1JA
Tel. 0171 403 3507
[Southwark, Bermondsey, Camberwell.]

Sutton Archives and Local Studies Section,
Central Library, St Nicholas Way,
Sutton,
Surrey SM1 1EA
Tel. 0181 770 4747
www.earl.org.uk/partners/sutton/archive.html
[Bedlington and Wallington, Sutton and
   Cheam, Carshalton.]

Tower Hamlets Local History Library and
   Archives,
Bancroft Library,

277 Bancroft Road,
London E1 4DQ
Tel. 0181 980 4366
[Bethnal Green, Poplar, Stepney.]

Waltham Forest Archives and Local
   History Library,
Vestry House Museum,
Vestry Road,
London E17 9NH
Tel. 0181 509 1917
[Chingford, Leyton and Walthamstow.]

Wandsworth Local History Collection,
Battersea Library,
265 Lavender Hill,
London SW11 1BJ
Tel. 0181 871 7467
[Wandsworth, Battersea.]

Westminster Archives Centre,
10 St Ann's Street,
London SW1P 2XR
Tel. 0171 798 2180
www.earl.org.uk/partners/westminster/
   index.html
[Westminster, Paddington, St Marylebone.]